Praise for the Sierra/Bates Java Programmer Stu

"Kathy Sierra is one of the few people in the world who can make complicated things seem damn simple. And as if that isn't enough, she can make boring things seem interesting. I always look forward to reading whatever Kathy writes—she's one of my favorite authors."

—*Paul Wheaton, Trail Boss JavaRanch.com*

"Who better to write a Java study guide than Kathy Sierra, the reigning queen of Java instruction? Kathy Sierra has done it again—here is a study guide that almost guarantees you a certification!"

—*James Cubeta, Systems Engineer, SGI*

"The thing I appreciate most about Kathy is her quest to make us all remember that we are teaching people and not just lecturing about Java. Her passion and desire for the highest quality education that meets the needs of the individual student is positively unparalleled at SunEd. Undoubtedly there are hundreds of students who have benefited from taking Kathy's classes."

—*Victor Peters, founder Next Step Education & Software Sun Certified Java Instructor*

"I want to thank Kathy for the EXCELLENT Study Guide. The book is well written, every concept is clearly explained using a real life example, and the book states what you specifically need to know for the exam. The way it's written, you feel that you're in a classroom and someone is actually teaching you the difficult concepts, but not in a dry, formal manner. The questions at the end of the chapters are also REALLY good, and I am sure they will help candidates pass the test. Watch out for this Wickedly Smart book."

—*Alfred Raouf, Web Solution Developer*

"The Sun Certification exam was certainly no walk in the park, but Kathy's material allowed me to not only pass the exam, but Ace it!"

—*Mary Whetsel, Sr. Technology Specialist,*
Application Strategy and Integration, The St. Paul Companies

"Bert has an uncanny and proven ability to synthesize complexity into simplicity offering a guided tour into learning what's needed for the certification exam."

—*Thomas Bender, President, Gold Hill Software Design, Inc.*

OCP Java SE 6 Programmer Practice Exams

(Exam 310-065)

OCP Java SE 6 Programmer Practice Exams

(Exam 310-065)

Bert Bates
Kathy Sierra

New York   Chicago   San Francisco   Lisbon   London   Madrid
Mexico City   Milan   New Delhi   San Juan   Seoul   Singapore   Sydney   Toronto

The McGraw·Hill Companies

Cataloging-in-Publication Data is on file with the Library of Congress

McGraw-Hill books are available at special quantity discounts to use as premiums and sales promotions, or for use in corporate training programs. To contact a representative, please e-mail us at bulksales@mcgraw-hill.com.

OCP Java SE 6 Programmer Practice Exams (Exam 310-065)

1234567890   DOC DOC   109876543210

ISBN   978-0-07-226088-5

MHID   0-07-226088-2

Sponsoring Editor Timothy Green	**Technical Editor** JavaRanch.com	**Composition** Glyph International
Editorial Supervisor Jody McKenzie	**Copy Editor** Mike McGee	**Illustration** Glyph International
Project Manager Madhu Bhardwaj, Glyph International	**Proofreader** Erica Orloff	**Art Director, Cover** Jeff Weeks
Acquisitions Coordinator Stephanie Evans	**Production Supervisor** James Kussow	

To all you Java folks who continue to doGoodStuff( )

ABOUT THE AUTHORS

Bert Bates was a lead developer for many of Sun's Java certification exams, including the SCJP exam. He is a forum moderator on JavaRanch.com and has been developing software for more than 20 years. Bert is the co-author of several best-selling Java books, and he was a founding member of Sun's original Java Champions program.

Kathy Sierra was a lead developer for the SCJP exam. Kathy worked as a Sun "master trainer," and in 1997, founded JavaRanch.com, the world's largest Java community web site. Her best-selling Java books have won multiple Software Development Magazine awards, and she was a founding member of Sun's original Java Champions program.

Technical Review Superstars

Once again, we called on a brilliant collection of JavaRanch.com moderators to provide the technical review (and technical editing) for this book. Wow! These guys are awesome, truly.

Roel

Devaka

Top honors go to **Roel De Nijs**. Roel has an amazing eye for detail (he claims to shoot a mean game of snooker, too). His many suggestions improved this book immeasurably. Roel, we can't thank you enough.

Coming in a close second, we have a tie between **Devaka Cooray** and **Jeanne Boyarsky**. Not only did Devaka do a fantastic job as a reviewer, he contributed some of the book's gnarliest questions. (If you find yourself banging your head over a really tough question, you might just have Devaka to ~~curse~~ thank.) He is truly a renaissance man. If he's not up to his ankles in some twisty bit of software architecture, he likes to relax over recreational mathematics.

Jeanne

Christophe

Jeanne, what can we say? Jeanne is tireless AND relentless. On the surface you might think that Jeanne is very mild mannered, but what you don't know is that in her off hours, she and her team of evil high school scientists are plotting to control the world with an army of killer, attack robots. Jeanne, thanks for all your help.

Also making some really great saves were **Christophe Verré**, **Martijn Verburg**, and **Deepak Bala**. Christophe has helped us before—now that's dedication!

Rounding out the team were **Henry Wong**, **Mark Spritzler**, **Jesper Young**, and **Fred Rosenberger**. Thanks for your help guys, and Mark and Fred, thanks for helping us out... again!

Stop the presses! At the last possible minute our old friend **Mikalai Zaikin** dropped in and saved the day with a few huge edits... thanks Mikalai!

CONTENTS

ACKNOWLEDGMENTS

Bert and Kathy would like to thank:

- All of our patient and generous friends at McGraw-Hill: Tim Green (have we really been doing this for eight years now?), Jody McKenzie (who put up with us, again), Stephanie Evans, Madhu Bhardwaj, Mike McGee, and Meghan Riley.
- Evelyn Cartagena, for getting us started in the certification biz.
- Eden and Skyler, for putting up with their parents' weird, author-y lifestyle.
- Paul Wheaton, for running JavaRanch. Oh, and for all the other moderators and ranchers at the ranch.
- Steinar and Lucy, for all your help in keeping our horsemanship passion alive. We promise we'll do more riding now that the writing is done!
- Our competition Icelandic horses (and buddies) Eyra, Vafi, and Draumur. And, of course, our emergency backup horses, Andi and Kara. Tolt on!
- Everyone else who adds so much to our lives: Jennifer, Annette, Cait, Steindor, Bryan and Kathy, Mary, Eric, Beth, Morgan and Alex, Gabriele, and of course Lenstar.
- Finally, to La Femme Nikita, rodent assassin.

INTRODUCTION

Just How Hard Is the OCP Java SE Programmer Exam?

Since you've decided to pick this book up, we're guessing that you're considering taking the OCP Java SE 6 Programmer exam.

The OCP Java SE Programmer exam is considered one of the hardest in the IT industry, and we can tell you from experience that a large percentage of exam candidates go in to the test unprepared. As programmers, we tend to learn only what we need to complete our current project, given the insane deadlines we're usually under. But this exam attempts to prove your complete understanding of the Java language, not just the parts of it you've become familiar with in your work.

Experience alone will rarely get you through this exam with a passing mark, because even the things you think you know might work just a little different than you imagined. It isn't enough to be able to get your code to work correctly; you must understand the core fundamentals in a deep way, and with enough breadth to cover virtually anything that could crop up in the course of using the language.

What this Book Is (and Is Not)

As we'll discuss again in Chapter 4, most successful candidates do three things:

- Study with a good study guide
- Take a lot of mock exams
- Write a lot of code

This book focuses on the last two items of the preceding list. It is NOT a study guide. If you haven't worked with a good study guide, and you find that you're scoring well on the practice exams in this book, count yourself unusual. Our experience, working with thousands of candidates, is that taking mock exams alone isn't enough to pass this exam. (Our main goal with this book is to supplement our study guide.)

The basic study plan we recommend is that you do a lot of reading and coding before taking the four full mock exams in this book.

How to Use this Book's Six Exams

This book begins with two short (14-question) assessment exams. These exams are meant to help you determine whether you've done enough preparation to tackle the book's remaining four full exams.

After the two assessment exams comes the first full (60-question) practice exam. After that, you'll find a short chapter that will give you some tips and ideas for coding exercises you can do to further your studies.

Finally, three more full 60-question practice exams are included. We recommend that after each exam you document the areas where you still need work, and do some more preparation before the next exam.

Study Tips

First and foremost, give yourself plenty of time to study. Java is a complex programming language, and you can't expect to cram what you need to know into a single study session. It is a field best learned over time, by studying a subject and then applying your knowledge. Build yourself a study schedule and stick to it, but be reasonable about the pressure you put on yourself, especially if you're studying in addition to your regular duties at work.

One easy technique to use in studying for certification exams is the 15-minutes-per-day effort. Simply study for a minimum of 15 minutes every day. It is a small but significant commitment. If you have a day where you just can't focus, then give up after 15 minutes. If you have a day where it flows completely for you, study longer. As long as you have more of the "flow days," your chances of succeeding are excellent.

We strongly recommend you use flash cards when preparing for the Programmer's exam. A flash card is simply a 3 × 5 or 4 × 6 index card with a question on the front, and the answer on the back. You construct these cards yourself as you go through a chapter, capturing any topic you think might need more memorization or practice time. You can drill yourself with them by reading the question, thinking through the answer, and then turning the card over to see if you're correct. Or you can get another person to help you by holding up the card with the question facing you, and then verifying your answer. Most of our students have found these to be tremendously helpful, especially because they're so portable that while you're in study mode, you can take them everywhere. Best not to use them while driving, though, except at red lights. We've taken ours everywhere—the doctor's office, restaurants, theaters, you name it.

Certification study groups are another excellent resource, and you won't find a larger or more willing community than on the JavaRanch.com Big Moose Saloon certification forums. If you have a question from this book, or any other mock exam question you may have stumbled upon, posting a question in a certification forum will get you an answer, in nearly all cases, within a day—usually, within a few hours. You'll find us (the authors) there several times a week, helping those just starting out on their exam preparation journey. (You won't actually think of it as anything as pleasant-sounding as a "journey" by the time you're ready to take the exam.)

Finally, we recommend that you write a lot of little Java programs! During the course of writing this book, we wrote hundreds of small programs, and if you listen to what the most successful candidates say (you know, those guys who got 98 percent), they almost always report that they wrote a lot of code.

Exam Taking Tips

As much as possible, we've tried to structure the questions in this book to match the "look and feel," the complexity, and the level of detail of the questions on the real exam. The following are a collection of fun facts relating to the real exam, and the practice exams in this book that should also help you feel like you're in familiar territory when you sit down to take the actual exam at a test center.

The Constraints of Worldwide Consistency

One of the great things about the OCP Java SE Programmer certification is that it's recognized globally. In order to achieve such recognition, the test centers throughout the world are as standardized as possible. While this is great from the perspective of fairness, it does impose some constraints:

- The test engine must run on the lowest common denominator hardware.
- The exam's question formats must be universally supported.

What this means to you is that the code samples you'll be analyzing are often poorly formatted (so that you can see a lot of code in a small space), or that you'll have to do a lot of scrolling up and down to see all the code for a given question. The questions in this book are formatted to emulate what you'll encounter at your actual test center.

Question Formats

The OCP Java SE Programmer exam has two styles of questions: Multiple Choice and Drag and Drop. Regardless of format, there is no **partial credit** for a given question. If you get most, but not all, of a question correct, you get zero credit for that question.

Multiple Choice   For each question, a scenario (often including some Java code) will be presented, followed by a list of possible answers. On the real exam, you will ALWAYS be told how many correct answers to choose. In this book, we often say: "Choose all that apply." We want to make it a bit tougher for you.

These exams typically number the lines of code in a question. When a code listing starts with line 1, it means you're looking at an entire source file. If a code listing starts at a line number greater than 1, that means you're looking at a partial source file. When looking at a partial source file, assume that the code you can't see is correct. (For instance, unless explicitly stated, you can assume that a partial source file will have the correct import and package statements.)

Drag and Drop   On the real exam, you should expect that about 20–25 percent of the questions you encounter will be drag-and-drop style. This book includes eight simulated drag-and-drop questions—enough to give you a rough idea of what you'll encounter on the real exam. Drag-and-drop questions typically consist of three components:

- **A scenario**   A short description of the task you are meant to complete.
- **A partially completed task**   A code listing, a table, or a directory tree. The partially completed task will contain empty slots, which are indicated with (typically yellow) boxes. These boxes need to be filled to complete the task.
- **A set of possible "fragment" answers**   You will click fragments (typically blue boxes) and drag and drop them into the correct empty slots. The question's scenario will tell you whether you can reuse fragments.

Most drag-and-drop questions will have anywhere from 4 to 10 empty slots to fill, and typically a few more fragments than are needed (usually some fragments are left unused). Drag-and-drop questions are often the most complex on the exam, and the number of possible answer combinations makes them almost impossible to guess.

INSIDE THE EXAM

In regards to drag-and-drop questions, there is a huge problem with the testing software at many of the testing centers worldwide. In general, the testing software allows you to review questions you've already answered as often as you'd like.

In the case of drag-and-drop questions, however, many candidates have reported that if they choose to review a question, the software will erase their previous answer! BE CAREFUL! Until this problem is corrected, we recommend you keep a list of which questions are drag and drop, so you won't review one unintentionally. Another good idea is to write down your drag-and-drop answers so that if one gets erased, it will be less painful to re-create the answer.

This brings us to another issue that some candidates have reported. The testing center is supposed to provide you with sufficient writing implements so you can work problems out "on paper." In some cases, the centers have provided inadequate markers and dry-erase boards that are too small and cumbersome to use effectively. We recommend you call ahead and verify that you will be supplied with actual pencils and several sheets of paper.

Time Management

The real exam has 60 questions (the same for the four full practice exams in this book). You need 35 correct questions to pass. (The online web site for the OCP Java SE Programmer exam states this, not too helpfully, as 58.33 percent.) As of this writing, you will be given three hours to complete the exam (three minutes per question), which should be more than enough time. Always check with the exam center before taking your exam because this information is subject to change.

You are allowed to answer questions in any order, and you can go back and check your answers after you've gone through the test. There are no penalties for wrong answers, so it's better to at least attempt an answer than to not give one at all.

A good strategy for taking the exam is to go through it once and answer all the questions that come to you quickly. You can then go back and do the others. Answering one question might jog your memory for how to answer a previous one.

The real exam is presented in full screen, with a single question per screen. Navigation buttons allow you to move forward and backward between questions. In the upper-right corner of the screen, counters show the number of questions and the time remaining. Most important, there is a Mark check box in the upper-left corner of the screen—this will prove to be a critical tool, as explained next.

As you're taking the exam, if you're not entirely confident in your answer to a question, answer it anyway, but check the Mark box to flag it for later review. In the event that you run out of time, at least you've provided a "first guess" answer, rather than leaving it blank.

Second, go back through the entire test, using the insight you gained from the first go-through. For example, if the entire test looks difficult, you'll know better than to spend more than a minute or two on each question. Create a pacing with small milestones—for example, "I need to answer 10 questions every 25 minutes."

At this stage, it's probably a good idea to skip past the time-consuming questions, marking them for the next pass. Try to finish this phase before you're 50–60 percent through the testing time.

Third, go back through all the questions you marked for review, using the Review Marked button in the question review screen. This step includes taking a second look at all the questions you were unsure of in previous passes, as well as tackling the time-consuming ones you deferred until now. Chisel away at this group of questions until you've answered them all.

If you're more comfortable with a previously marked question, unmark the Review Marked button now. Otherwise, leave it marked. Work your way through the time-consuming questions now, especially those requiring manual calculations. Unmark them when you're satisfied with the answer.

By the end of this step, you've answered every question in the test, despite having reservations about some of your answers. If you run out of time in the next step, at least you won't lose points for lack of an answer. You're in great shape if you still have 10–20 percent of your time remaining.

Technical Tips

Be very careful reading the code examples. Check for syntax errors first: count curly braces, semicolons, and parentheses, and then make sure there are as many left ones as right ones. Look for capitalization errors and other such syntax problems before trying to figure out what the code does.

Many of the questions on the exam will hinge on subtleties of syntax. You will need to have a thorough knowledge of the Java language in order to succeed.

1

Self-Assessment
Test 1

How Close Are You to Ready?

The 14-question assessment tests in this chapter and Chapter 2 are designed to help you answer the question: "How close am I to ready?" The best way to start answering the readiness question is to set aside 42 minutes (yes, 42!) and take the first assessment exam.

As we discussed in the introduction, many Java programmers with years of experience are surprised by the depth and breadth of topics covered in the OCP Java SE 6 Programmer exam. The assessment exams in this chapter and Chapter 2 are designed to help you determine how much more studying you'll need to do before you take the real exam. Each of the first two chapters includes a table to help you match your assessment test results to a rough study plan. In a nutshell, for each of the assessment exams, 8 (out of 14) correct questions is on the boundary of achieving a passing score.

The exams in this book are intended primarily for candidates who feel they've mostly completed their studies and want additional exam practice. If your scores on the assessment exams are not near the passing mark, we recommend you do more studying before trying any of the four full practice exams included in later chapters. In other words, this book's job is to help you put the final touches on your OCP Java SE 6 Programmer preparation. It's NOT intended to be your primary study guide.

With all that said, set your timer to 42 minutes and dive in. We'll see you on the other side...

ASSESSMENT TEST I

The real exam has 60 questions and you are given three hours. Since this assessment exam has only 14 questions, allow yourself only 42 minutes to complete this exam. On the real exam, and on all of the exams in this book, give yourself credit only for those questions that you answer 100 percent correctly. For instance, if a question has three correct answers and you get two of the three correct, you get zero credit. There is no partial credit. Good luck!

1. Given:

```
2. public class Bunnies {
3.    static int count = 0;
4.    Bunnies() {
5.       while(count < 10) new Bunnies(++count);
6.    }
7.    Bunnies(int x) { super(); }
8.    public static void main(String[] args) {
9.       new Bunnies();
10.      new Bunnies(count);
11.      System.out.println(count++);
12.   }
13. }
```

What is the result?

A. 9

B. 10

C. 11

D. 12

E. Compilation fails.

F. An exception is thrown at runtime.

2. Given:

```
2. public class Jail {
3.    private int x = 4;
4.    public static void main(String[] args) {
5.       protected int x = 6;
6.       new Jail().new Cell().slam();
7.    }
8.    class Cell {
9.       void slam() { System.out.println("throw away key " + x); }
10.   }
11. }
```

Which are true? (Choose all that apply.)

A. Compilation succeeds.

B. The output is "throw away key 4".

C. The output is "throw away key 6".

D. Compilation fails due to an error on line 5.

E. Compilation fails due to an error on line 6.

F. Compilation fails due to an error on line 9.

3. Given:

```
2. public class Fabric extends Thread {
3.    public static void main(String[] args) {
4.       Thread t = new Thread(new Fabric());
5.       Thread t2 = new Thread(new Fabric());
6.       t.start();
7.       t2.start();
8.    }
9.    public static void run() {
10.       for(int i = 0; i < 2; i++)
11.          System.out.print(Thread.currentThread().getName() + " ");
12.    }
13. }
```

Which are true? (Choose all that apply.)

A. Compilation fails.

B. No output is produced.

C. The output could be Thread-1 Thread-3 Thread-1 Thread-2

D. The output could be Thread-1 Thread-3 Thread-1 Thread-3

E. The output could be Thread-1 Thread-1 Thread-2 Thread-2

F. The output could be Thread-1 Thread-3 Thread-3 Thread-1

G. The output could be Thread-1 Thread-3 Thread-1 Thread-1

4. Given:

```
2. class Feline { }
3. public class BarnCat2 extends Feline {
4.    public static void main(String[] args) {
5.       Feline ff = new Feline();
6.       BarnCat2 b = new BarnCat2();
7.       // insert code here
8.    }
9. }
```

Which, inserted independently at line 7, compile? (Choose all that apply.)

A. `if (b instanceof ff) System.out.print("1 ");`

B. `if (b.instanceof(ff)) System.out.print("2 ");`

C. `if (b instanceof Feline) System.out.print("3 ");`

D. `if (b instanceOf Feline) System.out.print("4 ");`

E. `if (b.instanceof(Feline)) System.out.print("5 ");`

5. Given:

```
2. public class Choosy {
3.    public static void main(String[] args) {
4.       String result = "";
5.       int x = 7, y = 8;
6.       if (x == 3) { result += "1"; }
7.       else if (x > 9) { result += "2"; }
8.       else if (y < 9) { result += "3"; }
9.       else if (x == 7) { result += "4"; }
10.      else { result += "5"; }
11.      System.out.println(result);
12.   }
13. }
```

What is the result? (Choose all that apply.)

A. 3

B. 34

C. 35

D. 345

E. Compilation fails due to an error on line 5.

F. Compilation fails due to errors on lines 8 and 9.

G. Compilation fails due to errors on lines 7, 8, and 9.

6. Given:

```
1. public class Twine {
2.    public static void main(String[] args) {
3.       String s = "";
4.       StringBuffer sb1 = new StringBuffer("hi");
5.       StringBuffer sb2 = new StringBuffer("hi");
6.       StringBuffer sb3 = new StringBuffer(sb2);
7.       StringBuffer sb4 = sb3;
8.       if (sb1.equals(sb2)) s += "1 ";
9.       if (sb2.equals(sb3)) s += "2 ";
```

```
10.      if(sb3.equals(sb4)) s += "3 ";
11.      String s2 = "hi";
12.      String s3 = "hi";
13.      String s4 = s3;
14.      if(s2.equals(s3)) s += "4 ";
15.      if(s3.equals(s4)) s += "5 ";
16.      System.out.println(s);
17.    }
18. }
```

What is the result?

A. 1 3

B. 1 5

C. 1 2 3

D. 1 4 5

E. 3 4 5

F. 1 3 4 5

G. 1 2 3 4 5

H. Compilation fails.

7. Which are true? (Choose all that apply.)

A. All classes of Exception extend Error.

B. All classes of Error extend Exception.

C. All Errors must be handled or declared.

D. All classes of Exception extend Throwable.

E. All Throwables must be handled or declared.

F. All Exceptions must be handled or declared.

G. RuntimeExceptions need never be handled or declared.

8. Given:

```
2. import java.util.*;
3. public class Birthdays {
4.    public static void main(String[] args) {
5.      Map<Friends, String> hm = new HashMap<Friends, String>();
6.      hm.put(new Friends("Charis"), "Summer 2009");
7.      hm.put(new Friends("Draumur"), "Spring 2002");
8.      Friends f = new Friends(args[0]);
9.      System.out.println(hm.get(f));
10.    }
11. }
```

```
12. class Friends {
13.    String name;
14.    Friends(String n) { name = n; }
15. }
```

And the command line invocation:

```
java Birthdays Draumur
```

What is the result?

A. `null`

B. `Draumur`

C. `Spring 2002`

D. Compilation fails.

E. The output is unpredictable.

F. An exception is thrown at runtime.

G. `Friends@XXXX` (where XXXX is a representation of a hashcode)

9. Given:

```
2. import java.util.*;
3. class Cereal { }
4. public class Flakes extends Cereal {
5.    public static void main(String[] args) {
6.       List<Flakes> c0 = new List<Flakes>();
7.       List<Cereal> c1 = new ArrayList<Cereal>();
8.       List<Cereal> c2 = new ArrayList<Flakes>();
9.       List<Flakes> c3 = new ArrayList<Cereal>();
10.      List<Object> c4 = new ArrayList<Flakes>();
11.      ArrayList<Cereal> c5 = new ArrayList<Flakes>();
12.   }
13. }
```

Which are true? (Choose all that apply.)

A. Compilation succeeds.

B. Compilation fails due to an error on line 6.

C. Compilation fails due to an error on line 7.

D. Compilation fails due to an error on line 8.

E. Compilation fails due to an error on line 9.

F. Compilation fails due to an error on line 10.

G. Compilation fails due to an error on line 11.

10. Given:

```
3. public class RediMix extends Concrete {
4.    RediMix() { System.out.println("r "); }
5.    public static void main(String[] args) {
6.      new RediMix();
7.    }
8. }
9. class Concrete extends Sand {
10.   Concrete() { System.out.print("c "); }
11.   private Concrete(String s) { }
12. }
13. abstract class Sand {
14.   Sand() { System.out.print("s "); }
15. }
```

What is the result?

A. r

B. c r

C. r c

D. s c r

E. r c s

F. Compilation fails due to a single error in the code.

G. Compilation fails due to multiple errors in the code.

11. Which statement(s) are true? (Choose all that apply.)

A. Coupling is the OO principle most closely associated with hiding a class's implementation details.

B. Coupling is the OO principle most closely associated with making sure classes know about other classes only through their APIs.

C. Coupling is the OO principle most closely associated with making sure a class is designed with a single, well-focused purpose.

D. Coupling is the OO principle most closely associated with allowing a single object to be seen as having many types.

12. Given:

```
2. class Mosey implements Runnable {
3.    public void run() {
4.      for(int i = 0; i < 1000; i++) {
5.        System.out.print(Thread.currentThread().getId() + "-" + i + " ");
6. } } }
```

```
7.  public class Stroll {
8.    public static void main(String[] args) throws Exception {
9.      Thread t1 = new Thread(new Mosey());
10.     // insert code here
11.   }
12. }
```

Which of the following code fragments, inserted independently at line 10, will probably run most (or all) of the main thread's run() method invocation before running most of the t1 thread's run() method invocation? (Choose all that apply.)

A. ```
t1.setPriority(1);
new Mosey().run();
t1.start();
```

B. ```
t1.setPriority(9);
new Mosey().run();
t1.start();
```

C. ```
t1.setPriority(1);
t1.start();
new Mosey().run();
```

D. ```
t1.setPriority(8);
t1.start();
new Mosey().run();
```

13. Given:

```
37.   boolean b = false;
38.   int i = 7;
39.   double d = 1.23;
40.   float f = 4.56f;
41.
42.   // insert code here
```

Which line(s) of code, inserted independently at line 42, will compile and run without exception? (Choose all that apply.)

A. `System.out.printf(" %b", b);`

B. `System.out.printf(" %i", i);`

C. `System.out.format(" %d", d);`

D. `System.out.format(" %d", i);`

E. `System.out.format(" %f", f);`

14. Given:

```
1. import java.util.*;
2. public class MyPancake implements Pancake {
3.    public static void main(String[] args) {
4.      List<String> x = new ArrayList<String>();
5.      x.add("3");  x.add("7");  x.add("5");
6.      List<String> y = new MyPancake().doStuff(x);
7.      y.add("1");
8.      System.out.println(x);
9.    }
10.   List<String> doStuff(List<String> z) {
11.     z.add("9");
12.     return z;
13.   }
14. }
15. interface Pancake {
16.   List<String> doStuff(List<String> s);
17. }
```

What is the most likely result?

A. [3, 7, 5]

B. [3, 7, 5, 9]

C. [3, 7, 5, 9, 1]

D. Compilation fails.

E. An exception is thrown at runtime.

QUICK ANSWER KEY

1. B	**6.** E	**11.** B
2. D	**7.** D, G	**12.** A, B, C
3. A	**8.** A	**13.** A, D, E
4. C	**9.** B, D, E, F, G	**14.** D
5. A	**10.** D	

ASSESSMENT TEST 1: ANSWERS

1. Given:

```
2. public class Bunnies {
3.    static int count = 0;
4.    Bunnies() {
5.       while(count < 10) new Bunnies(++count);
6.    }
7.    Bunnies(int x) { super(); }
8.    public static void main(String[] args) {
9.       new Bunnies();
10.      new Bunnies(count);
11.      System.out.println(count++);
12.   }
13. }
```

What is the result?

A. 9

B. 10

C. 11

D. 12

E. Compilation fails.

F. An exception is thrown at runtime.

Answer (for Objective 5.4):

☑ **B** is correct. It's legal to invoke "new" from within a constructor, and it's legal to call super() on a class with no explicit superclass. On the real exam, it's important to watch out for pre- and post-incrementing.

☒ **A**, **C**, **D**, **E**, and **F** are incorrect based on the above.

2. Given:

```
2. public class Jail {
3.    private int x = 4;
4.    public static void main(String[] args) {
5.       protected int x = 6;
6.       new Jail().new Cell().slam();
7.    }
8.    class Cell {
9.       void slam() { System.out.println("throw away key " + x); }
10.   }
11. }
```

Which are true? (Choose all that apply.)

A. Compilation succeeds.

B. The output is "`throw away key 4`".

C. The output is "`throw away key 6`".

D. Compilation fails due to an error on line 5.

E. Compilation fails due to an error on line 6.

F. Compilation fails due to an error on line 9.

> Answer (for Objective 1.3):
>
> ☑ **D** is correct. Line 5 is declaring local variable "`x`", and local variables cannot have access modifiers. If line 5 read "`int x = 6`", the code would compile and the result would be "`throw away key 4`". Line 5 creates an anonymous `Jail` object, an anonymous `Cell` object, and invokes `slam()`. Inner classes have access to their enclosing class's `private` variables.
>
> ☒ **A, B, C, E,** and **F** are incorrect based on the above.

3. Given:

```
2. public class Fabric extends Thread {
3.    public static void main(String[] args) {
4.       Thread t = new Thread(new Fabric());
5.       Thread t2 = new Thread(new Fabric());
6.       t.start();
7.       t2.start();
8.    }
9.    public static void run() {
10.      for(int i = 0; i < 2; i++)
11.         System.out.print(Thread.currentThread().getName() + " ");
12.   }
13. }
```

Which are true? (Choose all that apply.)

A. Compilation fails.

B. No output is produced.

C. The output could be `Thread-1 Thread-3 Thread-1 Thread-2`

D. The output could be `Thread-1 Thread-3 Thread-1 Thread-3`

E. The output could be `Thread-1 Thread-1 Thread-2 Thread-2`

F. The output could be `Thread-1 Thread-3 Thread-3 Thread-1`

G. The output could be `Thread-1 Thread-3 Thread-1 Thread-1`

Answer (for Objective 4.1):

☑ **A** is correct. Fabric does not correctly extend Thread because the `run()` method cannot be `static`. If `run()` was correctly implemented, then **D**, **E**, and **F** would have been correct. Thread names do *NOT* have to be sequentially assigned.

☒ **C** is wrong even if `run()` is correct because only two threads are involved. **G** is wrong even if `run()` is correct, because `run()` is called only once per thread.

---

4. Given:

```
2. class Feline { }
3. public class BarnCat2 extends Feline {
4.    public static void main(String[] args) {
5.      Feline ff = new Feline();
6.      BarnCat2 b = new BarnCat2();
7.      // insert code here
8.    }
9. }
```

Which, inserted independently at line 7, compile? (Choose all that apply.)

A. `if(b instanceof ff) System.out.print("1 ");`

B. `if(b.instanceof(ff)) System.out.print("2 ");`

C. `if(b instanceof Feline) System.out.print("3 ");`

D. `if(b instanceOf Feline) System.out.print("4 ");`

E. `if(b.instanceof(Feline)) System.out.print("5 ");`

Answer (for Objective 7.6):

☑ **C** is the correct syntax.

☒ **A**, **B**, **D**, and **E** all use incorrect syntax for the `instanceof` operator.

---

5. Given:

```
2. public class Choosy {
3.    public static void main(String[] args) {
4.      String result = "";
5.      int x = 7, y = 8;
```

```
 6.      if(x == 3) { result += "1"; }
 7.      else if (x > 9) { result += "2"; }
 8.      else if (y < 9) { result += "3"; }
 9.      else if (x == 7) { result += "4"; }
10.      else { result += "5"; }
11.      System.out.println(result);
12.    }
13.  }
```

What is the result? (Choose all that apply.)

A. 3

B. 34

C. 35

D. 345

E. Compilation fails due to an error on line 5.

F. Compilation fails due to errors on lines 8 and 9.

G. Compilation fails due to errors on lines 7, 8, and 9.

Answer (for Objective 2.1):

☑ **A** is correct. It's legal to declare several variables on a single line, and it's legal to have multiple else-if statements. Once an else-if succeeds, the remaining else-if and else statements in the block are ignored.

☒ **B, C, D, E, F,** and **G** are incorrect based on the above.

6. Given:

```
 1. public class Twine {
 2.    public static void main(String[] args) {
 3.       String s = "";
 4.       StringBuffer sb1 = new StringBuffer("hi");
 5.       StringBuffer sb2 = new StringBuffer("hi");
 6.       StringBuffer sb3 = new StringBuffer(sb2);
 7.       StringBuffer sb4 = sb3;
 8.       if(sb1.equals(sb2)) s += "1 ";
 9.       if(sb2.equals(sb3)) s += "2 ";
10.       if(sb3.equals(sb4)) s += "3 ";
11.       String s2 = "hi";
12.       String s3 = "hi";
13.       String s4 = s3;
```

```
14.      if(s2.equals(s3)) s += "4 ";
15.      if(s3.equals(s4)) s += "5 ";
16.      System.out.println(s);
17.    }
18. }
```

What is the result?

A. 1 3

B. 1 5

C. 1 2 3

D. 1 4 5

E. 3 4 5

F. 1 3 4 5

G. 1 2 3 4 5

H. Compilation fails.

Answer (for Objective 3.1):

☑ **E** is correct. The `StringBuffer` class doesn't override the `equals()` method, so two different `StringBuffer` objects with the same value will not be equal according to the `equals()` method. On the other hand, the `String` class's `equals()` method has been overridden so that two different `String` objects with the same value will be considered equal according to the `equals()` method.

☒ **A, B, C, D, F, G,** and **H** are incorrect based on the above.

7. Which are true? (Choose all that apply.)

   A. All classes of Exception extend Error.

   B. All classes of Error extend Exception.

   C. All Errors must be handled or declared.

   D. All classes of Exception extend Throwable.

   E. All Throwables must be handled or declared.

   F. All Exceptions must be handled or declared.

   G. RuntimeExceptions need never be handled or declared.

Answer (for Objective 2.5):

☑ **D** and **G** are correct. While it's true that this is a strict memorization question, some facts are so essential that you just have to burn them into your brain. The class hierarchy relationships between Throwable, Error, Exception, and RuntimeException fall into that "gotta know 'em" category.

☒ **A, B, C, E,** and **F** are incorrect statements.

8. Given:

```
2. import java.util.*;
3. public class Birthdays {
4.    public static void main(String[] args) {
5.       Map<Friends, String> hm = new HashMap<Friends, String>();
6.       hm.put(new Friends("Charis"), "Summer 2009");
7.       hm.put(new Friends("Draumur"), "Spring 2002");
8.       Friends f = new Friends(args[0]);
9.       System.out.println(hm.get(f));
10.    }
11. }
12. class Friends {
13.    String name;
14.    Friends(String n) { name = n; }
15. }
```

And the command line invocation:

```
java Birthdays Draumur
```

What is the result?

A. `null`

B. `Draumur`

C. `Spring 2002`

D. Compilation fails.

E. The output is unpredictable.

F. An exception is thrown at runtime.

G. `Friends@XXXX` (where XXXX is a representation of a hashcode)

Answer (for Objective 6.2):

☑ **A** is correct. The `Friends` class doesn't override `equals()` and `hashCode()`, so the key to the `HashMap` is a specific instance of `Friends`, not the value of a given `Friends` instance's name.

☒ **B, C, D, E, F,** and **G** are incorrect based on the above.

9. Given:

```
2. import java.util.*;
3. class Cereal { }
4. public class Flakes extends Cereal {
5.    public static void main(String[] args) {
6.       List<Flakes> c0 = new List<Flakes>();
7.       List<Cereal> c1 = new ArrayList<Cereal>();
8.       List<Cereal> c2 = new ArrayList<Flakes>();
9.       List<Flakes> c3 = new ArrayList<Cereal>();
10.       List<Object> c4 = new ArrayList<Flakes>();
11.       ArrayList<Cereal> c5 = new ArrayList<Flakes>();
12.    }
13. }
```

Which are true? (Choose all that apply.)

A. Compilation succeeds.

B. Compilation fails due to an error on line 6.

C. Compilation fails due to an error on line 7.

D. Compilation fails due to an error on line 8.

E. Compilation fails due to an error on line 9.

F. Compilation fails due to an error on line 10.

G. Compilation fails due to an error on line 11.

Answer (for Objective 6.3):

☑ **B, D, E, F,** and **G** are correct because those lines of code will *NOT* compile. **B,** (line 6), is incorrect because List is abstract. **D, E, F,** and **G** are all incorrect because polymorphic assignments can't be applied to the generic type parameter.

☒ **A** is incorrect based on the above. **C** is incorrect because line 7 uses legal syntax.

10. Given:

```
3. public class RediMix extends Concrete {
4.    RediMix() { System.out.println("r "); }
5.    public static void main(String[] args) {
6.       new RediMix();
7.    }
8. }
9. class Concrete extends Sand {
10.    Concrete() { System.out.print("c "); }
11.    private Concrete(String s) { }
12. }
13. abstract class Sand {
14.    Sand() { System.out.print("s "); }
15. }
```

What is the result?

A. r

B. c r

C. r c

D. s c r

E. r c s

F. Compilation fails due to a single error in the code.

G. Compilation fails due to multiple errors in the code.

Answer (for Objective 1.5):

☑ **D** is correct. It's legal for abstract classes to have constructors, and it's legal for a constructor to be private. Normal constructor chaining is the result of this code.

☒ **A, B, C, E, F,** and **G** are incorrect based on the above.

11. Which statement(s) are true? (Choose all that apply.)

A. Coupling is the OO principle most closely associated with hiding a class's implementation details.

B. Coupling is the OO principle most closely associated with making sure classes know about other classes only through their APIs.

C. Coupling is the OO principle most closely associated with making sure a class is designed with a single, well-focused purpose.

D. Coupling is the OO principle most closely associated with allowing a single object to be seen as having many types.

Answer (for Objective 5.1):

☑   **B** is correct.

☒   **A** refers to encapsulation, **C** refers to cohesion, and **D** refers to polymorphism.

12. Given:

```
2. class Mosey implements Runnable {
3.    public void run() {
4.       for(int i = 0; i < 1000; i++) {
5.          System.out.print(Thread.currentThread().getId() + "-" + i + " ");
6. } } }
7. public class Stroll {
8.    public static void main(String[] args) throws Exception {
9.       Thread t1 = new Thread(new Mosey());
10.      // insert code here
11.   }
12. }
```

Which of the following code fragments, inserted independently at line 10, will probably run most (or all) of the main thread's `run()` method invocation before running most of the `t1` thread's `run()` method invocation? (Choose all that apply.)

A. ```
t1.setPriority(1);
new Mosey().run();
t1.start();
```

B.  ```
t1.setPriority(9);
new Mosey().run();
t1.start();
```

C. ```
t1.setPriority(1);
t1.start();
new Mosey().run();
```

D.  ```
t1.setPriority(8);
t1.start();
new Mosey().run();
```

Answer (for Objective 4.2):

☑   **A**, **B**, and **C** are correct. For **A** and **B**, the main thread executes the `run()` method before it starts `t1`. **C** is correct because `t1` is set to a low priority, giving the main thread scheduling priority.

☒   **D** is incorrect because by setting `t1`'s priority to 8, the `t1` thread will tend to execute mostly before the main thread.

13. Given:

```
37.  boolean b = false;
38.  int i = 7;
39.  double d = 1.23;
40.  float f = 4.56f;
41.
42.  // insert code here
```

Which line(s) of code, inserted independently at line 42, will compile and run without exception? (Choose all that apply.)

A. `System.out.printf(" %b", b);`

B. `System.out.printf(" %i", i);`

C. `System.out.format(" %d", d);`

D. `System.out.format(" %d", i);`

E. `System.out.format(" %f", f);`

Answer (for Objective 3.4):

☑ **A, D,** and **E** have the correct conversion characters for their respective argument. Remember that `printf()` and `format()` have the same functionality.

☒ **B** is incorrect because (as we can see with answer **D**), integers should use `%d`. **C** is incorrect because both floats and doubles should use `%f`.

14. Given:

```
1.  import java.util.*;
2.  public class MyPancake implements Pancake {
3.    public static void main(String[] args) {
4.      List<String> x = new ArrayList<String>();
5.      x.add("3"); x.add("7"); x.add("5");
6.      List<String> y = new MyPancake().doStuff(x);
7.      y.add("1");
8.      System.out.println(x);
9.    }
10.   List<String> doStuff(List<String> z) {
11.     z.add("9");
12.     return z;
13.   }
14. }
15. interface Pancake {
16.   List<String> doStuff(List<String> s);
17. }
```

What is the most likely result?

A.   [3, 7, 5]

B.   [3, 7, 5, 9]

C.   [3, 7, 5, 9, 1]

D.   Compilation fails.

E.   An exception is thrown at runtime.

Answer (for Objective 7.1):

☑   **D** is correct. `MyPancake.doStuff()` must be marked `public`. If it is, then **C** would be correct.

☒   **A, B, C**, and **E** are incorrect based on the above.

Analyzing Your Results

Now that you've taken this book's first assessment exam, it's time to look at your results and figure out what they mean and what to do next.

As of this writing, a passing score on the OCP Java SE 6 Programmer exam is 58.33 percent (35 out of 60 questions). Of course, this chapter's assessment exam had only 14 questions, so if you got 8.1 of the 14 questions correct, then in theory you passed!

Now for the bad news... We picked 14 of the easiest questions in the book to be on this first assessment exam. Based on the fact that we thought these were easier than average questions, Table 1-1 is a rough guide to where you are in your studies:

| TABLE 1-1 | What Your Score Means |

Number of Correct Answers	Recommended Plan
0–5	You should do a LOT of studying before taking more of the exams in this book.
6–8	You should do a little more studying before taking more of the exams in this book.
9–11	You're right on the "passing" boundary; the next assessment test will tell you more.
12–14	You're probably ready to use the five remaining exams in this book to polish your skills, but start with the second assessment exam to verify this conclusion.

Creating Your Exam Log

The more you can pinpoint your weaknesses, the more focused and efficient your studies will be. We recommend you create a written log for each of the exams in this book, and for any other practice exams you take. Once you've taken a practice exam and scored it, go back through the exam and make a log. We like the rough format shown in Table 1-2, but you should modify it to suit your learning style. Note that we filled in several example rows to illustrate how you might fill in your logs.

Table 1-2 is an example of what a partial exam log might look like after you've filled it in. The more honest you are with yourself, the more useful these logs will be. For example, if you guessed on a question, even a little bit, it will be helpful to you to acknowledge that guess in your log. Another way to be honest with yourself is to reflect on whether you knew a certain topic thoroughly, or whether the question just happened to hit on your strong point.

TABLE 1-2	Sample Exam Log

Test Name: *Self-Assessment Test 1*

Q#	Topic	Objective	Correct	Notes
1	"new" and super() in a constructor	5.4-constructors	no	Confused super() with overloading.
2	else if's	2.1-if / switch	yes	I guessed on the nested part.
3	formatting characters	3.5-regex	no	Wow, I don't have these memorized!
4	threads, run() signature	4.1-threads	yes	This one seemed easy.
...				

In addition, it will help you to fill out ALL the columns in the log. The very act of thinking through them and then writing down your own summary of each question will be a great learning exercise. Be precise with your terms! Here are some examples:

- Are you referring to an instance of a class or a class?
- Call them reference variables, not pointers.
- Think in terms of a method's "signature."
- Call them "chained constructors."
- Use the phrase "handle or declare," and so on.

The most successful OCP Java SE 6 Programmer candidates we've seen take the time to learn the phrases and terms that experienced Java programmers use. When you find yourself thinking in terms of that vernacular, know that you're in good company—so fill out your logs.

More Study Tips

Some of the following ideas were covered in the introduction and bear repeating. Some of these ideas, however, are new.

Write Lots of Code Almost every test question in this book has the hidden benefit of being a great starting point for small coding projects. It's almost universally true that the candidates who score well on the OCP Java SE 6 Programmer exam wrote lots and lots of small Java programs during their studies. We wrote lots of programs as we wrote this book. Take the code you see in a question, type it in, compile it, and run it. Then, tweak the code, compile it, and run it again. Add `System.out.print` statements. Try to break stuff.

Don't Use an IDE   The team that created the actual exam wrote their code using a basic text editor, and they compiled and ran their code from the command line. Once you've got your basics covered, IDEs are great tools. While you're studying for the exam, they're not. *Usually* an IDE will give you the same result as you get from the command line, but not always! And the trick is in knowing when your results will vary.

Get a Good Study Guide   We're fond of the study guide written by a couple of hackers named Kathy and Bert, but several good study guides are available. We recommend you visit "the bunkhouse" at JavaRanch.com. It has tons of excellent book reviews, and based on those reviews and comments you can get a good sense of the styles and quality of the books you're considering.

We understand that these study guides can be expensive, but consider the value of your time. A good study guide can easily save you hundreds of hours of poking around the Internet trying to find the documentation you need. Sure, you could probably find most of the information for "free" on the Web, but that takes time. A good study guide represents a single source compendium of all that good info that's scattered around the Internet.

Make and Revise Flash Cards   Earlier in the chapter, we recommended you create exam logs and "Topics to Study" lists. Based on those documents, you can make flash cards as described in the introduction. Your exam logs and "Topics to Study" lists should help you decide which of your existing flash cards you can retire, and which new ones you should make.

Focus Your API Studies   The Java APIs are huge. Even the few packages and classes listed in the OCP Java SE 6 Programmer objectives make a daunting list. The good news is that the API-related questions in this book will tend to focus you on the parts of the API you need to know. Similarly, the better study guides and practice exams will also do a good job of focusing on those parts of the API that you really need to know. As mentioned earlier, read the reviews! Some practice exams are known to be well focused, and some less so. If you're really focused on the OCP Java SE 6 Programmer exam, stick to those practice exams that are more focused.

Common Questions and Complaints, and Some Answers

Over the years, we've heard a lot of questions and complaints from candidates. Here are some of the most common concerns we hear, and (we hope) some decent answers.

Why Is the Code Formatting so Terrible?

Remember, when you go to a test center to take the official test, you're going to a center that more or less has to be replicated on a world-wide basis. In other words, the hardware and test engine you use is more or less the same as you would discover in any test center in the world. That means your computer monitor probably won't be a high-resolution monitor, and you may have to scroll up and down to see all the code you need to review for a given question. That's life. In order to minimize the pain associated with low-res monitors, the exam creators often jam a LOT of code into small spaces. So when you see code like this

```
3. public class VLA implements Comparator<VLA> {
4.   int dishSize;
5.   public static void main(String[] args) {
6.     VLA[] va = {new VLA(40), new VLA(200), new VLA(60)};
7.     for(VLA v: va) System.out.print(v.dishSize + " ");
8. } }
```

understand that the exam team knew this was horrible formatting (and not an example of "best practices coding"). They were trying to help you do less scrolling.

Why Is There so Much Memorization?

Let's break this question down into two parts: the API and the language.

API Memorization

We often hear programmers say, "In the real world, when I have to use something from the API, I'm going to look it up anyway, rather than just trust my memory. So why do I have to memorize API stuff for the exam?"

A couple of reasons. First, an OCP Java SE 6 Programmer should know *how* to use the API in general. Second, if you've studied the commonly used packages in the API, you'll remember their basic capabilities even if you don't remember the exact details. This knowledge will make you a much better programmer. For instance, when we wrote this book, we had forgotten some of the API details that we needed to write the questions. However, we remembered where the "gotchas" were, and we knew what basic capabilities existed, so we were able to use the APIs quickly. That's part of being an OCP Java SE 6 Programmer and part of being a good programmer.

Language Memorization

We hear similar complaints about having to memorize language details. You should know that in the current version(s) of the exam, great care was taken to remove questions that focused on seldom-used "corner cases" in the language. The exam team's strategy was to write questions that test the kinds of constructs you're likely to encounter in the real world when looking at someone else's code. The second reason is similar to the API discussion. You might not, for instance, remember the exact syntax for using a switch statement, but you will remember its capabilities—and when it's the right tool to use, you'll be able to use it quickly and correctly. The bottom line is this: after studying for this exam, you *will* be a better Java programmer, and you *will* use the language more like it was intended.

exam

ⓦatch

Although we said this in the introduction, it bears repeating. In the real exam, EVERY multiple choice question will ALWAYS tell you how many correct answers there are. In other words, the real exam will never say, "Choose all that apply." When you're taking the real exam, if you get to a question you're not quite sure of, knowing the number of correct answers can help you narrow down the choices and make a better guess. (And guessing wrong DOES NOT hurt your score!) But in this book, we want to toughen you up. We want you to be extra-prepared, so we often say, "Choose all that apply."

exam
ⓦatch

The real exam has two kinds of questions: (1) multiple choice and (2) drag and drop. On the real exam, you should expect 15 to 20 percent of your questions to be drag-and-drop style. In this book, we've created a few questions (more like 4 percent) that attempt to emulate the kinds of drag-and-drop questions you'll get on the real exam.

On both the real exam and in our drag-and-drop questions, there may be more than one correct answer. In both cases, you get full credit for any correct answer.

Preparing for Self-Assessment Test 2

When you feel you've done the appropriate amount of preparation, head to the next chapter and take a whack at the second assessment exam.

2

Self-Assessment
Test 2

How Close Are You to Ready?

The 14-question assessment test in this chapter is designed to help you answer the question: "How close am I to ready?" The best way to answer the readiness question is to set aside 42 minutes and take this exam... but wait!

How did you score on the first assessment exam? If you needed to do more studying, did you? We hope you'll find that the questions on this exam are tougher than the questions on the first exam. Given that, if your results on the first exam were borderline or worse, you should have put in some serious study time before trying this exam. On the other hand, if you did really well on the first assessment exam, then this one should give you a truer sense of your readiness for the real exam.

ASSESSMENT TEST 2

The real exam has 60 questions and you are given three hours. Since this assessment exam has only 14 questions, allow yourself only 42 minutes to complete this exam. On the real exam, and on all of the exams in this book, give yourself credit only for those questions that you answer 100 percent correctly. For instance, if a question has three correct answers and you get two of the three correct, you get zero credit. There is no partial credit. Good luck!

I. Given:

```
3. import java.util.*;
4. public class VLA2 implements Comparator<VLA2> {
5.    int dishSize;
6.    public static void main(String[] args) {
7.      VLA2[] va = {new VLA2(40), new VLA2(200), new VLA2(60)};
8.
9.      Arrays.sort(va, va[0]);
10.     int index = Arrays.binarySearch(va, new VLA2(40), va[0]);
11.     System.out.print(index + " ");
12.     index = Arrays.binarySearch(va, new VLA2(80), va[0]);
13.     System.out.print(index);
14.   }
15.   public int compare(VLA2 a, VLA2 b) {
16.     return b.dishSize - a.dishSize;
17.   }
18.   VLA2(int d) { dishSize = d; }
19. }
```

What is the result?

A. 0 -2

B. 0 -3

C. 2 -1

D. 2 -2

E. Compilation fails.

F. An exception is thrown at runtime.

2. Given a directory structure:

```
- baseDir
  - testDir
    - subDir2
      - Shackelton.txt
```

and given the following code:

```
12.    String name = "testDir" + File.pathSeparator + "subDir2"
                       + File.pathSeparator + "Shackelton.txt";
13.    File f = new File(name);
14.    System.out.println("exists " + f.exists());
```

Assuming the proper import statements and exception handling, which statements must be true in order for the output to be "exists true"? (Choose three.)

A. Line 12 is correct as it stands.

B. Line 14 is correct as it stands.

C. The program must be invoked from the baseDir directory.

D. The program must be invoked from the testDir directory.

E. Line 12 must use File.separator instead of File.pathSeparator.

F. Line 14 must use the method fileExists() instead of exists().

3. Given:

```
1. import java.io.*;
2. import java.util.*;
3. import static java.lang.Short.*;
4. import static java.lang.Long.*;
5. public class MathBoy {
6.    public static void main(String[] args) {
7.       long x = 123456789;
8.       short y = 22766;   // maximum value of a short is 32767
9.       System.out.printf("%1$+10d %2$010d ", x, MAX_VALUE - y);
10.      System.out.println(new Date());
11.    }
12. }
```

Which are true? (Choose all that apply.)

A. Compilation fails.

B. The output will include "+"

C. The output will include "10001"

D. The output will include "0000010001"

E. The output will include today's date.

F. The output will include the number of milliseconds from January 1, 1970 until today.

4. Given:

```
1. public class WeatherTest {
2.    static Weather w;
3.    public static void main(String[] args) {
```

```
4.        System.out.print(w.RAINY.count + " " + w.Sunny.count + " ");
5.    }
6. }
7. enum Weather {
8.    RAINY, Sunny;
9.    int count = 0;
10.    Weather() {
11.        System.out.print("c ");
12.        count++;
13.    }
14. }
```

What is the result?

A. c 1 c 1

B. c 1 c 2

C. c c 1 1

D. c c 1 2

E. c c 2 2

F. Compilation fails.

G. An exception is thrown at runtime.

5. Given:

```
2. import java.text.*;
3. public class Gazillion {
4.    public static void main(String[] args) throws Exception {
5.        String s = "123.456xyz";
6.        NumberFormat nf = NumberFormat.getInstance();
7.        System.out.println(nf.parse(s));
8.        nf.setMaximumFractionDigits(2);
9.        System.out.println(nf.format(s));
10.    }
11. }
```

Which are true? (Choose all that apply.)

A. Compilation fails.

B. The output will contain "123.45 ".

C. The output will contain "123.456".

D. The output will contain "123.456xyz".

E. An exception will be thrown at runtime.

6. Given that the current directory is `bigApp`, and the following directory structure:

```
bigApp
    |-- classes
            |-- com
                  |-- wickedlysmart
                              |-- BigAppMain.class
```

And the code:

```
package com.wickedlysmart;
public class BigAppMain {
  public static void main(String[] args) {
    System.out.println("big app");
  }
}
```

Which will invoke `BigAppMain`? (Choose all that apply.)

A. `java classes/com.wickedlysmart.BigAppMain`

B. `java classes com/wickedlysmart/BigAppMain`

C. `java classes.com.wickedlysmart.BigAppMain`

D. `java -cp classes com.wickedlysmart.BigAppMain`

E. `java -cp /classes com.wickedlysmart.BigAppMain`

F. `java -cp .:classes com.wickedlysmart.BigAppMain`

G. `java -cp classes/com/wickedlysmart com.wickedlysmart.BigAppMain`

7. Given:

```
2. class Game {
3.    static String s = "-";
4.    String s2 = "s2";
5.    Game(String arg) { s += arg; }
6. }
7. public class Go extends Game {
8.    Go() { super(s2); }
9.    { s += "i "; }
10.   public static void main(String[] args) {
11.     new Go();
12.     System.out.println(s);
13.   }
14.   static { s += "sb "; }
15. }
```

What is the result?

A. `-sb i s2`

B. `-sb s2 i`

C. `-s2 i sb`

D. `-s2 sb i`

E. Compilation fails.

F. An exception is thrown at runtime.

8. Given:

```
2. public class Salmon extends Thread {
3.    public static long id;
4.    public void run() {
5.      for(int i = 0; i < 4; i++) {
6.        // insert code here
7.          new Thread(new Salmon()).start();
8.          throw new Error();
9.        }
10.        System.out.print(i + " ");
11.   } }
12.   public static void main(String[] args) {
13.      Thread t1 = new Salmon();
14.      id = t1.getId();
15.      t1.start();
16. } }
```

And the two code fragments:

I. `if(i == 2 && id == Thread.currentThread().getId()) {`

II. `if(i == 2) {`

When inserting either fragment, independently at line 6, which are true? (Choose all that apply.)

A. Both fragments produce the same output.

B. Both fragments will end in about the same amount of time.

C. Compilation fails, regardless of which fragment is inserted.

D. Regardless of which fragment is inserted, output ends once the Error is thrown.

E. Regardless of which fragment is inserted, output continues after the Error is thrown.

9. Given:

```
2. public class Internet {
3.    private int y = 8;
4.    public static void main(String[] args) {
5.      new Internet().go();
6.    }
```

```
7.    void go() {
8.      int x = 7;
9.      TCPIP ip = new TCPIP();
10.     class TCPIP {
11.       void doit() { System.out.println(y + x); }
12.     }
13.     ip.doit();
14.   }
15. }
```

What is the result? (Choose all that apply.)

A. Compilation succeeds.

B. Compilation fails due to an error on line 3.

C. Compilation fails due to an error on line 8.

D. Compilation fails due to an error on line 9.

E. Compilation fails due to an error on line 10.

F. Compilation fails due to accessing x on line 11.

G. Compilation fails due to accessing y on line 11.

10. Given:

```
4. public static void main(String[] args) {
5.    try {
6.      if(args.length == 0)  throw new Exception();
7.    }
8.    catch (Exception e) {
9.      System.out.print("done ");
10.     doStuff();  // assume this method compiles
11.   }
12.   finally {
13.     System.out.println("finally ");
14.   }
15. }
```

Which are possible outputs? (Choose all that apply.)

A. "done "

B. "finally "

C. "done finally "

D. Compilation fails.

E. No output is produced.

11. Given:

```
3. class A { }
4. class B extends A { }
5. class C extends B { }
6. public class Carpet<V extends B> {
7.    public <X extends V> Carpet<? extends V> method(Carpet<? super X> e) {
8.      // insert code here
9. } }
```

Which, inserted independently at line 8, will compile? (Choose all that apply.)

A. `return new Carpet<X>();`

B. `return new Carpet<V>();`

C. `return new Carpet<A>();`

D. `return new Carpet<B>();`

E. `return new Carpet<C>();`

12. Given:

```
1. class One {
2.    int x = 0;
3.    { assert x == 1; }
4. }
5. public class Two {
6.    public static void main(String[] args) {
7.        int y = 0;
8.        assert y == 0;
9.        if(args.length > 0)
10.           new One();
11.    }
12. }
```

Which of the following will run without error? (Choose all that apply.)

A. `java Two`

B. `java Two x`

C. `java -ea Two`

D. `java -ea Two x`

E. `java -ea:One Two`

F. `java -ea:One Two x`

G. `java -ea:Two Two x`

13. Given:

```
2. class SafeDeposit {
3.    private static SafeDeposit singleton;
4.    public static SafeDeposit getInstance(int code) {
5.      if(singleton == null)
6.        singleton = new SafeDeposit(code);
7.      return singleton;
8.    }
9.    private int code;
10.   private SafeDeposit(int c) { code = c; }
11.   int getCode() { return code; }
12. }
13. public class BeSafe {
14.   // insert lots of code here
25. }
```

Which are true? (Choose all that apply.)

A. Compilation fails.

B. Class BeSafe can create many instances of SafeDeposit.

C. Class BeSafe CANNOT create any instances of SafeDeposit.

D. Class BeSafe can create only one instance of SafeDeposit.

E. Class BeSafe can create instances of SafeDeposit without using the getInstance() method.

F. Once class BeSafe has created an instance of SafeDeposit, it cannot change the value of the instance's "code" variable.

14. Given:

```
2. public class DMV implements Runnable {
3.    public static void main(String[] args) {
4.      DMV d = new DMV();
5.      new Thread(d).start();
6.      Thread t1 = new Thread(d);
7.      t1.start();
8.    }
9.    public void run() {
10.     for(int j = 0; j < 4; j++) {  do1();    do2();  }
11.   }
12.   void do1() {
13.     try { Thread.sleep(1000); }
14.     catch (Exception e) { System.out.print("e "); }
15.   }
16.   synchronized void do2() {
17.     try { Thread.sleep(1000); }
18.     catch (Exception e) { System.out.print("e "); }
19. } }
```

Which are true? (Choose all that apply.)

A. Compilation fails.

B. The program's minimum execution time is about 8 seconds.

C. The program's minimum execution time is about 9 seconds.

D. The program's minimum execution time is about 12 seconds.

E. The program's minimum execution time is about 16 seconds.

F. Un-synchronizing do2 () changes the program's minimum execution time by only a few milliseconds.

QUICK ANSWER KEY

1. D
2. B, C, E
3. A
4. C
5. C, E

6. D, F
7. E
8. E
9. D, F
10. A, B, C

11. A, B
12. A, B, C, E, G
13. B, F
14. C

ASSESSMENT TEST 2: ANSWERS

1. Given:

```
3.  import java.util.*;
4.  public class VLA2 implements Comparator<VLA2> {
5.    int dishSize;
6.    public static void main(String[] args) {
7.      VLA2[] va = {new VLA2(40), new VLA2(200), new VLA2(60)};
8.
9.      Arrays.sort(va, va[0]);
10.     int index = Arrays.binarySearch(va, new VLA2(40), va[0]);
11.     System.out.print(index + " ");
12.     index = Arrays.binarySearch(va, new VLA2(80), va[0]);
13.     System.out.print(index);
14.   }
15.   public int compare(VLA2 a, VLA2 b) {
16.     return b.dishSize - a.dishSize;
17.   }
18.   VLA2(int d) { dishSize = d; }
19. }
```

What is the result?

A. 0 -2

B. 0 -3

C. 2 -1

D. 2 -2

E. Compilation fails.

F. An exception is thrown at runtime.

Answer (for Objective 6.5):

☑ **D** is correct. If you answered **B**, don't feel too bad. A couple of things are going on here: The compare() method has swapped the normal ordering, so "arrays of VLA2" sort in descending sequence. Second, of course, is that when binarySearch() can't find an element it returns (-(insertion point) -1) to indicate where the element would have been placed if it had been found. Note that on line 9, we're sorting based on a Comparator (the 2nd argument).

☒ **A, B, C, E,** and **F** are incorrect based on the above.

2. Given a directory structure:

```
- baseDir
  - testDir
    - subDir2
      - Shackelton.txt
```

and given the following code:

```
12.   String name = "testDir" + File.pathSeparator + "subDir2"
                    + File.pathSeparator + "Shackelton.txt";
13.   File f = new File(name);
14.   System.out.println("exists " + f.exists());
```

Assuming the proper import statements and exception handling, which statements must be true in order for the output to be "exists true"? (Choose three.)

A. Line 12 is correct as it stands.

B. Line 14 is correct as it stands.

C. The program must be invoked from the baseDir directory.

D. The program must be invoked from the testDir directory.

E. Line 12 must use File.separator instead of File.pathSeparator

F. Line 14 must use the method fileExists() instead of exists()

Answer (for Objective 3.2):

☑ **B, C,** and **E** are correct. In order to find the Shackelton.txt file the program must be invoked from the baseDir directory. The pathSeparator field in the File class is used to separate path lists, not directories in paths, and the correct method is File.exists().

☒ **A, D,** and **F** are incorrect based on the above.

3. Given:

```
1. import java.io.*;
2. import java.util.*;
3. import static java.lang.Short.*;
4. import static java.lang.Long.*;
5. public class MathBoy {
6.    public static void main(String[] args) {
7.       long x = 123456789;
8.       short y = 22766;   // maximum value of a short is 32767
9.       System.out.printf("%1$+10d %2$010d ", x, MAX_VALUE - y);
10.      System.out.println(new Date());
11.   }
12. }
```

Which are true? (Choose all that apply.)

A. Compilation fails.

B. The output will include "+"

C. The output will include "10001"

D. The output will include "0000010001"

E. The output will include today's date.

F. The output will include the number of milliseconds from January 1, 1970 until today.

Answer (for Objective 7.1):

☑ **A** is correct. Both Short and Long have `static` MAX_VALUE fields, so the reference to MAX_VALUE in line 9 is ambiguous. (If line 4 was removed, the answer would be **B, C, D,** and **E**.)

☒ **B, C, D, E,** and **F** are incorrect based on the above.

4. Given:

```
1. public class WeatherTest {
2.    static Weather w;
3.    public static void main(String[] args) {
4.      System.out.print(w.RAINY.count + " " + w.Sunny.count + " ");
5.    }
6. }
7. enum Weather {
8.    RAINY, Sunny;
9.    int count = 0;
10.   Weather() {
11.     System.out.print("c ");
12.     count++;
13.   }
14. }
```

What is the result?

A. c 1 c 1

B. c 1 c 2

C. c c 1 1

D. c c 1 2

E. c c 2 2

F. Compilation fails.

G. An exception is thrown at runtime.

Answer (for Objective 1.1):

☑ **C** is correct. All of an enum's values are initialized at the same time, and an enum's variables are treated as if they were instance variables, not static variables.

☒ **A, B, D, E, F,** and **G** are incorrect, based on the above.

5. Given:

```
2. import java.text.*;
3. public class Gazillion {
4.   public static void main(String[] args) throws Exception {
5.     String s = "123.456xyz";
6.     NumberFormat nf = NumberFormat.getInstance();
7.     System.out.println(nf.parse(s));
8.     nf.setMaximumFractionDigits(2);
9.     System.out.println(nf.format(s));
10.  }
11. }
```

Which are true? (Choose all that apply.)

A. Compilation fails.

B. The output will contain `"123.45 "`

C. The output will contain `"123.456"`

D. The output will contain `"123.456xyz"`

E. An exception will be thrown at runtime.

Answer (for Objective 3.4):

☑ **C** and **E** are correct. The invocation of `parse()` will return 123.456. The invocation of `format()` will throw an exception.

☒ **A, B,** and **D** are incorrect based on the above.

6. Given that the current directory is `bigApp`, and the following directory structure:

```
bigApp
    |-- classes
            |-- com
                |-- wickedlysmart
                            |-- BigAppMain.class
```

And the code :

```
package com.wickedlysmart;
public class BigAppMain {
  public static void main(String[] args) {
    System.out.println("big app");
  }
}
```

Which will invoke `BigAppMain`? (Choose all that apply.)

A. `java classes/com.wickedlysmart.BigAppMain`

B. `java classes com/wickedlysmart/BigAppMain`

C. `java classes.com.wickedlysmart.BigAppMain`

D. `java -cp classes com.wickedlysmart.BigAppMain`

E. `java -cp /classes com.wickedlysmart.BigAppMain`

F. `java -cp .:classes com.wickedlysmart.BigAppMain`

G. `java -cp classes/com/wickedlysmart com.wickedlysmart.BigAppMain`

Answer (for Objective 7.2):

☑ **D** and **F** are correct. **F** will be a tiny bit slower than **D**, because the `.:` tells the JVM to look in the current directory (in this case `bigApp`), before looking in `classes`.

☒ **A, B, C, E,** and **G** use incorrect syntax, which will keep the JVM from finding the `.class` file.

7. Given:

```
2. class Game {
3.    static String s = "-";
4.    String s2 = "s2";
5.    Game(String arg) { s += arg; }
6. }
7. public class Go extends Game {
8.    Go() { super(s2); }
9.    { s += "i "; }
10.   public static void main(String[] args) {
11.      new Go();
12.      System.out.println(s);
13.   }
14.   static { s += "sb "; }
15. }
```

What is the result?

A. -sb i s2

B. -sb s2 i

C. -s2 i sb

D. -s2 sb i

E. Compilation fails.

F. An exception is thrown at runtime.

Answer (for Objective 5.4):

☑ **E** is correct. The s2 variable is an instance variable that can't be used in the call to super because the instance hasn't been created yet.

☒ **A, B, C, D,** and **F** are incorrect based on the above.

8. Given:

```
2. public class Salmon extends Thread {
3.    public static long id;
4.    public void run() {
5.      for(int i = 0; i < 4; i++) {
6.        // insert code here
7.          new Thread(new Salmon()).start();
8.          throw new Error();
9.        }
10.       System.out.print(i + " ");
11.    } }
12.    public static void main(String[] args) {
13.      Thread t1 = new Salmon();
14.      id = t1.getId();
15.      t1.start();
16. } }
```

And the two code fragments:

I. if(i == 2 && id == Thread.currentThread().getId()) {

II. if(i == 2) {

When inserting either fragment, independently at line 6, which are true? (Choose all that apply.)

A. Both fragments produce the same output.

B. Both fragments will end in about the same amount of time.

C. Compilation fails, regardless of which fragment is inserted.

D. Regardless of which fragment is inserted, output ends once the Error is thrown.

E. Regardless of which fragment is inserted, output continues after the Error is thrown.

Answer (for Objective 4.2):

☑ **E** is correct. In either case, before the Error is thrown a new thread is created, and the new thread will execute independently of the Error.

☒ **A** and **B** are incorrect because fragment II creates a sort of recursive, endless loop. **C** and **D** are incorrect based on the above.

9. Given:

```
2. public class Internet {
3.    private int y = 8;
4.    public static void main(String[] args) {
5.       new Internet().go();
6.    }
7.    void go() {
8.       int x = 7;
9.       TCPIP ip = new TCPIP();
10.       class TCPIP {
11.          void doit() { System.out.println(y + x); }
12.       }
13.       ip.doit();
14.    }
15. }
```

What is the result? (Choose all that apply.)

A. Compilation succeeds.

B. Compilation fails due to an error on line 3.

C. Compilation fails due to an error on line 8.

D. Compilation fails due to an error on line 9.

E. Compilation fails due to an error on line 10.

F. Compilation fails due to accessing x on line 11.

G. Compilation fails due to accessing y on line 11.

Answer (for Objective 1.5):

☑ **D** and **F** are correct. Method-local inner classes can use variables from their enclosing methods, only if they are marked `"final"`. A method-local inner class can be instantiated only after it has been declared. It is legal to use private members from the enclosing class.

☒ **A, B, C, E,** and **G** are incorrect based on the above.

10. Given:

```
4. public static void main(String[] args) {
5.    try {
6.       if(args.length == 0)  throw new Exception();
7.    }
8.    catch (Exception e) {
9.       System.out.print("done ");
10.      doStuff();  // assume this method compiles
11.    }
12.    finally {
13.       System.out.println("finally ");
14.    }
15. }
```

Which are possible outputs? (Choose all that apply.)

A. `"done "`

B. `"finally "`

C. `"done finally "`

D. Compilation fails.

E. No output is produced.

Answer (for Objective 2.4):

☑ **A, B,** and **C** are correct. Typically, if you invoked the program without a command-line argument, an exception would be thrown and the output would be `"done finally"`. If you invoked the program with a command-line argument, no exception would be thrown and the `finally` statement would produce the output: `"finally"`. If, however, `doStuff()` did something like call `System.exit(1)`, then a no-arg invocation could produce `"done"`.

☒ **D** and **E** are incorrect based on the above.

11. Given:

```
3. class A { }
4. class B extends A { }
5. class C extends B { }
6. public class Carpet<V extends B> {
7.   public <X extends V> Carpet<? extends V> method(Carpet<? super X> e) {
8.     // insert code here
9. } }
```

Which, inserted independently at line 8, will compile? (Choose all that apply.)

A. `return new Carpet<X>();`

B. `return new Carpet<V>();`

C. `return new Carpet<A>();`

D. `return new Carpet<B>();`

E. `return new Carpet<C>();`

Answer (for Objective 6.4):

☑ **A** and **B** are correct. The generic declaration at the class level says that `Carpet` can accept any type which is either B or a subtype of B. The generic declaration at the method level is "`<X extends V>`", which means that X is a type of V or a subtype of V, where the class type of V can vary at runtime—hence, the exact scopes of X and V are unknown at compile time. **A** and **B** are correct because X and V bind to the scope of `<? extends V>`, where X is known as a subtype of V as it's declared at the method level.

☒ **C**, **D**, and **E** are incorrect because it's illegal to use a concrete class type since the exact scope of V is unknown.

12. Given:

```
1. class One {
2.   int x = 0;
3.   { assert x == 1; }
4. }
5. public class Two {
6.   public static void main(String[] args) {
7.     int y = 0;
8.     assert y == 0;
9.     if(args.length > 0)
10.        new One();
11.  }
12. }
```

Which of the following will run without error? (Choose all that apply.)

A. `java Two`

B. `java Two x`

C. `java -ea Two`

D. `java -ea Two x`

E. `java -ea:One Two`

F. `java -ea:One Two x`

G. `java -ea:Two Two x`

Answer (for Objective 2.3):

☑ **A, B, C, E,** and **G** are correct. **A** and **B** run because assertions were not enabled. **C** and **E** run because an instance of class `One` is not created. **G** runs because assertions are enabled only for class `Two`.

☒ **D** throws an `AssertionError` because assertions were enabled and an instance of class One was created. **F** throws an `AssertionError` because assertions were enabled specifically for class `One`, and an instance of class One was created.

13. Given:

```
2. class SafeDeposit {
3.    private static SafeDeposit singleton;
4.    public static SafeDeposit getInstance(int code) {
5.       if(singleton == null)
6.          singleton = new SafeDeposit(code);
7.       return singleton;
8.    }
9.    private int code;
10.   private SafeDeposit(int c) { code = c; }
11.   int getCode() { return code; }
12. }
13. public class BeSafe {
14.    // insert lots of code here
25. }
```

Which are true? (Choose all that apply.)

A. Compilation fails.

B. Class `BeSafe` can create many instances of `SafeDeposit`.

C. Class BeSafe CANNOT create any instances of SafeDeposit.

D. Class BeSafe can create only one instance of SafeDeposit.

E. Class BeSafe can create instances of SafeDeposit without using the getInstance() method.

F. Once class BeSafe has created an instance of SafeDeposit, it cannot change the value of the instance's "code" variable.

Answer (for Objectives 5.3 and 4.3):

☑ **B** and **F** are correct. It's legal to have a private constructor. As long as class BeSafe doesn't use multiple threads, it can create only one instance of SafeDeposit. If BeSafe is multithreaded, it's possible for SafeDeposit's unsynchronized getInstance() method to return more than one instance of the class. **F** is correct because "code" is private and there is no setter. Note: expect to see questions that cover more than one objective!

☒ **A**, **C**, and **D** are incorrect based on the above. **E** is incorrect because SafeDeposit's only constructor is private.

14. Given:

```
2. public class DMV implements Runnable {
3.    public static void main(String[] args) {
4.       DMV d = new DMV();
5.       new Thread(d).start();
6.       Thread t1 = new Thread(d);
7.       t1.start();
8.    }
9.    public void run() {
10.      for(int j = 0; j < 4; j++) {   do1();   do2();   }
11.   }
12.   void do1() {
13.      try { Thread.sleep(1000); }
14.      catch (Exception e) { System.out.print("e "); }
15.   }
16.   synchronized void do2() {
17.      try { Thread.sleep(1000); }
18.      catch (Exception e) { System.out.print("e "); }
19. } }
```

Which are true? (Choose all that apply.)

A.   Compilation fails.

B.   The program's minimum execution time is about 8 seconds.

C.   The program's minimum execution time is about 9 seconds.

D.   The program's minimum execution time is about 12 seconds.

E.   The program's minimum execution time is about 16 seconds.

F.   Un-synchronizing do2() changes the program's minimum execution time by only a few milliseconds.

Answer (for Objective 4.3):

☑   **C** is correct. Both thread's first invocation of do1() will start at about the same time. After that second has elapsed, one of the threads will invoke do2(), and the other will have to wait. Once the thread that ran do2() first is done with do2(), the other thread can run do2(). Thereafter, the threads will alternate running do1() and do2(), but they are able to run mostly simultaneously.

☒   **A, B, D,** and **E** are incorrect based on the above. **F** is incorrect because un-synchronizing do2() will shave about 1000 milliseconds off the elapsed time.

Analyzing Your Results

It was our intention that the assessment exam in chapter 1 be a little easier than the rest of the book, and a little easier than the real exam. It's also our intention that this second assessment exam, and the exams in the rest of the book, be a little harder than the real exam.

As of this writing, a passing score on the OCP Java SE Programmer exam is 58.33 percent (35 out of 60 questions). Of course, this chapter's assessment exam had only 14 questions, so if you got 8.1 of the 14 questions correct, then in theory you passed! Table 2.1 is a rough guide to where you are in your studies.

| TABLE 2-1 | What Your Score Means |

Number of Correct Answers	Recommended Plan
0–5	You should do a LOT of studying before taking more of the exams in this book.
6–8	You should do some more studying before taking more of the exams in this book.
9–11	You're a little ahead of the "passing" boundary. We recommend you do a bit more studying.
12–14	You're probably ready to use the four remaining full exams in this book to polish your skills.

Preparing for Practice Exam I

When you feel you've done the appropriate amount of preparation, carve out a dedicated three hours and try the first full 60-question practice exam in the next chapter.

3

Practice Exam 1

A Few Thoughts

Here are a few thoughts before you start this practice exam.

Question Management

Before you start the clock, give yourself a few blank sheets of paper and a couple of pencils. You should keep a list of questions you need to return to, and of course you might want to make notes when you're trying to figure out a particularly tricky question.

exam

ⓦatch You will get some sort of writing equipment at the testing center. Unfortunately, not all testing centers have agreed on what the "writing equipment" standard is. If you can choose between a few centers that are close to you, call first. If one center offers you a small dry erase board, and another offers you pencils and paper, go for the pencil and paper, even if it means a longer commute! The advantages of pencil and paper over a small dry erase board are enormous!

Time Management

Some candidates report that three hours for the exam is plenty of time. Some candidates (even candidates who do well) report that they felt pressed for time. Remember, you'll have enough time to spend three minutes on each question. Of course, some questions will take very little time, but some questions (like threads and garbage collection) might take more. If you find yourself getting hung up on a particular question, add it to your list of "questions to return to" and move on. It's much better to miss a few tough questions than to not even get to some easy ones at the end of the exam.

exam

ⓦatch Before you go to the exam center, reread the caution in the intro concerning the Drag and Drop bug in the exam engine. It's crucial!

Drag and Drop

Each of the four full practice exams in this book have a couple of simulated Drag and Drop (D&D), style questions. As in the real exam, the instructions can vary slightly from one D&D to the next. For instance, sometimes you can use a fragment more than once, and sometimes you can't. Also, as in the real exam, sometimes there will be more than one way to correctly arrange the fragments. You will receive full credit for ANY of the correct answer arrangements.

PRACTICE EXAM I

The real exam has 60 questions and you are given three hours. It's the same with this exam.

1. Given:

```
2. public class Bang extends Thread {
3.    static Thread t1, t2, t3;
4.    public static void main(String[] args) throws Exception {
5.       t1 = new Thread(new Bang());
6.       t2 = new Thread(new Bang());
7.       t3 = new Thread(new Bang());
8.       t1.start();   t2.start();   t3.start();
9.    }
10.   public void run() {
11.      for(int i = 0; i < 500; i++) {
12.         System.out.print(Thread.currentThread().getId() + " ");
13.         if(i == 250)
14.            try {
15.               System.out.print("**" + t1.getId() + "**");
16.               t1.sleep(600);
17.            }
18.            catch (Exception e) { }
19. } } }
```

Which are true? (Choose all that apply.)

A. Compilation fails.

B. An exception is thrown at runtime.

C. Bang will execute for a second or two.

D. Bang will execute for at least 10 minutes.

E. Thread t1 will almost certainly be the last thread to finish.

F. Thread t1 will almost certainly be the first thread to finish.

G. It's difficult to predict which thread will be the last to finish.

2. Given:

```
3. public class Dec26 {
4.    public static void main(String[] args) {
5.       short a1 = 6;
6.       new Dec26().go(a1);
7.       new Dec26().go(new Integer(7));
8.    }
9.    void go(Short x) { System.out.print("S "); }
10.   void go(Long x) { System.out.print("L "); }
11.   void go(int x) { System.out.print("i "); }
12.   void go(Number n) { System.out.print("N "); }
13. }
```

What is the result?

A. i L

B. i N

C. S L

D. S N

E. Compilation fails.

F. An exception is thrown at runtime.

3. Given:

```
1. public class Fellowship {
2.    public static void main(String[] args) {
3.       // insert code here
4.    }
5. }
6. class Numinor {
7.    enum Members {
8.       HOBBITS(48), ELVES(74), DWARVES(50);
9.       int height;
10.      Members(int h) { height = h; }
11.      int getHeight() { return height; }
12.    }
13. }
```

And these four lines of code to be inserted, independently at line 3:

```
I.    int h0 = Numinor.Members.HOBBITS.getHeight();
II.   int h1 = Numinor.Members.getHeight();
III.  int h2 = Members.HOBBITS.getHeight();
IV.   int h3 = Members.height;
```

Which are true? (Choose all that apply.)

A. Line I will compile.

B. Line II will compile.

C. Line III will compile.

D. Line IV will compile.

E. Class Numinor will NOT compile.

4. Given:

```
2. public class Volume {
3.    Volume v;
4.    int size;
5.    public static void main(String[] args) {
6.       Volume myV = new Volume();
```

```
7.        final Volume v2;
8.        v2 = myV.doStuff(myV);
9.        v2.v.size = 7;
10.       System.out.print(v2.size);
11.    }
12.    Volume doStuff(Volume v3) {
13.       v3.size = 5;
14.       v3.v = new Volume();
15.       return v3;
16. } }
```

What is the result? (Choose all that apply.)

A. 5

B. 7

C. Compilation fails due to an error on line 8.

D. Compilation fails due to an error on line 9.

E. Compilation fails due to an error on line 13.

F. Compilation fails due to an error on line 14.

5. Given:

```
3. public class BirdHouse {
4.    public static void main(String[] args) {
5.       String r = "0";
6.       int x = -1, y = -5;
7.       if(x < 5)
8.       if(y > 0)
9.       if(x > y)
10.      r += "1";
11.      else r += "2";
12.      else r += "3";
13.      else r += "4";
14.      System.out.println(r);
15. } }
```

What is the result?

A. 0

B. 01

C. 02

D. 03

E. 013

F. 023

G. Compilation fails.

6. Given:

```
 1. class c1 { }
 2. class c2 { }
 3. interface i1 { }
 4. interface i2 { }
 5. class A extends c2 implements i1 { }
 6. class B implements i1 implements i2 { }
 7. class C implements c1 { }
 8. class D extends c1, implements i2 { }
 9. class E extends i1, i2 { }
10. class F implements i1, i2 { }
```

What is the result? (Choose all that apply.)

A. Class A does not compile.

B. Class B does not compile.

C. Class C does not compile.

D. Class D does not compile.

E. Class E does not compile.

F. Class F does not compile.

G. Compilation succeeds for all of the classes.

7. Given that `"it, IT"` and `"pt"` are valid `Locale` codes, and given:

```
41.    Date d = new Date();
42.    DateFormat df;
43.    Locale[] la = {new Locale("it", "IT"), new Locale("pt")};
44.    for(Locale l: la) {
45.      df = DateFormat.getDateInstance(DateFormat.FULL, l);
46.      System.out.println(d.format(df));
47.    }
```

Which are true? (Choose all that apply.)

A. An exception will be thrown at runtime.

B. Compilation fails due to an error on line 43.

C. Compilation fails due to an error on line 45.

D. Compilation fails due to an error on line 46.

E. Classes from the `java.text` package are used in this code.

F. Classes from the `java.util` package are used in this code.

8. Given:

```
 2. class SuperCool {
 3.    static String os = "";
 4.    void doStuff() { os += "super "; }
 5. }
 6. public class Cool extends SuperCool {
 7.    public static void main(String[] args) {
 8.      new Cool().go();
 9.    }
10.    void go() {
11.      SuperCool s = new Cool();
12.      Cool c = (Cool)s;
13.      // insert code here
14.    }
15.    void doStuff() { os += "cool "; }
16. }
```

If the rest of the code compiles, which line(s) of code, inserted independently at line 13, compile? (Choose all that apply.)

A. c.doStuff();

B. s.doStuff();

C. this.doStuff();

D. super.doStuff();

E. c.super.doStuff();

F. s.super.doStuff();

G. this.super.doStuff();

H. There are other errors in the code.

9. Given:

```
 5.    static String s = "";
 6.    public static void main(String[] args) {
 7.      try { doStuff(args); }
 8.      catch (Error e) { s += "e "; }
 9.      s += "x ";
10.      System.out.println(s);
11.    }
12.    static void doStuff(String[] args) {
13.      if(args.length == 0)
14.        throw new IllegalArgumentException();
15.      s += "d ";
16.    }
```

And, if the code compiles, and given a java invocation with no arguments, what is the result? (Choose all that apply.)

A. d x

B. e x

C. d e x

D. Compilation fails due to an error on line 8.

E. Compilation fails due to an error on line 12.

F. Compilation fails due to an error on line 14.

G. An uncaught IllegalArgumentException is thrown.

10. Given:

```
2. class Paratrooper implements Runnable {
3.    public void run() {
4.       System.out.print(Thread.currentThread().getName() + " ");
5. } }
6. public class Jump {
7.    static Paratrooper p;
8.    static { p = new Paratrooper(); }
9.    { Thread t1 = new Thread(p, "bob"); t1.start(); }
10.   public static void main(String[] args) {
11.      new Jump();
12.      new Thread(new Runnable() { public void run()
              { ; }}, "carol").start();
13.      new Thread(new Paratrooper(), "alice").start();
14.   }
15.   Jump() { Thread t2 = new Thread(p, "ted"); t2.start(); }
16. }
```

Which are true? (Choose all that apply.)

A. The output could be ted bob alice

B. The output could be bob alice carol

C. The output could be bob carol ted alice

D. Compilation fails due to an error on line 8.

E. Compilation fails due to an error on line 9.

F. Compilation fails due to an error on line 12.

G. Compilation fails due to an error on line 15.

11. Use the fragments below to fill in the blanks so that the code will compile, and when invoked with:

```
java Dropkick fish
```

will produce the output: "1 4 "

Note: All of the blanks must be filled, not all the fragments will be used, and fragments can be used only once.

Code:

```
public class Dropkick {
  public static void main(String[] args) {
    boolean test = false;
    String[] s = {"duck", null, "frog"};

    if((s[1] == null) ____ (s[1].length() == 0)) System.out.print("1 ");

    if((s[2] == null) ____ (test ____ true)) System.out.print("2 ");

    if((s[0].equals("duck")) ____ (args[0].equals("fish")))
       System.out.print("3 ");
    if((args[0] != null) && (_____)) System.out.print("4 ");
  }
}
```

Fragments:

```
|, ||, &, &&, ^, <, %, =, ==, !=, false, test, s[1]
```

12. Which are true? (Choose all that apply.)
    A. For a specific object, it's NOT possible for finalize() to be invoked more than once.
    B. It's possible for objects, on whom finalize() has been invoked by the JVM, to avoid the GC.
    C. Overriding finalize() ensures that objects of that type will always be GCed when they become eligible.
    D. The finalize() method is invoked only for GC-eligible objects that are NOT part of "islands of isolation."
    E. For every object that the GC considers collecting, the GC remembers whether finalize() has been invoked for that specific object.

13. Given that:
    Exception is the superclass of IOException and
    IOException is the superclass of FileNotFoundException
    and

```
2. import java.io.*;
3. class Author {
4.   protected void write() throws IOException { }
5. }
```

```
 6. public class Salinger extends Author {
 7.    private void write(int x) { }
 8.    protected void write(long x) throws FileNotFoundException { }
 9.    protected void write(boolean x) throws Exception { }
10.    protected int write(short x) { return 7; }
11.    public void write() { }
12. }
```

What is the result? (Choose all that apply.)

A. Compilation succeeds.

B. Compilation fails due to an error on line 7.

C. Compilation fails due to an error on line 8.

D. Compilation fails due to an error on line 9.

E. Compilation fails due to an error on line 10.

F. Compilation fails due to an error on line 11.

14. Given:

```
 2. class Chilis {
 3.    Chilis(String c, int h) { color = c; hotness = h; }
 4.    String color;
 5.    int hotness;
 6.    public boolean equals(Object o) {
 7.      if(this == (Chilis)o) return true;
 8.      return false;
 9.    }
10.    public String toString() { return color + " " + hotness; }
11. }
```

If instances of class Chilis are to be used as keys in a Map, which are true? (Choose all that apply.)

A. Without overriding hashCode(), the code will not compile.

B. As it stands, the equals() method has been legally overridden.

C. It's possible for such keys to find the correct entries in the Map.

D. It's NOT possible for such keys to find the correct entries in the Map.

E. As it stands, the Chilis class legally supports the equals() and hashCode() contracts.

F. If hashCode() was correctly overridden, it would make retrieving Map entries by key easier.

15. Given:

```
 2. public class Contact {
 3.    private String name;
 4.    private String city;
 5.    String getName() { return name; }
```

```
 6.    void setName(String n) { name = n; }
 7.    void setCity(String c) {
 8.      if(c == null) throw new NullPointerException();
 9.      city = c;
10.    }
11.    String getCity() { return city; }
12. }
```

Which are true? (Choose all that apply.)

A. Compilation fails.

B. The class is well encapsulated.

C. The setCity() method is an example of loose coupling.

D. The setCity() method has better encapsulation than setName().

E. The setCity() method is cohesive; the setName() method is not.

16. Given the current directory is bigApp, and the directory structure:

```
bigApp
    |-- classes
             |-- Cloned.class
```

And the file:

```
public class Cloned {
  public static void main(String[] args) {
    System.out.println("classes");
    assert(Integer.parseInt(args[0]) > 0);
} }
```

Which will produce the output "classes" followed by an AssertionError? (Choose all that apply.)

A. java -cp classes Cloned -4

B. java -cp classes -ea Cloned

C. java -ea-cp classes Cloned -4

D. java -ea -cp classes Cloned 4

E. java -ea, cp classes Cloned 4

F. java -ea -cp classes Cloned -4

G. java -cp classes Cloned -4 -ea

17. Given:

```
1. interface Syrupable {
2.   void getSugary();
3. }
```

```
4. abstract class Pancake implements Syrupable { }
5.
6. class BlueBerryPancake implements Pancake {
7.   public void getSugary() { ; }
8. }
9. class SourdoughBlueBerryPancake extends BlueBerryPancake {
10.   void getSugary(int s) { ; }
11. }
```

Which are true? (Choose all that apply.)

A. Compilation succeeds.

B. Compilation fails due to an error on line 2.

C. Compilation fails due to an error on line 4.

D. Compilation fails due to an error on line 6.

E. Compilation fails due to an error on line 7.

F. Compilation fails due to an error on line 9.

G. Compilation fails due to an error on line 10.

18. Given:

```
1. public class Endless {
2.   public static void main(String[] args) {
3.     int i = 0;
4.     short s = 0;
5.     for(int j = 0, k = 0; j < 3; j++) ;
6.     for(int j = 0; j < 3; counter(j)) ;
7.     for(int j = 0, int k = 0; j < 3; j++) ;
8.     for(; i < 5; counter(5), i++) ;
9.     for(i = 0; i < 3; i++, System.out.print("howdy ")) ;
10.   }
11.   static int counter(int y) { return y + 1; }
12. }
```

What is the result? (Choose all that apply.)

A. howdy howdy howdy

B. The code runs in an endless loop.

C. Compilation fails due to an error on line 5.

D. Compilation fails due to an error on line 6.

E. Compilation fails due to an error on line 7.

F. Compilation fails due to an error on line 8.

G. Compilation fails due to an error on line 9.

19. Given:

```
2. class Big {
3.    void doStuff(int x) { }
4. }
5. class Heavy extends Big {
6.    // void doStuff(byte b) { }
7.    // protected void doStuff(int x) throws Exception { }
8. }
9. public class Weighty extends Heavy {
10.   // void doStuff(int x) { }
11.   // String doStuff(int x) { return "hi"; }
12.   // public int doStuff(int x) { return 7; }
13.   // private int doStuff(char c) throws Error { return 1; }
14. }
```

Which method(s), if uncommented independently, compile? (Choose all that apply.)

A. Line 6

B. Line 7

C. Line 10

D. Line 11

E. Line 12

F. Line 13

20. Which are true? (Choose all that apply.)

A. A given `TreeSet`'s ordering cannot be changed once it's created.

B. The `java.util.Properties` class is conceptually more like a List than like a Map.

C. It's a reasonable design choice to use a `LinkedList` when you want to design queue-like functionality.

D. Of the main types of collections flavors (Lists, Sets, Maps), Queues are conceptually most like Sets.

E. It's programmatically easier to perform a non-destructive traversal of a `PriorityQueue` than a `LinkedList`.

F. Classes that implement the `Set` interface are usually well suited for applications that require access to a collection based on an index.

21. Given the following directory structure:

```
test -|
      | - Finder.class
      | - testdir -|
                   | - subdir
                   | - subdir2
                   | - testfile.txt
```

If test, testdir, subdir, and subdir2 are all directories, and Finder.class and testfile.txt are files, and given:

```
import java.io.*;
public class Finder {
   public static void main(String[] args) throws IOException {
      String[] files = new String[100];
      File dir = new File(args[0]);
      files = dir.list();
      System.out.println(files.length);
   } }
```

And, if the code compiles, the invocation:

```
java Finder testdir
```

What is the result?

A. 1

B. 2

C. 3

D. 4

E. 5

F. 100

G. Compilation fails.

H. An exception is thrown at runtime.

22. Given:

```
1. public class Grids {
2.    public static void main(String[] args) {
3.       int [][] ia2;
4.       int [] ia1 = {1,2,3};
5.       Object o = ia1;
6.       ia2 = new int[3][3];
7.       ia2[0] = (int[])o;
8.       ia2[0][0] = (int[])o;
9. } }
```

What is the result? (Choose all that apply.)

A. Compilation fails due to an error on line 4.

B. Compilation fails due to an error on line 5.

C. Compilation fails due to an error on line 6.

D. Compilation fails due to an error on line 7.

E.   Compilation fails due to an error on line 8.

F.   Compilation succeeds and the code runs without exception.

G.   Compilation succeeds and an exception is thrown at runtime.

23.   Given:

```
3. public class OffRamp {
4.   public static void main(String[] args) {
5.       int [] exits = {0,0,0,0,0,0};
6.       int x1 = 0;
7.
8.       for(int x = 0; x < 4; x++) exits[0] = x;
9.       for(int x = 0; x < 4; ++x) exits[1] = x;
10.
11.      x1 = 0; while(x1++ < 3) exits[2] = x1;
12.      x1 = 0; while(++x1 < 3) exits[3] = x1;
13.
14.      x1 = 0; do { exits[4] = x1; }  while(x1++ < 7);
15.      x1 = 0; do { exits[5] = x1; }  while(++x1 < 7);
16.
17.      for(int x: exits)
18.         System.out.print(x + " ");
19. } }
```

What is the result?

A.   3 3 2 2 6 6

B.   3 3 3 2 7 6

C.   3 3 3 2 7 7

D.   4 3 3 2 7 6

E.   4 3 3 2 7 7

F.   Compilation fails.

24.   Given:

```
2. import java.util.*;
3. public class HR {
4.   public static void main(String[] args) {
5.       List<Integer> i = new Vector<Integer>();
6.       i.add(3); i.add(2); i.add(5);
7.       int ref = 1;
8.       doStuff(ref);
9.       System.out.println(i.get(ref));
10.   }
11.   static int doStuff(int x) {
12.       return ++x;
13. } }
```

What is the result?

A. 2

B. 3

C. 5

D. Compilation fails.

E. An exception is thrown at runtime.

25. Given:

```
2. import java.util.*;
3. public class Vinegar {
4.    public static void main(String[] args) {
5.      Set<Integer> mySet = new HashSet<Integer>();
6.      do1(mySet, "0");  do1(mySet, "a");
7.      do2(mySet, "0");  do2(mySet, "a");
8.    }
9.    public static void do1(Set s, String st) {
10.     s.add(st);
11.     s.add(Integer.parseInt(st));
12.   }
13.   public static void do2(Set<Integer> s, String st) {
14.     s.add(st);
15.     s.add(Integer.parseInt(st));
16. } }
```

Which are true? (Choose all that apply.)

A. Compilation succeeds.

B. Compilation fails due to an error on line 6.

C. Compilation fails due to an error on line 13.

D. Compilation fails due to an error on line 14.

E. Compilation fails due to an error on line 15.

F. If only the line(s) of code that don't compile are removed, the code will run without exception.

G. If only the line(s) of code that don't compile are removed, the code will throw an exception.

26. Given:

```
3. class Employee {
4.    private String name;
5.    void setName(String n) { name = n; }
6.    String getName() { return name; }
7. }
8. interface Mungeable {
9.    void doMunging();
```

```
10. }
11. public class MyApp implements Mungeable {
12.   public void doMunging() { ; }
13.   public static void main(String[] args) {
14.     Employee e = new Employee();
15.     e.setName("bob");
16.     System.out.print(e.getName());
17. } }
```

Which are true? (Choose all that apply.)

A. MyApp is-a Employee.

B. MyApp is-a Mungeable.

C. MyApp has-a Employee.

D. MyApp has-a Mungeable.

E. The code is loosely coupled.

F. The Employee class is well encapsulated.

27. Given that `FileNotFoundException` extends `IOException`, and given:

```
2. import java.io.*;
3. public class MacPro extends Laptop {
4.   public static void main(String[] args) {
5.     new MacPro().crunch();
6.   }
7.   // insert code here
8. }
9. class Laptop {
10.   void crunch() throws IOException { }
11. }
```

Which method(s), inserted independently at line 7, compile? (Choose all that apply.)

A. `void crunch() { }`

B. `void crunch() throws Exception { }`

C. `void crunch(int x) throws Exception { }`

D. `void crunch() throws RuntimeException { }`

E. `void crunch() throws FileNotFoundException { }`

28. Given:

```
2. class Horse {
3.   String hands = "15";
4. }
5. class GaitedPony extends Horse {
6.   static String hands = "14";
```

```
 7.   public static void main(String[] args) {
 8.      String hands = "13.2";
 9.      String result = new GaitedPony().getSize(hands);
10.      System.out.println(" " + result);
11.   }
12.   String getSize(String s) {
13.      System.out.print("hands: " + s);
14.      return hands;
15. } }
```

What is the result?

A. 14

B. 15

C. hands: 13.2 14

D. hands: 13.2 15

E. Compilation fails.

F. An exception is thrown at runtime.

29. Given:

```
 2. public class Humping {
 3.   public static void main(String[] args) {
 4.      String r = "-";
 5.      char[] c = {'a', 'b', 'c', 'z'};
 6.      for(char c1: c)
 7.        switch (c1) {
 8.           case 'a': r += "a";
 9.           case 'b': r += "b"; break;
10.           default: r += "X";
11.           case 'z': r+= "z";
12.        }
13.      System.out.println(r);
14. } }
```

What is the result?

A. -abXz

B. -abbXz

C. -abbXzz

D. -abbXzXz

E. Compilation fails due to a single error.

F. Compilation fails due to multiple errors.

30. Given:

```
1. import java.util.*;
2. public class Garage {
3.   public static void main(String[] args) {
4.     Map<String, String> hm = new HashMap<String, String>();
5.     String[] k = {null, "2", "3", null, "5"};
6.     String[] v = {"a", "b", "c", "d", "e"};
7.
8.     for(int i=0; i<5; i++) {
9.       hm.put(k[i], v[i]);
10.       System.out.print(hm.get(k[i]) + " ");
11.     }
12.     System.out.print(hm.size() + " " + hm.values() + "\n");
13.   } }
```

What result is most likely?

A. a b c a e 4 [c, b, a, e]

B. a b c d e 4 [c, b, a, e]

C. a b c d e 4 [c, d, b, e]

D. a b c, followed by an exception.

E. An exception is thrown with no other output.

F. Compilation fails due to error(s) in the code.

31. Given:

```
2. class Jiggy extends Thread {
3.   Jiggy(String n) { super(n); }
4.   public void run() {
5.     for(int i = 0; i < 100; i++) {
6.       if("t1".equals(Thread.currentThread().getName()) && i == 5) {
7.         new Jiggy("t3").start();
8.         throw new Error();
9.       }
10.       if("t2".equals(Thread.currentThread().getName()) && i == 5) {
11.         new Jiggy("t4").start();
12.         throw new Error();
13.       }
14.       System.out.print(Thread.currentThread().getName() + "-");
15.     }
16.   }
17.   public static void main(String[] args) {
18.     Thread t1 = new Jiggy("t1");
19.     Thread t2 = new Jiggy("t2");
20.     t1.setPriority(1);  t2.setPriority(9);
21.     t2.start();  t1.start();
22. } }
```

Which are true? (Choose all that apply.)

A. Compilation fails.

B. After throwing error(s), t3 will most likely complete before t4.

C. After throwing error(s), t4 will most likely complete before t3.

D. The code will throw one error and then no more output will be produced.

E. The code will throw two errors and then no more output will be produced.

F. After throwing error(s) it's difficult to determine whether t3 or t4 will complete first.

32. Given:

```
3. class Stereo { void makeNoise() { assert false; } }
4. public class BoomBox extends Stereo {
5.    public static void main(String[] args) {
6.       new BoomBox().go(args);
7.    }
8.    void go(String[] args) {
9.       if(args.length > 0)  makeNoise();
10.      if(!args[0].equals("x")) System.out.println("!x");
11. } }
```

And, if the code compiles, the invocation:

```
java -ea BoomBox
```

What is the result?

A. !x

B. Compilation fails.

C. An AssertionError is thrown.

D. A NullPointerException is thrown.

E. An IllegalArgumentException is thrown.

F. An ArrayIndexOutOfBoundsException is thrown.

33. Given:

```
1. public class LaSelva extends Beach {
2.    LaSelva() { s = "LaSelva"; }
3.    public static void main(String[] args) { new LaSelva().go(); }
4.     void go() {
5.       Beach[] ba = { new Beach(), new LaSelva(), (Beach) new LaSelva() };
6.       for(Beach b: ba)  System.out.print(b.getBeach().s + " ");
7.    }
8.    LaSelva getBeach() { return this; }
9. }
10. class Beach {
```

```
11.    String s;
12.    Beach() { s = "Beach"; }
13.    Beach getBeach() { return this; }
14. }
```

What is the result?

A. `Beach LaSelva Beach`

B. `Beach LaSelva LaSelva`

C. `Beach LaSelva` followed by an exception.

D. Compilation fails due to an error at line 5.

E. Compilation fails due to an error at line 6.

F. Compilation fails due to an error at line 8.

G. Compilation fails due to an error at line 13.

34. When using the `java.io.Console` class, which are true? (Choose all that apply.)

A. Objects of type `java.io.Console` are created using a constructor from the same class.

B. Objects of type `java.io.Console` are created using a method from the `java.io.File` class.

C. Objects of type `java.io.Console` are created using a method from the `java.lang.System` class.

D. Objects of type `java.io.Console` are created using a method from the `java.lang.Object` class.

E. The method(s) designed to read passwords can optionally disable the echoing of user input.

F. The method(s) designed to read passwords return a `char[]`.

35. Given:

```
3. public class Stealth {
4.    public static void main(String[] args) {
5.       Integer i = 420;
6.       Integer i2;
7.       Integer i3;
8.       i2 = i.intValue();
9.       i3 = i.valueOf(420);
10.      System.out.println((i == i2) + " " + (i == i3));
11. } }
```

What is the result?

A. `true true`

B. `true false`

C. `false true`

D. false false

E. Compilation fails.

F. An exception is thrown at runtime.

36. Given:

```
2. import java.io.*;
3. interface Risky {
4.    String doStuff() throws Exception;
5.    Risky doCrazy();
6.    void doInsane();
7. }
8. class Bungee implements Risky {
9.    public String doStuff() throws IOException {
10.      throw new IOException();
11.    }
12.    public Bungee doCrazy() { return new Bungee(); }
13.    public void doInsane() throws NullPointerException {
14.      throw new NullPointerException();
15. } }
```

What is the result? (Choose all that apply.)

A. Compilation succeeds.

B. The Risky interface will not compile.

C. The Bungee.doStuff() method will not compile.

D. The Bungee.doCrazy() method will not compile.

E. The Bungee.doInsane() method will not compile.

37. Given that IllegalArgumentException extends RuntimeException, and given:

```
11.  static String s = "";
12.  public static void main(String[] args) {
13.    try { doStuff(); }
14.    catch (Exception ex) { s += "c1 "; }
15.    System.out.println(s);
16.  }
17.  static void doStuff() throws RuntimeException {
18.    try {
19.      s += "t1 ";
20.      throw new IllegalArgumentException();
21.    }
22.    catch (IllegalArgumentException ie) { s += "c2 "; }
23.    throw new IllegalArgumentException();
24.  }
```

What is the result?

A. c1 t1 c2

B. c2 t1 c1

C. t1 c1 c2

D. t1 c2 c1

E. Compilation fails.

F. An uncaught exception is thrown at runtime.

38. Given:

```
1. public class Networking {
2.    public static void main(String[] args) {
3.       List<Integer> i = new LinkedList<Integer>();
4.       i.add(4); i.add(2); i.add(5);
5.       int r = 1;
6.       doStuff(r);
7.       System.out.println(i.get(r));
8.    }
9.    static int doStuff(int x) {
10.      return ++x;
11. } }
```

What is the result?

A. 2

B. 4

C. 5

D. Compilation fails.

E. An exception is thrown at runtime.

39. Given:

```
1. import java.util.*;
2. public class Unturned {
3.    public static void main(String[] args) {
4.       String[] towns = {"aspen", "vail", "t-ride", "dillon"};
5.       MySort ms = new MySort();
6.       Arrays.sort(towns, ms);
7.       System.out.println(Arrays.binarySearch(towns, "dillon"));
8.    }
9.    static class MySort implements Comparator<String> {
10.      public int compare(String a, String b) {
11.         return b.compareTo(a);
12. } } }
```

What is the most likely result?

A. -1

B. 1

C. 2

D. 3

E. Compilation fails.

F. An exception is thrown at runtime.

40. Given:

```
2. class Weed {
3.    protected static String s = "";
4.    final void grow() { s += "grow "; }
5.    static final void growFast() { s += "fast "; }
6. }
7. public class Thistle extends Weed {
8.    void grow() { s += "t-grow "; }
9.    void growFast() { s+= "t-fast "; }
10. }
```

Which are the FEWEST change(s) required for this code to compile? (Choose all that apply.)

A. s must be marked public.

B. Thistle.grow() must be marked final.

C. Weed.grow() must NOT be marked final.

D. Weed.growFast() must NOT be marked final.

E. Weed.growFast() must NOT be marked static.

F. Thistle.growFast() must be removed from the class.

41. Given:

```
2. import java.util.regex.*;
3. public class Decaf {
4.    public static void main(String[] args) {
5.        Pattern p = Pattern.compile(args[0]);
6.        Matcher m = p.matcher(args[1]);
7.        while(m.find())
8.            System.out.print(m.group() + " ");
9. } }
```

And the three command-line invocations:

I. java Decaf "0([0-7])?" "1012 0208 430"

II. java Decaf "0([0-7])*" "1012 0208 430"

III. java Decaf "0([0-7])+" "1012 0208 430"

Which are true? (Choose all that apply.)

A. All three invocations will return valid octal numbers.

B. None of the invocations will return valid octal numbers.

C. Only invocations II and III will return valid octal numbers.

D. All three invocations will return the same set of valid octal numbers.

E. Of those invocations that return only valid octal numbers, each invocation will return a different set of valid octal numbers.

42. Given:

```
1. class Locker extends Thread {
2.    private static Thread t;
3.    public void run() {
4.      if(Thread.currentThread() == t) {
5.        System.out.print("1 ");
6.        synchronized(t) { doSleep(2000); }
7.        System.out.print("2 ");
8.      } else {
9.        System.out.print("3 ");
10.       synchronized(t) { doSleep(1000); }
11.       System.out.print("4 ");
12.     }
13.   }
14.   private void doSleep(long delay) {
15.     try { Thread.sleep(delay); } catch(InterruptedException ie) { ; }
16.   }
17.   public static void main(String args[]) {
18.     t = new Locker();
19.     t.start();
20.     new Locker().start();
21. } }
```

Assuming that `sleep()` sleeps for about the amount of time specified in its argument, and that all other code runs almost instantly, which are true? (Choose all that apply.)

A. Compilation fails.

B. An exception could be thrown.

C. The code could cause a deadlock.

D. The output could be 1 3 4 2

E. The output could be 1 3 2 4

F. The output could be 3 1 4 2

G. The output could be 3 1 2 4

43. Fill in the blanks using the fragments below, so that the code compiles and produces the output: "1 3 2 3 2 "

Note: You might not need to fill in all of the blanks. Also, you won't use all of the fragments, and each fragment can be used only once.

Code:

```
interface Gadget { }
class Watch {
  class Workings implements Gadget {
    Workings() _____

    void tick() _____


    _____    _____
  }
  _____    _____
}
public class Timer {
  public static void main(String[] args) {
    Watch w = new Watch();

    _____ ww = w.new Workings();

    _____
} }
```

Fragments:

```
{ System.out.print("2 "); }          w.tick();
{ Workings in = new Workings(); }    Watch()
{ System.out.print("3 "); }          Watch.Workings
{ System.out.print("1 "); }          Workings
ww.tick();              Workings()
w.Workings              void tock()
```

44. Given:

```
2. public class Later {
3.    public static void main(String[] args) {
4.       boolean earlyExit = new Later().test1(args);
5.       if(earlyExit) assert false;
6.       new Later().test2(args);
7.    }
8.    boolean test1(String[] a) {
9.       if (a.length == 0) return false;
```

```
10.       return true;
11.    }
12.    private void test2(String[] a) {
13.      if (a.length == 2) assert false;
14. } }
```

Which are true? (Choose all that apply.)

A. Compilation fails.

B. The assertion on line 5 is appropriate.

C. The assertion on line 13 is appropriate.

D. "java -ea Later" will run without error.

E. "java -ea Later x" will run without error.

F. "java -ea Later x y" will run without error.

G. "java -ea Later x y z" will run without error.

45. Given:

```
343.   String s = "1234";
344.   StringBuilder sb =
345.     new StringBuilder(s.substring(2).concat("56").replace("7","6"));
346.   System.out.println(sb.append("89").insert(3,"x"));
```

What is the result?

A. 34x5689

B. 345x689

C. 345x789

D. 23x45689

E. 23x45789

F. Compilation fails.

46. Given the following pseudo-code design for a new accounting system:

```
class Employee
  maintainEmployeeInfo()
  connectToRDBMS()

class Payroll
  setStateTaxCodes()
  findEmployeesByState()

class Utilities
  getNetworkPrinter()
```

Assuming the class and method names provide good definitions of their own functionalities, which are probably true? (Choose all that apply.)

A.   These classes appear to have low cohesion.

B.   These classes appear to have high cohesion.

C.   These classes appear to have weak validation.

D.   These classes appear to have strong validation.

E.   These classes appear to have weak encapsulation.

F.   These classes appear to have strong encapsulation.

47.   Given:

```
2. class Dog {
3.    void makeNoise() { System.out.print("bark "); }
4.    static void play() { System.out.print("catching "); }
5. }
6. class Bloodhound extends Dog {
7.    void makeNoise() { System.out.print("howl "); }
8.    public static void main(String[] args) {
9.       new Bloodhound().go();
10.       super.play();
11.       super.makeNoise();
12.    }
13.    void go() {
14.       super.play();
15.       makeNoise();
16.       super.makeNoise();
17. } }
```

What is the result? (Choose all that apply.)

A.   `catching howl bark catching bark`

B.   `catching howl howl catching howl`

C.   `catching howl bark`, then an exception.

D.   Compilation fails due to an error on line 10.

E.   Compilation fails due to an error on line 11.

F.   Compilation fails due to an error on line 14.

48.   Given:

```
3. public class Baskin {
4.    public static void main(String[] args) {
5.       int i = 4;
6.       int j = 1;
7.
```

```
8.       assert(i > Integer.valueOf(args[0]));
9.       assert(j > Integer.valueOf(args[0])): "error 1";
10.      assert(j > i): "error 2": "passed";
11. } }
```

And, if the code compiles, given the following two command-line invocations:

I. `java -ea Baskin 2`

II. `java -ea Baskin 0`

Which are true? (Choose all that apply.)

A. Compilation fails.

B. Invocations I and II will throw an `AssertionError` that will add `String` data to the program's execution log.

C. Invocations I and II will throw an `AssertionError` that will add `String` data to the program's stack trace.

D. Not all of the `assert` statements use assertions appropriately.

49. Given:

```
1. import java.util.*;
2. class Priorities {
3.   public static void main(String[] args) {
4.     PriorityQueue toDo = new PriorityQueue();
5.     toDo.add("dishes");
6.     toDo.add("laundry");
7.     toDo.add("bills");
8.     toDo.offer("bills");
9.     System.out.print(toDo.size() + " " + toDo.poll());
10.    System.out.print(" " + toDo.peek() + " " + toDo.poll());
11.    System.out.println(" " + toDo.poll() + " " + toDo.poll());
12. } }
```

What is the result?

A. `3 bills dishes laundry null null`

B. `3 bills bills dishes laundry null`

C. `3 dishes dishes laundry bills null`

D. `4 bills bills dishes laundry null`

E. `4 bills bills bills dishes laundry`

F. `4 dishes laundry laundry bills bills`

G. Compilation fails.

H. An exception is thrown at runtime.

50. Given that the working directory is `bigApp`, and the following directory structure:

```
bigApp
     |-- classes
     |         |-- com
     |              |-- wickedlysmart
     |-- source
               |-- com
                    |-- wickedlysmart
                                   |-- BigAppClass2.java
```

And the code:

```
1. public class BigAppClass2 { int doMore() { return 17; } }
```

And the following command-line invocations:

I. `javac -d source/com/wickedlysmart/BigAppClass2.java`

II. `javac -d classes source/com/wickedlysmart/BigAppClass2.java`

III. `javac -d classes/com/wickedlysmart source/com/wickedlysmart/BigAppClass2.java`

Which are true? (Choose all that apply.)

A. Invocation I will compile the file and place the .class file in the `bigApp` directory.

B. Invocation II will compile the file and place the .class file in the `classes` directory.

C. Invocation I will compile the file and place the .class file in the `wickedlysmart` directory.

D. Invocation II will compile the file and place the .class file in the `wickedlysmart` directory.

E. Invocation III will compile the file and place the .class file in the `wickedlysmart` directory.

51. Given:

```
 1. class Contact {
 2.    String doStuff() { return "howdy "; }
 3. }
 4. class Supplier extends Contact {
 5.    String doStuff() { return "send money "; }
 6.    public static void main(String[] args) {
 7.       Supplier s1 = new Supplier();
 8.       Contact c3 = new Contact();
 9.       Contact c1 = s1;
10.       Supplier s2 = (Supplier) c1;
11.       Supplier s3 = (Supplier) c3;
12.       Supplier s4 = new Contact();
13. } }
```

Which are true? (Choose all that apply.)

A. Compilation succeeds.

B. The code runs without exception.

C. If the line(s) of code that do NOT compile (if any) are removed, the code runs without exception.

D. If the line(s) of code that do NOT compile (if any) are removed, the code throws an exception at runtime.

52. Given that `Integer.parseInt()` throws `NumberFormatException`, and given:

```
3. public class Ladder {
4.    public static void main(String[] args) {
5.       try {
6.          System.out.println(doStuff(args));
7.       }
8.       catch (Exception e) { System.out.println("exc"); }
9.       doStuff(args);
10.   }
11.   static int doStuff(String[] args) {
12.      return Integer.parseInt(args[0]);
13. } }
```

And, if the code compiles, given the invocation:

```
java Ladder x
```

What is the result? (Choose all that apply.)

A. 0

B. exc

C. "exc" followed by an uncaught exception.

D. Compilation fails due to an error on line 4.

E. Compilation fails due to an error on line 9.

F. Compilation fails due to an error on line 11.

G. An uncaught exception is thrown with no other output.

53. Given the proper imports and given:

```
81.    String in = "1234,77777,689";
82.    Scanner sc = new Scanner(in);
83.    sc.useDelimiter(",");
84.    while(sc.hasNext())
85.       System.out.print(sc.nextInt() + " ");
86.    while(sc.hasNext())
87.       System.out.print(sc.nextShort() + " ");
```

What is the result?

A.   `1234 77777 689`

B.   Compilation fails.

C.   `1234 77777 689 1234 77777 689`

D.   `1234` followed by an exception.

E.   `1234 77777 689` followed by an exception.

F.   `1234 77777 689 1234` followed by an exception.

54.   Given:

```
1. public class Glank implements Vonk { Jooker[] j; }
2. abstract class Bostron { String yoodle; Bostron b; }
3. interface Protefor { }
4. interface Vonk extends Protefor { int x = 7; }
5. class Jooker { Bostron b; }
```

Which are true? (Choose all that apply.)

A.   Glanks have a Bostron.

B.   Jookers implement Protefors.

C.   Glanks implement Bostrons.

D.   Jookers have a String.

E.   Bostrons implement Vonks.

F.   Bostrons have a Bostron.

55.   Given that the root directory contains a subdirectory called `"office"` that contains some files for a Java application, if `"X"` and `"Y"` are unknown arguments, and the following command is invoked from the root directory in order to create a JAR file containing the `office` directory:

```
jar -cf X Y
```

Which are true? (Choose all that apply.)

A.   X should be the file name of the JAR file, and Y should be `"office"`.

B.   X should be `"office"`, and Y should be the file name of the JAR file.

C.   Specifying a file name of the JAR file here is optional.

D.   If a file name is not specified here, a file named `office.jar` will be created.

E.   The file name, if specified, must be ended with `.jar` extension.

F.   It is required that the `"office"` directory must initially have a subdirectory called `"META-INF"`.

G.   All of the files other than .java and .class files must be initially placed in the `META-INF` directory.

56. Given a partial API:

Final class Items implements no interfaces and has one constructor:

```
Items(String name, int value)
```

And given that you want to make collections of Items objects and sort them (using classes and interfaces in java.lang or java.util), sometimes by name, and sometimes by value, which are true? (Choose all that apply.)

A. It's likely that you'll use the Arrays class.

B. It's likely that you'll use the Collections class.

C. It's likely that you'll implement Comparable at least twice.

D. It's likely that you'll implement Comparator at least twice.

E. It's likely that you'll implement the compare() method at least twice.

F. It's likely that you'll implement the compareTo() method at least twice.

57. Given:

```
1.  import java.util.*;
2.  public class Drunken {
3.    public static void main(String[] args) {
4.      Set<Stuff> s = new HashSet<Stuff>();
5.      s.add(new Stuff(3));  s.add(new Stuff(4));  s.add(new Stuff(4));
6.      s.add(new Stuff(5));  s.add(new Stuff(6));
7.      s = null;
8.      // do more stuff
9.    }
10. }
11. class Stuff {
12.   int value;
13.   Stuff(int v) { value = v; }
14. }
```

When line 8 is reached, how many objects are eligible for garbage collection?

A. 4

B. 5

C. 6

D. 8

E. 10

F. 12

58. Given:

```
1. public class Hose <E extends Hose> {
2.   E innerE;
3.   public static E doStuff(E e, Hose<E> e2) {
4.     // insert code here
5.   }
6.   public E getE() {
7.     return innerE;
8. } }
```

Which can be inserted, independently at line 4, for the code to compile? (Choose all that apply.)

A. return e;

B. return e.getE();

C. return e2;

D. return e2.getE();

E. return new Hose().getE();

F. Compilation fails regardless of which return is inserted.

59. Given the following method signatures from `ArrayList`:

```
boolean add(E e)
protected void removeRange(int fromIndexInclusive, int toIndexExclusive)
int size()
```

and given:

```
2. import java.util.*;
3. public class MyUtil extends ArrayList {
4.   public static void main(String[] args) {
5.     MyUtil m = new MyUtil();
6.     m.add("w"); m.add("x"); m.add("y"); m.add("z");
7.     m.removeRange(1,3);
8.     System.out.print(m.size() + " ");
9.     MyUtil m2 = new MyUtil2().go();
10.    System.out.println(m2.size());
11.   }
12. }
13. class MyUtil2 {
14.   MyUtil go() {
15.     MyUtil m2 = new MyUtil();
16.     m2.add("1"); m2.add("2"); m2.add("3");
17.     m2.removeRange(1,2);
18.     return m2;
19. } }
```

What is the result?

A. 1 1

B. 1 2

C. 2 1

D. 2 2

E. An exception is thrown at runtime.

F. Compilation fails due to a single error.

G. Compilation fails due to multiple errors.

60. Given:

```
2. public class Hug implements Runnable {
3.    static Thread t1;
4.    static Hold h, h2;
5.    public void run() {
6.       if(Thread.currentThread().getId() == t1.getId()) h.adjust();
7.       else h2.view();
8.    }
9.    public static void main(String[] args) {
10.      h = new Hold();
11.      h2 = new Hold();
12.      t1 = new Thread(new Hug());
13.      t1.start();
14.      new Thread(new Hug()).start();
15. } }
16. class Hold {
17.    static int x = 5;
18.    synchronized void adjust() {
19.      System.out.print(x-- + " ");
20.      try { Thread.sleep(200); } catch (Exception e) { ; }
21.      view();
22.    }
23.    synchronized void view() {
24.      try { Thread.sleep(200); } catch (Exception e) { ; }
25.      if(x > 0) adjust();
26. } }
```

Which are true? (Choose all that apply.)

A. Compilation fails.

B. The program could deadlock.

C. The output could be 5 4 3 2 1

D. The program could produce thousands of characters of output.

E. If the `sleep()` invocations were removed the chances of deadlock would decrease.

F. If the `view()` method was not synchronized the chances of deadlock would decrease.

QUICK ANSWER KEY

1.	C, G	21.	C	41.	A, E
2.	B	22.	E	42.	D, E, F, G
3.	A	23.	B	43.	Drag and Drop
4.	A	24.	A	44.	D
5.	D	25.	D, G	45.	B
6.	B, C, D, E	26.	B, E, F	46.	A, E
7.	D, E, F	27.	A, D	47.	D, E
8.	A, B, C, D	28.	C	48.	A, D
9.	G	29.	C	49.	E
10.	A	30.	C	50.	B, E
11.	Drag and Drop	31.	C	51.	D
12.	B and E	32.	F	52.	C
13.	A	33.	B	53.	A
14.	B, C, E	34.	C, F	54.	A, D, F
15.	B	35.	D	55.	A
16.	F	36.	A	56.	B, D, E
17.	D	37.	D	57.	C
18.	E	38.	D	58.	F
19.	A, C, F	39.	A	59.	F
20.	A, C	40.	C, F	60.	C

PRACTICE EXAM 1: ANSWERS

1. Given:

```
2. public class Bang extends Thread {
3.    static Thread t1, t2, t3;
4.    public static void main(String[] args) throws Exception {
5.       t1 = new Thread(new Bang());
6.       t2 = new Thread(new Bang());
7.       t3 = new Thread(new Bang());
8.       t1.start();   t2.start();   t3.start();
9.    }
10.   public void run() {
11.      for(int i = 0; i < 500; i++) {
12.         System.out.print(Thread.currentThread().getId() + " ");
13.         if(i == 250)
14.            try {
15.               System.out.print("**" + t1.getId() + "**");
16.               t1.sleep(600);
17.            }
18.            catch (Exception e) { }
19. } } }
```

Which are true? (Choose all that apply.)

A. Compilation fails.

B. An exception is thrown at runtime.

C. Bang will execute for a second or two.

D. Bang will execute for at least 10 minutes.

E. Thread `t1` will almost certainly be the last thread to finish.

F. Thread `t1` will almost certainly be the first thread to finish.

G. It's difficult to predict which thread will be the last to finish.

Answer (for Objective 4.2):

☑ **C** and **G** are correct. The `sleep()` method's argument is in milliseconds. E is incorrect because `sleep` will be called once on each of the three threads, not on `Thread t1` three times. Remember, the `sleep()` method is `static` and operates on whichever thread is the currently running thread.

☒ **A, B, D, E,** and **F** are incorrect based on the above.

2. Given:

```
3. public class Dec26 {
4.    public static void main(String[] args) {
5.      short a1 = 6;
6.      new Dec26().go(a1);
7.      new Dec26().go(new Integer(7));
8.    }
9.    void go(Short x) { System.out.print("S "); }
10.   void go(Long x) { System.out.print("L "); }
11.   void go(int x) { System.out.print("i "); }
12.   void go(Number n) { System.out.print("N "); }
13. }
```

What is the result?

A. i L

B. i N

C. S L

D. S N

E. Compilation fails.

F. An exception is thrown at runtime.

Answer (for Objective 3.1):

☑ **B** is correct. First, code written before Java 5 shouldn't be affected by new Java features like autoboxing, therefore widening is preferred to boxing, producing "i". Second, you can't widen from one wrapper to another. In this case, Integer is-Not-a Long, but Integer is-a Number.

☒ **A, C, D, E,** and **F** are incorrect based on the above.

---

3. Given:

```
1. public class Fellowship {
2.    public static void main(String[] args) {
3.      // insert code here
4.    }
5. }
6. class Numinor {
7.    enum Members {
8.      HOBBITS(48), ELVES(74), DWARVES(50);
9.      int height;
10.     Members(int h) { height = h; }
```

```
11.     int getHeight() { return height; }
12.   }
13. }
```

And these four lines of code to be inserted, independently at line 3:

```
I.    int h0 = Numinor.Members.HOBBITS.getHeight();
II.   int h1 = Numinor.Members.getHeight();
III.  int h2 = Members.HOBBITS.getHeight();
IV.   int h3 = Members.height;
```

Which are true? (Choose all that apply.)

A. Line I will compile.

B. Line II will compile.

C. Line III will compile.

D. Line IV will compile.

E. Class `Numinor` will NOT compile.

Answer (for Objective 1.1):

☑ **A** is the correct syntax to access the `height` variable.

☒ **B, C,** and **D** are incorrect syntax, and **E** is incorrect because enums can have variables, constructors, and methods.

4. Given:

```
2. public class Volume {
3.    Volume v;
4.    int size;
5.    public static void main(String[] args) {
6.       Volume myV = new Volume();
7.       final Volume v2;
8.       v2 = myV.doStuff(myV);
9.       v2.v.size = 7;
10.      System.out.print(v2.size);
11.   }
12.   Volume doStuff(Volume v3) {
13.      v3.size = 5;
14.      v3.v = new Volume();
15.      return v3;
16. } }
```

What is the result? (Choose all that apply.)

A. 5

B. 7

C. Compilation fails due to an error on line 8.

D. Compilation fails due to an error on line 9.

E. Compilation fails due to an error on line 13.

F. Compilation fails due to an error on line 14.

Answer (for Objective 7.3):

☑ **A** is correct. A reference variable marked `"final"` cannot reference a different object, but the object it references can be changed.

☒ **B, C, D, E,** and **F** are incorrect based on the above.

5. Given:

```
3. public class BirdHouse {
4.    public static void main(String[] args) {
5.       String r = "0";
6.       int x = -1, y = -5;
7.       if(x < 5)
8.       if(y > 0)
9.       if(x > y)
10.      r += "1";
11.      else r += "2";
12.      else r += "3";
13.      else r += "4";
14.      System.out.println(r);
15. } }
```

What is the result?

A. 0

B. 01

C. 02

D. 03

E. 013

F. 023

G. Compilation fails.

Answer (for Objective 2.1):

☑ **D** is correct. Obviously, this is horrible code—we're trying to toughen you up for the real thing! Work these nested `if` statements from the inside out. The innermost `"if"` block is lines 9–11. The next set is lines 8 and 12, and finally lines 7 and 13. Given that, the first `"if"` is true, so the second `"if"` is evaluated. Since the second `"if"` test is false, its associated `"else"` (line 12) is executed.

☒ **A, B, C, E, F**, and **G** are incorrect based on the above.

6. Given:

```
 1. class c1 { }
 2. class c2 { }
 3. interface i1 { }
 4. interface i2 { }
 5. class A extends c2 implements i1 { }
 6. class B implements i1 implements i2 { }
 7. class C implements c1 { }
 8. class D extends c1, implements i2 { }
 9. class E extends i1, i2 { }
10. class F implements i1, i2 { }
```

What is the result? (Choose all that apply.)

A. Class A does not compile.

B. Class B does not compile.

C. Class C does not compile.

D. Class D does not compile.

E. Class E does not compile.

F. Class F does not compile.

G. Compilation succeeds for all of the classes.

Answer (for Objective 1.2):

☑ **B, C, D**, and **E** are correct, as those classes will NOT compile. For class B, it's okay to implement two interfaces, but the syntax is incorrect. For class C, classes extend other classes, they don't implement them. For class D, it's okay to extend AND implement, but the syntax is wrong. For class E, it's legal to implement more than one interface, but interfaces are implemented, not extended.

☒ **A** and **F** are declared correctly, and option **G** is incorrect based on the above.

7. Given that `"it, IT"` and `"pt"` are valid `Locale` codes, and given:

```
41.    Date d = new Date();
42.    DateFormat df;
43.    Locale[] la = {new Locale("it", "IT"), new Locale("pt")};
44.    for(Locale l: la) {
45.       df = DateFormat.getDateInstance(DateFormat.FULL, l);
46.       System.out.println(d.format(df));
47.    }
```

Which are true? (Choose all that apply.)

A. An exception will be thrown at runtime.

B. Compilation fails due to an error on line 43.

C. Compilation fails due to an error on line 45.

D. Compilation fails due to an error on line 46.

E. Classes from the `java.text` package are used in this code.

F. Classes from the `java.util` package are used in this code.

Answer (for Objective 3.3):

☑ **D, E,** and **F** are correct. It's okay to mix the two types of `Locale` on line 43. On line 46, we should use the `DateFormat` instance to invoke the `format()` method on the `Date` instance. The rest of the code is legal.

☒ **A, B,** and **C** are incorrect based on the above.

8. Given:

```
2. class SuperCool {
3.    static String os = "";
4.    void doStuff() { os += "super "; }
5. }
6. public class Cool extends SuperCool {
7.    public static void main(String[] args) {
8.       new Cool().go();
9.    }
10.    void go() {
11.       SuperCool s = new Cool();
12.       Cool c = (Cool)s;
13.       // insert code here
14.    }
15.    void doStuff() { os += "cool "; }
16. }
```

If the rest of the code compiles, which line(s) of code, inserted independently at line 13, compile? (Choose all that apply.)

A. `c.doStuff();`

B. `s.doStuff();`

C. `this.doStuff();`

D. `super.doStuff();`

E. `c.super.doStuff();`

F. `s.super.doStuff();`

G. `this.super.doStuff();`

H. There are other errors in the code.

Answer (for Objective 5.2):

☑ **A, B, C,** and **D** are correct. **A, B,** and **C** will invoke `Cool`'s version of `doStuff()`, and **D** will invoke `SuperCool`'s version of `doStuff()`.

☒ **E, F,** and **G** are all illegal syntax to try to invoke `SuperCool`'s version of `doStuff()`. **H** is incorrect because the rest of the code is legal.

9. Given:

```
5.   static String s = "";
6.   public static void main(String[] args) {
7.     try { doStuff(args); }
8.     catch (Error e) { s += "e "; }
9.     s += "x ";
10.    System.out.println(s);
11.  }
12.  static void doStuff(String[] args) {
13.    if(args.length == 0)
14.      throw new IllegalArgumentException();
15.    s += "d ";
16.  }
```

And, if the code compiles, and given a `java` invocation with no arguments, what is the result? (Choose all that apply.)

A. `d x`

B. `e x`

C. d e x

D. Compilation fails due to an error on line 8.

E. Compilation fails due to an error on line 12.

F. Compilation fails due to an error on line 14.

G. An uncaught `IllegalArgumentException` is thrown.

> Answer (for Objective 2.5):
>
> ☑ **G** is correct. It's legal, although uncommon to catch Errors. It's legal to shadow the variable name `"args"`. It's legal to throw a runtime exception without handling it or declaring it. And finally, the `catch` block doesn't catch the exception because exceptions don't extend from `Error`.
>
> ☒ **A, B, C, D, E,** and **F** are incorrect based on the above.

10. Given:

```
2. class Paratrooper implements Runnable {
3.    public void run() {
4.       System.out.print(Thread.currentThread().getName() + " ");
5. } }
6. public class Jump {
7.    static Paratrooper p;
8.    static { p = new Paratrooper(); }
9.    { Thread t1 = new Thread(p, "bob"); t1.start(); }
10.    public static void main(String[] args) {
11.       new Jump();
12.       new Thread(new Runnable() { public void run()
             { ; }}, "carol").start();
13.       new Thread(new Paratrooper(), "alice").start();
14.    }
15.    Jump() { Thread t2 = new Thread(p, "ted"); t2.start(); }
16. }
```

Which are true? (Choose all that apply.)

A. The output could be `ted bob alice`

B. The output could be `bob alice carol`

C. The output could be `bob carol ted alice`

D. Compilation fails due to an error on line 8.

E. Compilation fails due to an error on line 9.

F. Compilation fails due to an error on line 12.

G. Compilation fails due to an error on line 15.

Answer (for Objective 4.1):

☑ **A** is correct. As shown in this code, threads can be started in init blocks, constructors, and inner classes. The thread started in the inner class uses a `run()` method that doesn't print the thread's name, so `"carol"` is not in the output.

☒ **B, C, D, E, F,** and **G** are incorrect based on the above.

11. Use the fragments below to fill in the blanks so that the code will compile, and when invoked with:

```
java Dropkick fish
```

will produce the output: `"1 4 "`

Note: All of the blanks must be filled, not all the fragments will be used, and fragments can be used only once.

Code:

```
public class Dropkick {
   public static void main(String[] args) {
      boolean test = false;
      String[] s = {"duck", null, "frog"};

      if((s[1] == null) ____ (s[1].length() == 0)) System.out.print("1 ");

      if((s[2] == null) ____ (test ____ true)) System.out.print("2 ");

      if((s[0].equals("duck")) ____ (args[0].equals("fish")))
         System.out.print("3 ");
      if((args[0] != null) && (_____)) System.out.print("4 ");
   }
}
```

Fragments:

```
|, ||, &, &&, ^, <, %, =, ==, !=, false, test, s[1]
```

One possible answer (for Objective 7.6):

```
public class Dropkick {
  public static void main(String[] args) {
    boolean test = false;
    String[] s = {"duck", null, "frog"};
    if((s[1] == null) || (s[1].length() == 0)) System.out.print("1 ");
    if((s[2] == null) & (test = true)) System.out.print("2 ");
    if((s[0].equals("duck")) ^ (args[0].equals("fish")))
        System.out.print("3 ");
    if((args[0] != null) && (test)) System.out.print("4 ");
  }
}
```

12. Which are true? (Choose all that apply.)

A. For a specific object, it's NOT possible for `finalize()` to be invoked more than once.

B. It's possible for objects, on whom `finalize()` has been invoked by the JVM, to avoid the GC.

C. Overriding `finalize()` ensures that objects of that type will always be GCed when they become eligible.

D. The `finalize()` method is invoked only for GC-eligible objects that are NOT part of "islands of isolation."

E. For every object that the GC considers collecting, the GC remembers whether `finalize()` has been invoked for that specific object.

Answer (for Objective 7.4):

☑ **B** and **E** are correct. **B** is correct because `finalize()` itself might send a reference to a live thread, thus "uneligible-izing" the object. **E** is just correct.

☒ **A** is incorrect because while the JVM will invoke `finalize()` no more than once per object, your code is free to invoke `finalize()`. **C** and **D** are incorrect because no such rules exist.

13. Given that:

`Exception` is the superclass of `IOException` and

`IOException` is the superclass of `FileNotFoundException`

and

```
2. import java.io.*;
3. class Author {
4.    protected void write() throws IOException { }
5. }
6. public class Salinger extends Author {
7.    private void write(int x) { }
8.    protected void write(long x) throws FileNotFoundException { }
9.    protected void write(boolean x) throws Exception { }
10.    protected int write(short x) { return 7; }
11.    public void write() { }
12. }
```

What is the result? (Choose all that apply.)

A. Compilation succeeds.

B. Compilation fails due to an error on line 7.

C. Compilation fails due to an error on line 8.

D. Compilation fails due to an error on line 9.

E. Compilation fails due to an error on line 10.

F. Compilation fails due to an error on line 11.

Answer (for Objective 1.4):

☑ **A** is correct. All of the overrides and overloads are legal.

☒ **B, C, D, E,** and **F** are incorrect because it's legal for overloaded methods to have different return types, throw different exceptions, and have different access modifiers. Overridden methods have stricter requirements, but lines 7–10 are overloaded methods. Line 11 is an overridden method, and it's legal for overridden methods to have fewer exceptions and less restrictive access modifiers.

14. Given:

```
2. class Chilis {
3.    Chilis(String c, int h) { color = c; hotness = h; }
4.    String color;
5.    int hotness;
6.    public boolean equals(Object o) {
7.       if(this == (Chilis)o) return true;
8.       return false;
9.    }
10.    public String toString() { return color + " " + hotness; }
11. }
```

If instances of class `Chilis` are to be used as keys in a Map, which are true? (Choose all that apply.)

A. Without overriding `hashCode()`, the code will not compile.

B. As it stands, the `equals()` method has been legally overridden.

C. It's possible for such keys to find the correct entries in the Map.

D. It's NOT possible for such keys to find the correct entries in the Map.

E. As it stands, the `Chilis` class legally supports the `equals()` and `hashCode()` contracts.

F. If `hashCode()` was correctly overridden, it would make retrieving Map entries by key easier.

Answer (for Objective 6.2):

☑ **B, C,** and **E** are correct. If a class does NOT override `equals()` and `hashCode()`, class `Object` provides a default implementation. The default implementation's logic is that only two references to THE SAME OBJECT will be considered equal.

Given that, it might appear that `equals()` has been overridden, but in practice this overridden `equals()` method performs exactly as the default method performs. Therefore, the `equals()` and `hashCode()` methods will support their contracts, although it will be hard for a programmer to use this class for keys in a Map.

☒ **A** is incorrect because the code compiles. **D** is incorrect based on the above. **F** is incorrect because in practice `equals()` hasn't really been overridden.

15. Given:

```
2. public class Contact {
3.    private String name;
4.    private String city;
5.    String getName() { return name; }
6.    void setName(String n) { name = n; }
7.    void setCity(String c) {
8.       if(c == null) throw new NullPointerException();
9.       city = c;
10.    }
11.    String getCity() { return city; }
12. }
```

Which are true? (Choose all that apply.)

A. Compilation fails.

B. The class is well encapsulated.

C. The setCity() method is an example of loose coupling.

D. The setCity() method has better encapsulation than setName().

E. The setCity() method is cohesive; the setName() method is not.

Answer (for Objective 5.1):

☑ **B** is correct. The setCity() method includes argument validation, which is a good thing. It's not, by itself, an example of coupling or cohesion. Also, validation doesn't make a method more encapsulated.

☒ **A** is incorrect because it's legal to throw a NullPointerException without handling or declaring it. **C**, **D**, and **E** are incorrect based on the above.

---

16. Given the current directory is bigApp, and the directory structure:

```
bigApp
    |-- classes
              |-- Cloned.class
```

And the file:

```
public class Cloned {
  public static void main(String[] args) {
    System.out.println("classes");
    assert(Integer.parseInt(args[0]) > 0);
} }
```

Which will produce the output "classes" followed by an AssertionError? (Choose all that apply.)

A. java -cp classes Cloned -4

B. java -cp classes -ea Cloned

C. java -ea-cp classes Cloned -4

D. java -ea -cp classes Cloned 4

E. java -ea, cp classes Cloned 4

F. java -ea -cp classes Cloned -4

G. java -cp classes Cloned -4 -ea

Answer (for Objective 7.2):

☑ **F** is the correct syntax for the `java` command.

☒ **A** and **G** do not enable assertions (in **G**, the `-ea` is seen as the second argument). **B** throws an `ArrayIndexOutOfBoundsException`. **C** and **E** are invalid syntax. **D** passes the assert test.

17. Given:

```
1. interface Syrupable {
2.    void getSugary();
3. }
4. abstract class Pancake implements Syrupable { }
5.
6. class BlueBerryPancake implements Pancake {
7.    public void getSugary() { ; }
8. }
9. class SourdoughBlueBerryPancake extends BlueBerryPancake {
10.    void getSugary(int s) { ; }
11. }
```

Which are true? (Choose all that apply.)

A. Compilation succeeds.

B. Compilation fails due to an error on line 2.

C. Compilation fails due to an error on line 4.

D. Compilation fails due to an error on line 6.

E. Compilation fails due to an error on line 7.

F. Compilation fails due to an error on line 9.

G. Compilation fails due to an error on line 10.

Answer (for Objective 1.1):

☑ **D** is correct. Classes extend abstract classes, they don't implement them.

☒ **A, B, C, E, F,** and **G** are incorrect. The method on line 10 doesn't need to be declared `public` because it's an overload of the parent method, not an override.

18. Given:

```
1. public class Endless {
2.    public static void main(String[] args) {
3.       int i = 0;
```

```
4.      short s = 0;
5.      for(int j = 0, k = 0; j < 3; j++) ;
6.      for(int j = 0; j < 3; counter(j)) ;
7.      for(int j = 0, int k = 0; j < 3; j++) ;
8.      for(; i < 5; counter(5), i++) ;
9.      for(i = 0; i < 3; i++, System.out.print("howdy ")) ;
10.   }
11.   static int counter(int y) { return y + 1; }
12. }
```

What is the result? (Choose all that apply.)

A. howdy howdy howdy

B. The code runs in an endless loop.

C. Compilation fails due to an error on line 5.

D. Compilation fails due to an error on line 6.

E. Compilation fails due to an error on line 7.

F. Compilation fails due to an error on line 8.

G. Compilation fails due to an error on line 9.

Answer (for Objective 2.2):

☑ **E** is correct. When defining multiple variables in a `for` loop, line 5 uses the correct syntax.

☒ **A** is incorrect, although if other issues were fixed in the code, line 9 would create that output. **B** is incorrect, although if line 7 was fixed, line 6 would cause an endless loop because the `counter()` method is not incrementing the `for` loop's "j" variable. **C, D, F,** and **G** are incorrect because the rest of the code's syntax is correct.

19. Given:

```
2. class Big {
3.    void doStuff(int x) { }
4. }
5. class Heavy extends Big {
6.    // void doStuff(byte b) { }
7.    // protected void doStuff(int x) throws Exception { }
8. }
9. public class Weighty extends Heavy {
10.   // void doStuff(int x) { }
11.   // String doStuff(int x) { return "hi"; }
12.   // public int doStuff(int x) { return 7; }
13.   // private int doStuff(char c) throws Error { return 1; }
14. }
```

Which method(s), if uncommented independently, compile? (Choose all that apply.)

A. Line 6

B. Line 7

C. Line 10

D. Line 11

E. Line 12

F. Line 13

Answer (for Objective 5.4):

☑ **A, C**, and **F** are correct. **A** and **F** are valid overloads of `Big.doStuff()`, and **C** is a valid override of `Big.doStuff()`.

☒ **B, D**, and **E** are all illegal overrides of `Big.doStuff()`.

---

20. Which are true? (Choose all that apply.)

    A. A given `TreeSet`'s ordering cannot be changed once it's created.

    B. The `java.util.Properties` class is conceptually more like a List than like a Map.

    C. It's a reasonable design choice to use a `LinkedList` when you want to design queue-like functionality.

    D. Of the main types of collections flavors (Lists, Sets, Maps), Queues are conceptually most like Sets.

    E. It's programmatically easier to perform a non-destructive traversal of a `PriorityQueue` than a `LinkedList`.

    F. Classes that implement the `Set` interface are usually well suited for applications that require access to a collection based on an index.

Answer (for Objective 6.1):

☑ **A** and **C** are correct statements.

☒ **B** is incorrect because the `Properties` class is very Map-like. **D** is incorrect because Queues are most like Lists. **E** is incorrect because the `PriorityQueue` class itself provides no non-destructive traversal methods. **F** is incorrect because Lists are much better than Sets at index-based retrieval.

21. Given the following directory structure:

```
test -|
      | - Finder.class
      | - testdir -|
                   | - subdir
                   | - subdir2
                   | - testfile.txt
```

If `test`, `testdir`, `subdir`, and `subdir2` are all directories, and `Finder.class` and `testfile.txt` are files, and given:

```
import java.io.*;
public class Finder {
  public static void main(String[] args) throws IOException {
    String[] files = new String[100];
    File dir = new File(args[0]);
    files = dir.list();
    System.out.println(files.length);
} }
```

And, if the code compiles, the invocation:

```
java Finder testdir
```

What is the result?

A. 1

B. 2

C. 3

D. 4

E. 5

F. 100

G. Compilation fails.

H. An exception is thrown at runtime.

Answer (for Objective 3.2):

☑ **C** is correct. File I/O stuff is risky, but it's okay for `main()` to throw an exception. The `list()` method returns a `String[]` that contains the names of both the files AND subdirectories within the directory specified. Note that the current directory and its contents are not included.

☒ **A, B, D, E, F, G,** and **H** are incorrect based on the above.

22. Given:

```
1. public class Grids {
2.    public static void main(String[] args) {
3.       int [][] ia2;
4.       int [] ia1 = {1,2,3};
5.       Object o = ia1;
6.       ia2 = new int[3][3];
7.       ia2[0] = (int[])o;
8.       ia2[0][0] = (int[])o;
9. } }
```

What is the result? (Choose all that apply.)

A. Compilation fails due to an error on line 4.

B. Compilation fails due to an error on line 5.

C. Compilation fails due to an error on line 6.

D. Compilation fails due to an error on line 7.

E. Compilation fails due to an error on line 8.

F. Compilation succeeds and the code runs without exception.

G. Compilation succeeds and an exception is thrown at runtime.

Answer (for Objective 1.3):

☑ **E** is correct. Remember that arrays are objects, and that each array dimension is a separate type. So, for instance, `ia2` is of type "two dimensional int array", which is a different type than `ia1`. Line 8 attempts to assign a one-dimensional array into an `int`.

☒ **A, B, C,** and **D** are incorrect because lines 4–7 perform legal array manipulations. **F** and **G** are incorrect based on the above.

23. Given:

```
3. public class OffRamp {
4.    public static void main(String[] args) {
5.       int [] exits = {0,0,0,0,0,0};
6.       int x1 = 0;
7.
8.       for(int x = 0; x < 4; x++) exits[0] = x;
9.       for(int x = 0; x < 4; ++x) exits[1] = x;
10.
11.      x1 = 0; while(x1++ < 3) exits[2] = x1;
```

```
12.        x1 = 0; while(++x1 < 3) exits[3] = x1;
13.
14.        x1 = 0; do { exits[4] = x1; }  while(x1++ < 7);
15.        x1 = 0; do { exits[5] = x1; }  while(++x1 < 7);
16.
17.        for(int x: exits)
18.           System.out.print(x + " ");
19. } }
```

What is the result?

A. 3 3 2 2 6 6

B. 3 3 3 2 7 6

C. 3 3 3 2 7 7

D. 4 3 3 2 7 6

E. 4 3 3 2 7 7

F. Compilation fails.

Answer (for Objective 2.2):

☑ **B** is correct. With "for" loops, the last things that happen are the iteration expression and then the conditional expression. With "while" loops, the body only executes if the expression is true. With "do" loops, the body executes first, before the expression is evaluated. The final loop is a legal "for each" loop.

☒ **A, C, D, E,** and **F** are incorrect based on the above.

24. Given:

```
2. import java.util.*;
3. public class HR {
4.    public static void main(String[] args) {
5.       List<Integer> i = new Vector<Integer>();
6.       i.add(3); i.add(2); i.add(5);
7.       int ref = 1;
8.       doStuff(ref);
9.       System.out.println(i.get(ref));
10.   }
11.   static int doStuff(int x) {
12.      return ++x;
13. } }
```

What is the result?

A. 2

B. 3

C. 5

D. Compilation fails.

E. An exception is thrown at runtime.

Answer (for Objective 7.3):

☑ **A** is correct. The variable `"x"` is a copy of `ref`, and when `"x"` gets incremented, `ref` does not. Also, the list index is zero-based and instances of `Vector` aren't automatically sorted.

☒ **B, C, D,** and **E** are incorrect based on the above.

25. Given:

```
 2. import java.util.*;
 3. public class Vinegar {
 4.   public static void main(String[] args) {
 5.     Set<Integer> mySet = new HashSet<Integer>();
 6.     do1(mySet, "0");  do1(mySet, "a");
 7.     do2(mySet, "0");  do2(mySet, "a");
 8.   }
 9.   public static void do1(Set s, String st) {
10.     s.add(st);
11.     s.add(Integer.parseInt(st));
12.   }
13.   public static void do2(Set<Integer> s, String st) {
14.     s.add(st);
15.     s.add(Integer.parseInt(st));
16. } }
```

Which are true? (Choose all that apply.)

A. Compilation succeeds.

B. Compilation fails due to an error on line 6.

C. Compilation fails due to an error on line 13.

D. Compilation fails due to an error on line 14.

E. Compilation fails due to an error on line 15.

F. If only the line(s) of code that don't compile are removed, the code will run without exception.

G. If only the line(s) of code that don't compile are removed, the code will throw an exception.

Answer (for Objective 6.3):

☑ **D** and **G** are correct. It's legal to pass a generic collection to a method that's expecting a non-generic collection. In `do2()`, the compiler knows that `"s"` can contain only `Integers` and that `st` is a `String`. If this line of code is removed, the `parseInt()` invocation will throw a `NumberFormatException` when it is passed `"a"`.

☒ **A, B, C, E,** and **F** are incorrect based on the above.

26. Given:

```
 3. class Employee {
 4.    private String name;
 5.    void setName(String n) { name = n; }
 6.    String getName() { return name; }
 7. }
 8. interface Mungeable {
 9.    void doMunging();
10. }
11. public class MyApp implements Mungeable {
12.    public void doMunging() { ; }
13.    public static void main(String[] args) {
14.       Employee e = new Employee();
15.       e.setName("bob");
16.       System.out.print(e.getName());
17. } }
```

Which are true? (Choose all that apply.)

A. MyApp is-a Employee.

B. MyApp is-a Mungeable.

C. MyApp has-a Employee.

D. MyApp has-a Mungeable.

E. The code is loosely coupled.

F. The Employee class is well encapsulated.

Answer (for Objective 5.5):

☑ **B, E,** and **F** are correct statements about the code.

☒ **A** and **C** are incorrect because the MyApp class "uses" the Employee class, but MyApp isn't in Employee's class hierarchy, and MyApp doesn't "have" an Employee as part of its state. **D** is similarly incorrect because MyApp doesn't "have" a Mungeable as part of its state.

27. Given that `FileNotFoundException` extends `IOException`, and given:

```
2. import java.io.*;
3. public class MacPro extends Laptop {
4.    public static void main(String[] args) {
5.      new MacPro().crunch();
6.    }
7.    // insert code here
8. }
9. class Laptop {
10.    void crunch() throws IOException { }
11. }
```

Which method(s), inserted independently at line 7, compile? (Choose all that apply.)

A. `void crunch() { }`

B. `void crunch() throws Exception { }`

C. `void crunch(int x) throws Exception { }`

D. `void crunch() throws RuntimeException { }`

E. `void crunch() throws FileNotFoundException { }`

Answer (for Objective 2.4):

☑   **A** and **D** are correct. It's legal for an overriding method to throw fewer exceptions, and runtime exceptions are in a class hierarchy separate from checked exceptions.

☒   **C** would be correct if the invocation on line 5 was either handled or declared because it's not an override. **B** is wrong because it's a broader exception. **E** would be correct if the invocation on line 5 was either handled or declared.

28. Given:

```
2. class Horse {
3.    String hands = "15";
4. }
5. class GaitedPony extends Horse {
6.    static String hands = "14";
7.    public static void main(String[] args) {
8.      String hands = "13.2";
9.      String result = new GaitedPony().getSize(hands);
10.      System.out.println(" " + result);
11.    }
12.    String getSize(String s) {
13.      System.out.print("hands: " + s);
14.      return hands;
15. } }
```

What is the result?

A. 14

B. 15

C. hands: 13.2 14

D. hands: 13.2 15

E. Compilation fails.

F. An exception is thrown at runtime.

Answer (for Objective 1.3):

☑ **C** is correct. This code shows a kind of variable "shadowing." In the getSize() method, the question is whether to use the class's static "hands" variable, or to use the superclass's instance "hands" variable. The variable in the same class is used.

☒ **A, B, D, E,** and **F** are incorrect based on the above.

29. Given:

```
2. public class Humping {
3.    public static void main(String[] args) {
4.       String r = "-";
5.       char[] c = {'a', 'b', 'c', 'z'};
6.       for(char c1: c)
7.          switch (c1) {
8.             case 'a': r += "a";
9.             case 'b': r += "b"; break;
10.            default: r += "X";
11.            case 'z': r+= "z";
12.         }
13.      System.out.println(r);
14. } }
```

What is the result?

A. -abXz

B. -abbXz

C. -abbXzz

D. -abbXzXz

E. Compilation fails due to a single error.

F. Compilation fails due to multiple errors.

Answer (for Objective 2.1):

☑ **C** is correct. Remember that a matching case represents the entry point for code execution, not the only point that will be executed. Also, even though the default comes before case "z", when the switch variable equals "z" the switch will skip the default and choose case "z".

☒ **A, B, D, E,** and **F** are incorrect based on the above.

30. Given:

```
1.  import java.util.*;
2.  public class Garage {
3.    public static void main(String[] args) {
4.      Map<String, String> hm = new HashMap<String, String>();
5.      String[] k = {null, "2", "3", null, "5"};
6.      String[] v = {"a", "b", "c", "d", "e"};
7.
8.      for(int i=0; i<5; i++) {
9.        hm.put(k[i], v[i]);
10.       System.out.print(hm.get(k[i]) + " ");
11.     }
12.     System.out.print(hm.size() + " " + hm.values() + "\n");
13. } }
```

What result is most likely?

A. a b c a e 4 [c, b, a, e]

B. a b c d e 4 [c, b, a, e]

C. a b c d e 4 [c, d, b, e]

D. a b c, followed by an exception.

E. An exception is thrown with no other output.

F. Compilation fails due to error(s) in the code.

Answer (for Objective 6.1):

☑ **C** is correct. It's legal for a HashMap to have one null key, and if you invoke put() using an existing key, the new value replaces the old value. The values() method does NOT guarantee any ordering.

☒ **A, B, D, E,** and **F** are incorrect based on the above.

31. Given:

```
2. class Jiggy extends Thread {
3.    Jiggy(String n) { super(n); }
4.    public void run() {
5.      for(int i = 0; i < 100; i++) {
6.        if("t1".equals(Thread.currentThread().getName()) && i == 5) {
7.          new Jiggy("t3").start();
8.          throw new Error();
9.        }
10.       if("t2".equals(Thread.currentThread().getName()) && i == 5) {
11.         new Jiggy("t4").start();
12.         throw new Error();
13.       }
14.       System.out.print(Thread.currentThread().getName() + "-");
15.     }
16.   }
17.   public static void main(String[] args) {
18.     Thread t1 = new Jiggy("t1");
19.     Thread t2 = new Jiggy("t2");
20.     t1.setPriority(1);  t2.setPriority(9);
21.     t2.start();  t1.start();
22. } }
```

Which are true? (Choose all that apply.)

A. Compilation fails.

B. After throwing error(s), t3 will most likely complete before t4.

C. After throwing error(s), t4 will most likely complete before t3.

D. The code will throw one error and then no more output will be produced.

E. The code will throw two errors and then no more output will be produced.

F. After throwing error(s) it's difficult to determine whether t3 or t4 will complete first.

Answer (for Objective 4.2):

☑ **C** is correct. Threads can be constructed with a name. The errors will stop t1 and t2, but t3 and t4 will continue. The thread t4 will complete before t3 because it more or less "inherits" its priority from the thread that created it, t2.

☒ **A, B, D, E,** and **F** are incorrect based on the above.

32. Given:

```
3. class Stereo { void makeNoise() { assert false; } }
4. public class BoomBox extends Stereo {
5.    public static void main(String[] args) {
6.      new BoomBox().go(args);
7.    }
8.    void go(String[] args) {
9.      if(args.length > 0)  makeNoise();
10.      if(!args[0].equals("x")) System.out.println("!x");
11. } }
```

And, if the code compiles, the invocation:

```
java -ea BoomBox
```

What is the result?

A. !x

B. Compilation fails.

C. An AssertionError is thrown.

D. A NullPointerException is thrown.

E. An IllegalArgumentException is thrown.

F. An ArrayIndexOutOfBoundsException is thrown.

Answer (for Objective 2.6):

☑ **F** is correct. The java invocation passes no arguments to main(), so the args array has a length of 0, makeNoise() is not called, and line 10 throws an exception.

☒ **A, B, C, D,** and **E** are incorrect based on the above.

33. Given:

```
1. public class LaSelva extends Beach {
2.    LaSelva() { s = "LaSelva"; }
3.    public static void main(String[] args) { new LaSelva().go(); }
4.     void go() {
5.      Beach[] ba = { new Beach(), new LaSelva(), (Beach) new LaSelva() };
6.      for(Beach b: ba)  System.out.print(b.getBeach().s + " ");
7.    }
8.    LaSelva getBeach() { return this; }
9. }
10. class Beach {
11.    String s;
```

```
12.    Beach() { s = "Beach"; }
13.    Beach getBeach() { return this; }
14. }
```

What is the result?

A. `Beach LaSelva Beach`

B. `Beach LaSelva LaSelva`

C. `Beach LaSelva` followed by an exception.

D. Compilation fails due to an error at line 5.

E. Compilation fails due to an error at line 6.

F. Compilation fails due to an error at line 8.

G. Compilation fails due to an error at line 13.

Answer (for Objective 1.4):

☑ **B** is correct. Line 5 is declaring a `Beach` array and assigning three `Beach`-ish objects to it. The third object created in line 5 was created as type `LaSelva`, and then upcast to type `Beach`, but the value of its `String` didn't change when it was upcast. Next, `LaSelva`'s overriding `getBeach()` method is using a legal (as of Java 5) covariant return.

☒ **A, C, D, E, F**, and **G** are incorrect based on the above.

34. When using the `java.io.Console` class, which are true? (Choose all that apply.)

A. Objects of type `java.io.Console` are created using a constructor from the same class.

B. Objects of type `java.io.Console` are created using a method from the `java.io.File` class.

C. Objects of type `java.io.Console` are created using a method from the `java.lang.System` class.

D. Objects of type `java.io.Console` are created using a method from the `java.lang.Object` class.

E. The method(s) designed to read passwords can optionally disable the echoing of user input.

F. The method(s) designed to read passwords return a `char []`.

Answer (for Objective 3.2):

☑ **C** and **F** are correct.

☒ **A, B**, and **D** describe nonexistent approaches. **E** is incorrect because the `readPassword()` methods always disable the echoing of user input.

35. Given:

```
3. public class Stealth {
4.   public static void main(String[] args) {
5.     Integer i = 420;
6.     Integer i2;
7.     Integer i3;
8.     i2 = i.intValue();
9.     i3 = i.valueOf(420);
10.    System.out.println((i == i2) + " " + (i == i3));
11. } }
```

What is the result?

A. true true

B. true false

C. false true

D. false false

E. Compilation fails.

F. An exception is thrown at runtime.

Answer (for Objective 7.6):

☑ **D** is correct. In this code, lines 8 and 9 each create a new `Integer` object, and `==` tests whether two references refer to the same object.

☒ **A, B, C, E,** and **F** are incorrect based on the above.

36. Given:

```
2. import java.io.*;
3. interface Risky {
4.   String doStuff() throws Exception;
5.   Risky doCrazy();
6.   void doInsane();
7. }
8. class Bungee implements Risky {
9.   public String doStuff() throws IOException {
10.    throw new IOException();
11.  }
12.  public Bungee doCrazy() { return new Bungee(); }
13.  public void doInsane() throws NullPointerException {
14.    throw new NullPointerException();
15. } }
```

What is the result? (Choose all that apply.)

A. Compilation succeeds.

B. The Risky interface will not compile.

C. The Bungee.doStuff() method will not compile.

D. The Bungee.doCrazy() method will not compile.

E. The Bungee.doInsane() method will not compile.

Answer (for Objective 1.2):

☑ **A** is correct, the code is all legal. It's okay for an interface method to declare an exception. It's okay for an implementing method to throw either a narrower exception or runtime exception. Finally, it's okay for an implementing method to use a covariant return (as in line 12).

☒ **B, C, D,** and **E** are incorrect based on the above.

37. Given that IllegalArgumentException extends RuntimeException, and given:

```
11.   static String s = "";
12.   public static void main(String[] args) {
13.     try { doStuff(); }
14.     catch (Exception ex) { s += "c1 "; }
15.     System.out.println(s);
16.   }
17.   static void doStuff() throws RuntimeException {
18.     try {
19.       s += "t1 ";
20.       throw new IllegalArgumentException();
21.     }
22.     catch (IllegalArgumentException ie) { s += "c2 "; }
23.     throw new IllegalArgumentException();
24.   }
```

What is the result?

A. c1 t1 c2

B. c2 t1 c1

C. t1 c1 c2

D. t1 c2 c1

E. Compilation fails.

F. An uncaught exception is thrown at runtime.

Answer (for Objective 2.4):

☑ **D** is correct. The first exception is handled in doStuff(); the second is declared in doStuff() and handled in main().

☒ **A, B, C, E,** and **F** are incorrect based on the above.

38. Given:

```
1. public class Networking {
2.    public static void main(String[] args) {
3.       List<Integer> i = new LinkedList<Integer>();
4.       i.add(4); i.add(2); i.add(5);
5.       int r = 1;
6.       doStuff(r);
7.       System.out.println(i.get(r));
8.    }
9.    static int doStuff(int x) {
10.       return ++x;
11. } }
```

What is the result?

A. 2

B. 4

C. 5

D. Compilation fails.

E. An exception is thrown at runtime.

Answer (for Objective 7.1):

☑ **D** is correct. Of course, you need to import some stuff for this program to compile. This is an easy question if you spot the problem. If you don't, it'll seem tricky, so watch out for these on the real exam. With the proper import statements in place, **A** would be correct.

☒ **A, B, C,** and **E** are incorrect based on the above.

39. Given:

```
1. import java.util.*;
2. public class Unturned {
3.    public static void main(String[] args) {
4.       String[] towns = {"aspen", "vail", "t-ride", "dillon"};
5.       MySort ms = new MySort();
```

```
6.        Arrays.sort(towns, ms);
7.        System.out.println(Arrays.binarySearch(towns, "dillon"));
8.     }
9.   static class MySort implements Comparator<String> {
10.     public int compare(String a, String b) {
11.        return b.compareTo(a);
12. } } }
```

What is the most likely result?

A. -1

B. 1

C. 2

D. 3

E. Compilation fails.

F. An exception is thrown at runtime.

Answer (for Objective 6.5):

☑ **A** is correct. The binarySearch() method gives meaningful results only if it uses the same Comparator as the one used to sort the array. The static inner class is legal, and on the real exam expect to find inner classes sprinkled throughout questions that are focused on other objectives.

☒ **B, C, D, E,** and **F** are incorrect based on the above.

40. Given:

```
2. class Weed {
3.    protected static String s = "";
4.    final void grow() { s += "grow "; }
5.    static final void growFast() { s += "fast "; }
6. }
7. public class Thistle extends Weed {
8.    void grow() { s += "t-grow "; }
9.    void growFast() { s+= "t-fast "; }
10. }
```

Which are the FEWEST change(s) required for this code to compile? (Choose all that apply.)

A. s must be marked public.

B. Thistle.grow() must be marked final.

C. `Weed.grow()` must NOT be marked `final`.

D. `Weed.growFast()` must NOT be marked `final`.

E. `Weed.growFast()` must NOT be marked `static`.

F. `Thistle.growFast()` must be removed from the class.

Answer (for Objective 5.3):

☑ **C** and **F** are correct. `Thistle` can already access s. If `Weed.grow()` is NOT `final`, then `Thistle` can override it. In order for `Weed.growFast()` to be overridden, two changes (**D** and **E**), must occur, so for this question, it would require FEWER changes to remove `Thistle.growFast()` and not attempt an override.
Note: We don't like this kind of question either, but you may encounter some like it on the real exam.

☒ **A, B, D**, and **E** are incorrect based on the above.

41. Given:

```
2. import java.util.regex.*;
3. public class Decaf {
4.    public static void main(String[] args) {
5.       Pattern p = Pattern.compile(args[0]);
6.       Matcher m = p.matcher(args[1]);
7.       while(m.find())
8.          System.out.print(m.group() + " ");
9. } }
```

And the three command-line invocations:

I. `java Decaf "0([0-7])?" "1012 0208 430"`

II. `java Decaf "0([0-7])*" "1012 0208 430"`

III. `java Decaf "0([0-7])+" "1012 0208 430"`

Which are true? (Choose all that apply.)

A. All three invocations will return valid octal numbers.

B. None of the invocations will return valid octal numbers.

C. Only invocations II and III will return valid octal numbers.

D. All three invocations will return the same set of valid octal numbers.

E. Of those invocations that return only valid octal numbers, each invocation will return a different set of valid octal numbers.

Answer (for Objective 3.4):

☑ **A** and **E** are correct. The three invocations will return:

I. - 01 02 0 0

II. - 012 020 0

III. - 012 020

Of course, the key to this question is to remember how the three quantifiers (?, *, and +) work.

☒ **B, C,** and **D** are incorrect based on the output given above.

42. Given:

```
1. class Locker extends Thread {
2.    private static Thread t;
3.    public void run() {
4.       if(Thread.currentThread() == t) {
5.          System.out.print("1 ");
6.          synchronized(t) { doSleep(2000); }
7.          System.out.print("2 ");
8.       } else {
9.          System.out.print("3 ");
10.         synchronized(t) { doSleep(1000); }
11.         System.out.print("4 ");
12.      }
13.   }
14.   private void doSleep(long delay) {
15.      try { Thread.sleep(delay); } catch(InterruptedException ie) { ; }
16.   }
17.   public static void main(String args[]) {
18.      t = new Locker();
19.      t.start();
20.      new Locker().start();
21. } }
```

Assuming that `sleep()` sleeps for about the amount of time specified in its argument, and that all other code runs almost instantly, which are true? (Choose all that apply.)

A. Compilation fails.

B. An exception could be thrown.

C. The code could cause a deadlock.

D. The output could be 1 3 4 2

E. The output could be 1 3 2 4

F. The output could be 3 1 4 2

G. The output could be 3 1 2 4

Answer (for Objective 4.3):

☑ **D, E, F,** and **G** are correct. When one thread prints `"1"`, the other thread prints `"3"` and then either thread could hold the monitor lock of `"t"`. The other thread will wait until the lock is released and both threads will continue to normal completion.

☒ **A, B,** and **C** are incorrect based on the above.

43. Fill in the blanks using the fragments below, so that the code compiles and produces the output: `"1 3 2 3 2 "`

Note: You might not need to fill in all of the blanks. Also, you won't use all of the fragments, and each fragment can be used only once.

Code:

```
interface Gadget { }
class Watch {
   class Workings implements Gadget {
      Workings() _____

      void tick() _____


      _____      _____
   }
   _____      _____
}
public class Timer {
   public static void main(String[] args) {
      Watch w = new Watch();

      _____ ww = w.new Workings();


      _____
} }
```

Fragments:

```
{ System.out.print("2 "); }          w.tick();
{ Workings in = new Workings(); }     Watch()
{ System.out.print("3 "); }          Watch.Workings
{ System.out.print("1 "); }          Workings
ww.tick();              Workings()
w.Workings              void tock()
```

Answer (for Objective 1.5):

```
interface Gadget { }
class Watch {
  class Workings implements Gadget {
    Workings() { System.out.print("2 "); }
    void tick() { Workings in = new Workings();  }
    { System.out.print("3 "); }
  }
  Watch() { System.out.print("1 "); }
}
public class Timer {
  public static void main(String[] args) {
    Watch w = new Watch();
    Watch.Workings ww = w.new Workings();
    ww.tick();
  }
} }
```

Answer Notes: It's legal for inner classes to implement interfaces, have constructors, and have initialization blocks.

44. Given:

```
2. public class Later {
3.    public static void main(String[] args) {
4.       boolean earlyExit = new Later().test1(args);
5.       if(earlyExit) assert false;
6.       new Later().test2(args);
7.    }
8.    boolean test1(String[] a) {
9.       if (a.length == 0) return false;
10.      return true;
11.   }
12.   private void test2(String[] a) {
13.      if (a.length == 2) assert false;
14. } }
```

Which are true? (Choose all that apply.)

A. Compilation fails.

B. The assertion on line 5 is appropriate.

C. The assertion on line 13 is appropriate.

D. `"java -ea Later"` will run without error.

E. `"java -ea Later x"` will run without error.

F. `"java -ea Later x y"` will run without error.

G. `"java -ea Later x y z"` will run without error.

> Answer (for Objective 2.3):
>
> ☑ **D** is correct. This invocation will run without error.
>
> ☒ **A, B,** and **C** are incorrect because the code compiles, and neither assertion is appropriate because ultimately they are testing the `args` of `main()`. **E, F,** and **G** are incorrect. Each will throw an `AssertionError`.

45. Given:

```
343.   String s = "1234";
344.   StringBuilder sb =
345.      new StringBuilder(s.substring(2).concat("56").replace("7","6"));
346.   System.out.println(sb.append("89").insert(3,"x"));
```

What is the result?

A.   34x5689

B.   345x689

C.   345x789

D.   23x45689

E.   23x45789

F.   Compilation fails.

> Answer (for Objective 3.1):
>
> ☑ **B** is correct. The keys to remember are that indexes are 0-based, and that chained methods work from left to right. Also, the `replace()` method's first argument is the character to be replaced, so in this case the `replace()` invocation has no effect on the `StringBuilder`.
>
> ☒ **A, C, D, E,** and **F** are incorrect based on the above.

46. Given the following pseudo-code design for a new accounting system:

```
class Employee
  maintainEmployeeInfo()
  connectToRDBMS()

class Payroll
  setStateTaxCodes()
  findEmployeesByState()

class Utilities
  getNetworkPrinter()
```

Assuming the class and method names provide good definitions of their own functionalities, which are probably true? (Choose all that apply.)

A.   These classes appear to have low cohesion.

B.   These classes appear to have high cohesion.

C.   These classes appear to have weak validation.

D.   These classes appear to have strong validation.

E.   These classes appear to have weak encapsulation.

F.   These classes appear to have strong encapsulation.

Answer (for Objective 5.1):

☑   **A** and **E** are correct. Although somewhat subjective, **A** is correct because a method like `connectToRDBMS()` seems better placed in a utility class. As it stands, it makes the `Employee` class have low cohesion. **E** is probably correct because the `findEmployeesByState()` method should probably be placed in the `Employee` class. As it stands, the location of this method doesn't absolutely predict weak encapsulation, but it seems a likely outcome.

☒   **B** and **F** are incorrect based on the above. **C** and **D** are incorrect because there is no way to determine the degree of validation based on the data provided.

47.   Given:

```
2. class Dog {
3.   void makeNoise() { System.out.print("bark "); }
4.   static void play() { System.out.print("catching "); }
5. }
6. class Bloodhound extends Dog {
7.   void makeNoise() { System.out.print("howl "); }
8.   public static void main(String[] args) {
9.     new Bloodhound().go();
10.    super.play();
11.    super.makeNoise();
12.   }
13.   void go() {
14.     super.play();
15.     makeNoise();
16.     super.makeNoise();
17. } }
```

What is the result? (Choose all that apply.)

A. `catching howl bark catching bark`

B. `catching howl howl catching howl`

C. `catching howl bark`, then an exception.

D. Compilation fails due to an error on line 10.

E. Compilation fails due to an error on line 11.

F. Compilation fails due to an error on line 14.

Answer (for Objective 5.4):

☑ **D** and **E** are correct. Remember `"super"` is an instance variable, so it CANNOT be used from the `static` context of `main()`.

☒ **A, B, C**, and **F** are incorrect based on the above.

---

48. Given:

```
3. public class Baskin {
4.    public static void main(String[] args) {
5.       int i = 4;
6.       int j = 1;
7.
8.       assert(i > Integer.valueOf(args[0]));
9.       assert(j > Integer.valueOf(args[0])): "error 1";
10.      assert(j > i): "error 2": "passed";
11. } }
```

And, if the code compiles, given the following two command-line invocations:

I. `java -ea Baskin 2`

II. `java -ea Baskin 0`

Which are true? (Choose all that apply.)

A. Compilation fails.

B. Invocations I and II will throw an `AssertionError` that will add `String` data to the program's execution log.

C. Invocations I and II will throw an `AssertionError` that will add `String` data to the program's stack trace.

D. Not all of the `assert` statements use assertions appropriately.

Answer (for Objective 2.3):

☑ **A** and **D** are correct. The syntax on line 10 is invalid and will not compile. The `assert` statements on lines 8 and 9 are testing the arguments of a `public` method, which is considered an inappropriate use of assertions. If the syntax on line 10 was fixed, then option **C** would be correct.

☒ **B** and **C** are incorrect based on the above.

49. Given:

```
1. import java.util.*;
2. class Priorities {
3.   public static void main(String[] args) {
4.       PriorityQueue toDo = new PriorityQueue();
5.       toDo.add("dishes");
6.       toDo.add("laundry");
7.       toDo.add("bills");
8.       toDo.offer("bills");
9.       System.out.print(toDo.size() + " " + toDo.poll());
10.      System.out.print(" " + toDo.peek() + " " + toDo.poll());
11.      System.out.println(" " + toDo.poll() + " " + toDo.poll());
12. } }
```

What is the result?

A. `3 bills dishes laundry null null`

B. `3 bills bills dishes laundry null`

C. `3 dishes dishes laundry bills null`

D. `4 bills bills dishes laundry null`

E. `4 bills bills bills dishes laundry`

F. `4 dishes laundry laundry bills bills`

G. Compilation fails.

H. An exception is thrown at runtime.

Answer (for Objective 6.2):

☑ **E** is correct. The `add()` and `offer()` methods have the same functionality, and it's okay for `PriorityQueues` to have duplicate elements. Remembering that `PriorityQueues` are sorted, the `poll()` method removes the first element in the queue and returns it. The `peek()` method returns the first element from the queue but does NOT remove it.

☒ **A, B, C, D, F, G**, and **H** are incorrect based on the above.

50. Given that the working directory is `bigApp`, and the following directory structure:

```
bigApp
    |-- classes
    |        |-- com
    |             |-- wickedlysmart
    |-- source
             |-- com
                  |-- wickedlysmart
                             |-- BigAppClass2.java
```

And the code:

```
1. public class BigAppClass2 { int doMore() { return 17; } }
```

And the following command-line invocations:

I. `javac -d source/com/wickedlysmart/BigAppClass2.java`

II. `javac -d classes source/com/wickedlysmart/BigAppClass2.java`

III. `javac -d classes/com/wickedlysmart source/com/wickedlysmart/BigAppClass2.java`

Which are true? (Choose all that apply.)

A. Invocation I will compile the file and place the .class file in the `bigApp` directory.

B. Invocation II will compile the file and place the .class file in the `classes` directory.

C. Invocation I will compile the file and place the .class file in the `wickedlysmart` directory.

D. Invocation II will compile the file and place the .class file in the `wickedlysmart` directory.

E. Invocation III will compile the file and place the .class file in the `wickedlysmart` directory.

Answer (for Objective 7.2):

☑ **B** and **E** correctly describe the results that the `-d` option will produce. Note that the `BigAppClass2` class doesn't have a package statement.

☒ **A** and **C** will not compile. Option **D** is incorrect based on the above.

---

51. Given:

```
1. class Contact {
2.    String doStuff() { return "howdy "; }
3. }
4. class Supplier extends Contact {
5.    String doStuff() { return "send money "; }
```

```
6.    public static void main(String[] args) {
7.        Supplier s1 = new Supplier();
8.        Contact c3 = new Contact();
9.        Contact c1 = s1;
10.       Supplier s2 = (Supplier) c1;
11.       Supplier s3 = (Supplier) c3;
12.       Supplier s4 = new Contact();
13. } }
```

Which are true? (Choose all that apply.)

A. Compilation succeeds.

B. The code runs without exception.

C. If the line(s) of code that do NOT compile (if any) are removed, the code runs without exception.

D. If the line(s) of code that do NOT compile (if any) are removed, the code throws an exception at runtime.

Answer (for Objective 5.2):

☑ **D** is correct. Once line 12 is removed, the code will compile but throw a `ClassCastException` at line 11.

☒ **A**, **B**, and **C** are incorrect based on the above.

52. Given that `Integer.parseInt()` throws `NumberFormatException`, and given:

```
3. public class Ladder {
4.    public static void main(String[] args) {
5.        try {
6.            System.out.println(doStuff(args));
7.        }
8.        catch (Exception e) { System.out.println("exc"); }
9.        doStuff(args);
10.   }
11.   static int doStuff(String[] args) {
12.       return Integer.parseInt(args[0]);
13. } }
```

And, if the code compiles, given the invocation:

```
java Ladder x
```

What is the result? (Choose all that apply.)

A. 0

B. exc

C. "exc" followed by an uncaught exception.

D. Compilation fails due to an error on line 4.

E. Compilation fails due to an error on line 9.

F. Compilation fails due to an error on line 11.

G. An uncaught exception is thrown with no other output.

Answer (for Objective 2.5):

☑ **C** is correct. When "x" is the argument, a NumberFormatException (NFE) is thrown at line 12. Because this is a runtime exception, it doesn't have to be declared, and it's still propagated up to main(). The first time doStuff() is invoked, the NFE is handled in main(); the second time it is not handled.

☒ **A, B, D, E, F,** and **G** are incorrect based on the above.

53. Given the proper imports and given:

```
81.     String in = "1234,77777,689";
82.     Scanner sc = new Scanner(in);
83.     sc.useDelimiter(",");
84.     while(sc.hasNext())
85.       System.out.print(sc.nextInt() + " ");
86.     while(sc.hasNext())
87.       System.out.print(sc.nextShort() + " ");
```

What is the result?

A. 1234 77777 689

B. Compilation fails.

C. 1234 77777 689 1234 77777 689

D. 1234 followed by an exception.

E. 1234 77777 689 followed by an exception.

F. 1234 77777 689 1234 followed by an exception.

Answer (for Objective 3.4):

☑ **A** is correct. The first `while` loop "consumes" the `Scanner` object, so the second `while` loop has nothing to process. If the first `while` loop didn't exist, the second `while` loop would throw an out of range exception because shorts cannot be larger than 32767.

☒ **B, C, D, E**, and **F** are incorrect based on the above.

54. Given:

```
1. public class Glank implements Vonk { Jooker[] j; }
2. abstract class Bostron { String yoodle; Bostron b; }
3. interface Protefor { }
4. interface Vonk extends Protefor { int x = 7; }
5. class Jooker { Bostron b; }
```

Which are true? (Choose all that apply.)

A. Glanks have a Bostron.

B. Jookers implement Protefors.

C. Glanks implement Bostrons.

D. Jookers have a String.

E. Bostrons implement Vonks.

F. Bostrons have a Bostron.

Answer (for Objective 5.5):

☑ **A, D**, and **F** correctly describe some of the relationships within the code. Glanks have Bostrons indirectly through Jookers. Jookers have Strings indirectly through Bostrons, and Bostrons have Bostrons because it's very common to want to make linked lists with your Bostrons.

☒ **B** and **E** are incorrect because no such hierarchies exist in the code. **C** is incorrect because Glanks "have" Bostrons (indirectly), but they don't implement them.

55. Given that the root directory contains a subdirectory called `"office"` that contains some files for a Java application, if `"X"` and `"Y"` are unknown arguments, and the following command is invoked from the root directory in order to create a JAR file containing the `office` directory:

```
jar -cf X Y
```

Which are true? (Choose all that apply.)

A. "X" should be the file name of the JAR file, and "Y" should be "office"

B. "X" should be "office", and "Y" should be the file name of the JAR file.

C. Specifying a file name of the JAR file here is optional.

D. If a file name is not specified here, a file named office.jar will be created.

E. The file name, if specified, must be ended with .jar extension.

F. It is required that the "office" directory must initially have a subdirectory called "META-INF"

G. All of the files other than .java and .class files must be initially placed in the META-INF directory.

Answer (for Objective 7.5):

☑ A describes the correct syntax, therefore B is incorrect.

☒ C and D are incorrect because when the "f" option is used, you must specify a file name for the JAR file. E is incorrect because it's not required that the file name end with ".jar". F and G are incorrect because the META-INF directory is automatically created by this command.

56. Given a partial API:

Final class Items implements no interfaces and has one constructor:

```
Items(String name, int value)
```

And given that you want to make collections of Items objects and sort them (using classes and interfaces in java.lang or java.util), sometimes by name, and sometimes by value, which are true? (Choose all that apply.)

A. It's likely that you'll use the Arrays class.

B. It's likely that you'll use the Collections class.

C. It's likely that you'll implement Comparable at least twice.

D. It's likely that you'll implement Comparator at least twice.

E. It's likely that you'll implement the compare() method at least twice.

F. It's likely that you'll implement the compareTo() method at least twice.

Answer (for Objective 6.5):

☑ **B, D,** and **E** are correct. The most natural way to use the Java API in this case would be to create two classes, each of which implements `Comparator`. Each class that implements `Comparator` will implement a `compare()` method. Once this is done, you'd use `Collections.sort()` to sort the collections.

☒ **A, C,** and **F** are incorrect based on the above.

57. Given:

```
1. import java.util.*;
2. public class Drunken {
3.    public static void main(String[] args) {
4.       Set<Stuff> s = new HashSet<Stuff>();
5.       s.add(new Stuff(3));  s.add(new Stuff(4));  s.add(new Stuff(4));
6.       s.add(new Stuff(5));  s.add(new Stuff(6));
7.       s = null;
8.       // do more stuff
9.    }
10. }
11. class Stuff {
12.    int value;
13.    Stuff(int v) { value = v; }
14. }
```

When line 8 is reached, how many objects are eligible for garbage collection?

A. 4

B. 5

C. 6

D. 8

E. 10

F. 12

Answer (for Objective 7.4):

☑ **C** is correct. Because `Stuff` doesn't override `equals()`, there are five objects in the `HashSet`, plus the `HashSet` is also an object. The `int` primitive associated with each `Stuff` object is not an object. Note: Even if `equals()` was overridden, six objects would be eligible. The duplicate `Stuff` object, while not in the Set, would still be eligible.

☒ **A, B, D, E,** and **F** are incorrect based on the above.

58. Given:

```
1. public class Hose <E extends Hose> {
2.    E innerE;
3.    public static E doStuff(E e, Hose<E> e2) {
4.       // insert code here
5.    }
6.    public E getE() {
7.       return innerE;
8. } }
```

Which can be inserted, independently at line 4, for the code to compile? (Choose all that apply.)

A. `return e;`

B. `return e.getE();`

C. `return e2;`

D. `return e2.getE();`

E. `return new Hose().getE();`

F. Compilation fails regardless of which return is inserted.

Answer (for Objective 6.4):

☑ **F** is correct. The generic type `"E"`, which is declared at the class level, will be associated with each instance of `Hose`, and is not accessible to `static` methods. If `doStuff()` was non-static, **A** and **D** would be correct.

☒ **A, B, C, D,** and **E** are incorrect based on the above.

59. Given the following method signatures from `ArrayList`:

```
boolean add(E e)
protected void removeRange(int fromIndexInclusive, int toIndexExclusive)
int size()
```

and given:

```
2. import java.util.*;
3. public class MyUtil extends ArrayList {
4.    public static void main(String[] args) {
5.       MyUtil m = new MyUtil();
6.       m.add("w");  m.add("x");  m.add("y");  m.add("z");
7.       m.removeRange(1,3);
8.       System.out.print(m.size() + " ");
9.       MyUtil m2 = new MyUtil2().go();
```

```
10.      System.out.println(m2.size());
11.    }
12. }
13. class MyUtil2 {
14.    MyUtil go() {
15.      MyUtil m2 = new MyUtil();
16.      m2.add("1");  m2.add("2");  m2.add("3");
17.      m2.removeRange(1,2);
18.      return m2;
19. } }
```

What is the result?

A. 1 1

B. 1 2

C. 2 1

D. 2 2

E. An exception is thrown at runtime.

F. Compilation fails due to a single error.

G. Compilation fails due to multiple errors.

Answer (for Objective 5.3):

☑ **F** is correct. The `removeRange()` method is protected and so cannot be accessed from the `MyUtil2` class. The rest of the code is legal.

☒ **A, B, C, D, E**, and **G** are incorrect based on the above.

60. Given:

```
2. public class Hug implements Runnable {
3.    static Thread t1;
4.    static Hold h, h2;
5.    public void run() {
6.      if(Thread.currentThread().getId() == t1.getId()) h.adjust();
7.      else h2.view();
8.    }
9.    public static void main(String[] args) {
10.     h = new Hold();
11.     h2 = new Hold();
12.     t1 = new Thread(new Hug());
13.     t1.start();
```

```
14.       new Thread(new Hug()).start();
15. } }
16. class Hold {
17.    static int x = 5;
18.    synchronized void adjust() {
19.       System.out.print(x-- + " ");
20.       try { Thread.sleep(200); } catch (Exception e) { ; }
21.       view();
22.    }
23.    synchronized void view() {
24.       try { Thread.sleep(200); } catch (Exception e) { ; }
25.       if(x > 0) adjust();
26. } }
```

Which are true? (Choose all that apply.)

A.   Compilation fails.

B.   The program could deadlock.

C.   The output could be: 5 4 3 2 1

D.   The program could produce thousands of characters of output.

E.   If the `sleep()` invocations were removed the chances of deadlock would decrease.

F.   If the `view()` method was not synchronized the chances of deadlock would decrease.

Answer (for Objective 4.3):

☑   **C** is correct. It might look like this code could deadlock, but it can't. The two `Hug` threads are both using the same synchronized methods, but they aren't trying to use each other's instances.

☒   **A, B, D, E,** and **F** are incorrect based on the above. [If the chance of deadlock is already zero, it can't decrease. :)]

Analyzing Your Results

As of this writing, a passing score on the OCP Java SE Programmer exam is 58.33 percent (35 out of 60 questions). Table 3-1 offers a rough guide to where you are in your studies.

| TABLE 3-1 | What Your Score Means |

Number of Correct Answers	Recommended Plan
0–28	You should do a LOT of studying before taking more of the exams in this book.
29–35	You should do a bit more studying before taking more of the exams in this book.
36–44	You're a little ahead of the "passing" boundary, but we recommend you do a bit more studying.
45–60	You're probably ready to use the three remaining full exams in this book to polish your skills.

If you got less than 45 questions correct, the next chapter could be a big help. We're going to describe some small programming projects you can do that should help your understanding of the topics in the exam.

4

Coding Exercises

Studying for the OCP Java SE Programmer exam can be a grueling task. If you're happy with your progress, happy with your practice test results so far, and happy with your study plan, then you might not need to read this chapter. On the other hand, if you're feeling like you could use a (possibly) fresh perspective on how to approach studying for this exam, then read on.

Passing the Exam in Three Steps

As moderators at JavaRanch.com, we've had the opportunity to read suggestions given by thousands of programmers who have passed the old SCJP, now called OCP Java SE Programmer exam. The following three suggestions are by far the most common:

1. Use a good study guide. (Notice us not inserting a shameless plug here.)
2. Take lots of practice exams. (Just like in this book. ☺)
3. Write lots of code.

Code, Code, Code

This chapter is about step number 3: writing lots of code. Of course, not all code is equally good as a study aid. In general, we don't mean you should write "production" code or a big desktop application with lots of Swing. What we DO mean is that you should write lots of small programs. On the real exam, most of the questions contain less than 13 lines of code. (To be sure, on the real exam you'll often just see snippets of code that presumably exist in a larger program.) But while we were creating the questions for this book, we seldom wrote a program longer than 30 lines.

We recommend you write lots of "small" programs. There's nothing magical about the 30-line limit, but there is a little bit of magic in setting up some sort of size constraint. If, when you are writing your test code, you keep it short, you'll find that it helps you focus on exactly the Java idea you're researching. The other benefit of short programs is that they're easier to debug and fiddle with. If you study the questions in this book, you'll see that, for the most part, they are very focused. You won't see many getters or setters.

Tips for Creating Prototype "Study" Code

The good news about the kind of coding we're suggesting is that it's very similar to the kinds of coding that lots of agile-ish software development methodologies use at certain stages of on-the-job software development. We'll try to stay methodology-agnostic, but what we will say is that we're recommending that you write code that's very similar to code you might write if you were doing rapid prototyping or if you were in the early stages of an iterative development process. We understand that our readers have a wide range of experience, so please don't be offended if you know everything in the following list.

Your Goal   Write down your goal for the prototype code you want to create. As you develop and test the code, you might discover that you should have had a different intermediate goal... That's great. Go with the flow.

Focusing   Find the "sweet spot" for your goals. In general, you want your goals to be as focused as possible. At the same time, you want your goal to test something interesting. For instance, your goal might be "Create a separate thread in an inner class." It might turn out that once you've done that you wonder whether you can create a thread in a constructor, or in an init block. Cool! Try it. In the list of coding projects that follows, we tried to create tasks that were in the "sweet spot"—not too easy, but also not too broad.

Reference Materials   Unlike prototyping on the job, try to start each project without using the API or any other reference material. There's another kind of "sweet spot" here. Ideally, you want to spend some time trying different approaches, but you don't want to get stuck either. So, go easy on yourself—if your first iteration of code doesn't work, but you have a couple of ideas, go ahead and try them, too. As long as you're feeling positive and creative, keep experimenting. When you think you've hit a brick wall, don't punish yourself—go ahead and look something up. When you find you need to look something up, that's okay, but make a note of it. Perhaps make a new flashcard about the thing you needed to look up. The idea is to not get hung up trying to remember some little factoid.

Misunderstandings   A couple of closely related "meta-goals" should be part of all the prototype code you create: you want to discover misunderstandings, and you want to discover lacks of understanding. Sometimes, when you start prototyping, you'll discover that you mostly know what's going on, but that you got a few details wrong—in other words, a misunderstanding. Other times, you'll quickly discover that you've got no idea how to proceed—in other words, a lack of understanding. As you might guess, our advice is to keep a log of these topics so you'll know which topics need the most attention. Again, don't get hung up on any given topic.

Code Formatting   Unlike prototyping on the job, sometimes you should use the horrible "exam style" code formatting that you'll encounter in the real exam and (as you've discovered) in practice exams. Again, use moderation. You want to emulate "exam style" code enough so that you're comfortable reading it, but not enough so it seeps into your real-life code. Here are a couple of examples:

- Chain methods and/or constructors:

```
new TestCode().go("2");
```

- Eliminate curly braces:

```
for(String s: names) s += s;
```

- "Scrunch" your code. Here's an example of some Java-style code transmogrifying into "exam style":

  Standard Java (a.k.a., "1TBS" ["The One True Brace Style"]):

```
class MyStuff {
    int doStuff() {
        return 7;
    }
}
```

  Becomes "exam style":

```
class MyStuff { int doStuff() { return 7; } }
```

- Put several related statements on a single line:

```
s.add("a");  s.add("c");  s.add("b");
```

Creating Errors   As you iterate through your prototypes, one of your sub-goals should be to *break* stuff. You want to understand what causes compiler errors, what throws exceptions, and so on.

Keeping Errors   When you do break something, keep track of it! Instead of deleting the code that breaks, keep it inline and comment it out. For example, you'll see examples of questions in this book in which you're meant to determine which of several "code fragments" compile, or work a certain way. It's a good bet that those fragments exist in comments, somewhere in our prototype code. And, of course, erroneous code can be a great topic for a flashcard.

S.O.P.s   Yet another sweet spot here... `System.out.println()` statements (S.O.P.s) are a great way for you to debug your prototypes. But, unlike on the job, you also want to test your knowledge and learn stuff. In general, we'd recommend that in your first code iteration you don't add debugging-oriented `println()`s. When the code does something unexpected, study it for a bit before rushing in and adding a bunch of `println()`s. On the other hand, don't get too stuck. Usually when you're studying, you should avoid getting bogged down on any particular point.

Debugging 101   If you're really new to debugging, or to Java, common places you should consider adding S.O.P.s are:

- In your methods and constructors ("I got to method X").
- Inside any loops.
- To check the state of your data: What's the value of x? How many entries are in my collection?

Typing It   You'll remember stuff better if you've typed it in rather than cutting and pasting it. It's kind of like muscle memory for your brain.

Don't Use an IDE   We've said it a million times. The exam was created and tested using simple text editors and the command line. During the course of writing this book, we discovered a discrepancy between the compiler and a very common IDE. Also, even if you knew that your IDE would always agree with the compiler, IDEs are supposed to "help" by doing stuff for you behind the scenes. Once you've got your certification, go ahead and crank up your IDE; you'll be more efficient. But don't do it while you're studying. (Okay, if you get really really stuck, you could use it once in a while as a last resort.)

Memorizing APIs   We get a lot of grief about having the APIs on the exam. Candidates rightfully claim that they would never trust their memory of an API in production code, so why should they have to memorize API stuff for the exam? The exam creation team had a couple of very specific goals in mind for the API portions of the exam:

- Demonstrate your basic understanding of how common classes work.
- Demonstrate your ability to use the API.

For example, let's say that a year from now you have to use the `Date` and `Calendar` classes. The exam creation team will be happy if you say to yourself: "I don't remember exactly how to do this stuff, but I do remember that some of these classes use factory methods, and that there's something tricky about Locales being immutable."

Mangling Practice Questions At the end of this chapter we're going to list some possible prototyping projects for you. But never forget that almost every practice exam question you encounter is probably a great place to start a prototyping project. So in a way, in addition to the projects listed in this chapter, this book contains about 260 more prototyping projects, at no extra charge.

Prototype / Research / Study Projects

The following sections contain a list of "coding exercises" or "prototyping projects." We recommend you use them selectively. If you know you're weak in certain topics, feel free to jump to that section of the list first. If you want to do an overall assessment of your readiness, read through the list and try to honestly evaluate how difficult (or easy) it would be for you to complete the various projects. As you work through your coding projects, go out of your way to prove to yourself that you're really getting the results you think you're getting. If you can't verify that your code is doing what you think it's doing, then (with a few exceptions like garbage collection) your task isn't done.

How about reference materials? As we mentioned earlier, don't be too Draconian with yourself. Try to do the exercises without using reference materials. When you DO use reference material, make a note of it. Did you just need to check on a method signature, or did you completely forget a class's capabilities? Adjust your study plans accordingly.

Finally, the following list probably doesn't completely cover every topic you might find on the real exam. Use this list as a template to create your own coding projects that focus on areas you want to explore more thoroughly.

Section 1: Declarations, Initialization, Scoping

- **1.a** Create an interface that has methods and a constant. Create an abstract class with an abstract method, a non-abstract method, and an instance variable. Create a concrete class that uses both of the above.

■ **1.b**   Create a directory structure, and a couple of classes, in different packages, to demonstrate the differences between default and protected access rules.

■ **1.c**   Create a class, a subclass, and a sub-subclass. Create at least two constructors in each class and use `super()` and `this()` to access (one way or another) all of the constructors, based on invoking `new()` on the grandchild class.

■ **1.d**   Create a class that uses static initialization blocks, instance initialization blocks and a constructor, and prove the sequence in which they get called when the class is invoked and a new object is created.

■ **1.e**   Create a 2D array and a 3D array. Copy the 2D array into a part of the 3D array.

■ **1.f**   Create an enum that has a variable, a constructor, a method, and a constant class body. Create a class that exercises each of the enum's members.

■ **1.g**   Create a class, a subclass, and a sub-subclass:

■ Make overridden versions of methods in those classes.

■ Make an array of instances of the three and loop through them polymorphically.

■ Do the same with a collection instead of an array.

■ **1.h**   Create a class that has a static inner class and a method local inner class. Make instances of each inner class. Create code that accesses the inner classes' members from the outer class. Create code that accesses the outer class's members from within the inner classes.

■ **1.i**   Write a program that has variables of all four scopes. Try to access them out of their scope.

Section 2: Flow Control

■ **2.a**   Write a method that includes an if-else that's inside a while loop that's inside a for loop that's inside a do loop. Then add a labeled break and continue to the for loop.

■ **2.b**   Make a switch using an enum that contains a default case. Test the switch statement by iterating through the enum.

■ **2.c** Write code that deliberately throws the following exceptions, without using the "`throw`" keyword:

- ■ `ClassCastException`
- ■ `NullPointerException`
- ■ `ArrayIndexOutOfBoundsException`
- ■ `StackOverflowError`
- ■ `AssertionError`
- ■ `NumberFormatException`

■ **2.d** Catch all of the preceding exceptions and print some subsequent output outside of any error-handling code.

■ **2.e** Write a try-catch-finally and demonstrate it doing a try-catch-finally and then a try-finally.

■ **2.f** Write code that demonstrates how handle or declare rules are different for runtime exceptions, compile time exceptions, and errors.

■ **2.g** Write code that demonstrates handling some exceptions, and declaring some others.

■ **2.h** Create an assertion that passes or fails based on a command-line argument.

■ **2.i** Attempt to compile working assertion code with old versions of Java.

Section 3: APIs

■ **3.a** Create code that uses an `xxxValue()` method, a `parseXxx()` method, and a `valueOf()` method.

■ **3.b** Create code that invokes `String.concat()` and "loses" the result, and then show an invocation of `concat()` that saves the result.

■ **3.c** Create code that instantiates instances of two different numeric wrapper classes, adds the values of the two instances together, and then creates a third numeric wrapper instance whose value is the sum.

■ **3.d** Create code that makes a new directory on your hard drive, adds a text file to that directory, writes several lines of text data to the file, closes the file, reopens the file, reads data from the file and prints out the data.

■ **3.e** Create a program that instantiates a Date object whose date represents the two billionth second after the Java epoch (1/1/1970). Determine, based on your JVM's locale, what day of the week (first, second...) the two billionth second occurs. Next, add 15 months to that date and print the new date.

■ **3.f** Write a program that instantiates a `NumberFormat` object. Using methods available to the `NumberFormat` object, and given the String "345.67", create two `Number` objects; one with the value 345.67 and one with the value 345.

■ **3.g** Using classes from `java.util.regex`, and given the String a4 0x12 5b _x_ 056 092 0x5g, write a program that does the following: finds all occurrences of digits in the String, and all occurrences of word characters in the String. Next, write code that finds all occurrences of hexadecimal numbers in the String. Finally, write code that finds all occurrences of octal numbers in the String.

■ **3.h** Use `String.split()` to tokenize the following String: 3.14, 0x17-5b, cat.dog.
Your program must tokenize using three different delimiters—the dot(.), the comma, and a space character—all of which must be handed to the program via a command-line argument.

■ **3.i** Using classes from `java.util.regex`, write a program that returns whether a given String contains either all alphabetic characters, or all numeric characters, or whether the String is mixed.

Section 4: Concurrency

■ **4.a** Create a class that starts one thread from an initialization block, that starts another thread from an inner class, and that starts a third thread from a constructor.

■ **4.b** Create code that starts threads using `java.lang.Thread` and `java.lang.Runnable`.

■ **4.c** Create code that demonstrates how `sleep()`, `join()`, `setPriority()`, and `interrupt()` can affect how threads interact with each other.

■ **4.d** Create code that has a method named `atomic()`. Demonstrate in code how two threads can, sometimes, invoke `atomic()` concurrently. Next, make a version of the code in which the two threads CANNOT invoke `atomic()` concurrently.

■ **4.e** Create code in which two threads sometimes deadlock.

■ **4.f** Create code that demonstrates that when two threads invoke the same synchronized method—but against different objects—the threads runs concurrently.

Section 5: OO Concepts

■ **5.a** Write code in which overloaded methods try to "box then widen." Then try to "widen then box."

■ **5.b** Create a class and a subclass and perform legal reference variable upcasting and downcasting. Next, write code that won't compile due to casting errors. Finally, write code that will throw an exception when attempting a cast.

■ **5.c** Create legal overriding methods that change the following aspects of the method they override: the return type, the access modifier, exceptions thrown.

■ **5.d** Write code that accesses constructors with all four access modifiers.

■ **5.e** Write a singleton class.

■ **5.f** Write a superclass that requires any of its subclasses to create a no-arg constructor. Write a subclass for this superclass.

■ **5.g** Write two classes that interact with each other's "state" and maintain loose coupling.

■ **5.h** Write several classes such that there is an "is-a" relationship and a separate "has-a" relationship.

Section 6: Collections/Generics

■ **6.a** Create an "Items" class that has a String name, and an int value. Note that you will use this class in several of this section's exercises, and you may need to enhance this class as you go along. For all of **6.a**, use classes in java.util whenever possible:

  ■ Write a class that makes a collection of Items that guarantees no duplicates.

  ■ Write a class that makes a collection of Items that can be accessed in the order in which they were added to the collection.

■ Write a class that creates a collection in which a given instance of Items can be retrieved using a different associated String called "buyer".

■ Write a program that uses some combination of java.util .Comparator and java.lang.Comparable to sort a collection of Items either by name or by value.

■ **6.b** Create an array of Strings and use method(s) in the Arrays class to search the array for the location of specific Strings. Demonstrate an unsuccessful search. Next, sort the array in reverse order and perform another search.

■ **6.c** Create a collection of Strings and use method(s) in the Collections class to search the collection. Demonstrate successful and unsuccessful searches.

■ **6.d** Create a List of Longs. Create an array that "backs" the List. Change a value in the List and display the contents of the array. Change a value in the array and display the contents of the List. Attempt to add a new entry to the List.

■ **6.e** Create code that uses an Iterator to print the contents of a collection.

■ **6.f** Create a Set such that only Items can be added. Prove it.

■ **6.g** Create a Map such that only Strings can be keys and only Items can be values. Prove it.

■ **6.h** Create a non-generic collection and retrieve elements from it.

■ **6.i** Make a subclass of Items. Create a method that takes only Items or the Items subclass. Prove it.

■ **6.j** Write code such that the compiler issues a warning when you mix generic and non-generic collections.

■ **6.k** Write a method that takes an instance of any type, makes an ArrayList of that type, and then adds the original instance to the ArrayList.

Section 7: Fundamentals

■ **7.a** Create a compiler error concerning a final primitive. Create an error concerning a final reference variable. Attempt to change the state of an instance whose reference variable is final.

■ **7.b**   Write code that proves a short-circuit operator is short-circuiting, and that a non-short-circuit operator isn't short-circuiting.

■ **7.c**   Write code that determines whether the integer value of args[0] is evenly divisible by the integer value of args[1].

■ **7.d**   Write code that uses a ternary operator to populate a String with either "success" or "failure" based on whether args[0] can be parsed to an `int`.

■ **7.e**   Write code that demonstrates how postfix operators affect loop operations differently than prefix operators.

■ **7.f**   Write a program that adds two name-value pairs to `java.util` `.Properties`: one pair via a command-line option and one via a method in `Properties`. Next, print all the system's properties to verify that the two new properties were added.

■ **7.g**   Although difficult to prove, write code that creates instances of a class that are referred to by other instances, and yet are still eligible for garbage collection.

■ **7.h**   Create a class that has a method such that the first time the garbage collector attempts to collect a given instance, this method will keep the garbage collector from collecting that instance at that point.

■ **7.i**   Create code that passes primitives and reference variables into methods, demonstrating how "pass by value" works for primitives and reference variables.

■ **7.j**   Although not strictly on the exam, create a class and put it in a JAR file. Create a second class that uses the class in the JAR file.

■ **7.k**   Write a class that uses a static import.

■ **7.l**   Write a class that lives in a package. Write another class in another package that successfully uses methods from the first class.

5

Practice Exam 2

How Close Are You to Ready?

As you take this exam, and perhaps the rest of the exams in this book, you might want to keep a test log. In this log, you should record which questions you guessed on and which ones you knew without a doubt. On these exams and on the real exam, it's sometimes possible to use a "process of elimination" or other test-taking techniques to help you guess a correct answer. In practice, when you get to the real exam you'll want to do this if you hit a question that stumps you. But for these practice exams, guessing defeats the whole purpose! So, keep your log.

PRACTICE EXAM 2

The real exam has 60 questions and you are given three hours to complete it. Use the same time limits for this exam. On the real exam, and on all of the exams in this book, give yourself credit only for those questions that you answer 100 percent correctly. For instance, if a question has three correct answers and you get two of the three correct, you get zero credit. There is no partial credit. Good luck!

1. Concerning Java's Garbage Collector (GC), which are true? (Choose all that apply.)

   A. If Object X has a reference to Object Y, then Object Y cannot be GCed.

   B. A Java program can request that the GC runs, but such a request does NOT guarantee that the GC will actually run.

   C. If the GC decides to delete an object, and if `finalize()` has never been invoked for that object, it is guaranteed that the GC will invoke `finalize()` for that object before the object is deleted.

   D. Once the GC invokes `finalize()` on an object, it is guaranteed that the GC will delete that object once `finalize()` has completed.

   E. When the GC runs, it decides whether to remove objects from the heap, the stack, or both.

2. Given:

```
1. public class BackHanded {
2.    int state = 0;
3.    BackHanded(int s) { state = s; }
4.    public static void main(String... hi) {
5.       BackHanded b1 = new BackHanded(1);
6.       BackHanded b2 = new BackHanded(2);
7.       System.out.println(b1.go(b1) + " " + b2.go(b2));
8.    }
9.    int go(BackHanded b) {
10.      if(this.state == 2) {
11.         b.state = 5;
12.         go(this);
13.      }
14.      return ++this.state;
15. } }
```

What is the result?

   A. 1 2

   B. 1 3

   C. 1 6

   D. 1 7

   E. 2 6

F. 2 7

G. Compilation fails.

H. An exception is thrown at runtime.

3. Given:

```
42.    String s = "";
43.    if(011 == 9) s += 4;
44.    if(0x11 == 17) s += 5;
45.    Integer I = 12345;
46.    if(I.intValue() == Integer.valueOf("12345")) s += 6;
47.    System.out.println(s);
```

What is the result?

A. 5

B. 45

C. 46

D. 56

E. 456

F. Compilation fails.

G. An exception is thrown at runtime.

4. Given:

```
3. class Sport {
4.    Sport play() { System.out.print("play "); return new Sport(); }
5.    Sport play(int x) { System.out.print("play x "); return new Sport(); }
6. }
7. class Baseball extends Sport {
8.    Baseball play() { System.out.print("baseball "); return new Baseball(); }
9.    Sport play(int x) { System.out.print("sport "); return new Sport(); }
10.
11.    public static void main(String[] args) {
12.       new Baseball().play();
13.       new Baseball().play(7);
14.       super.play(7);
15.       new Sport().play();
16.       Sport s = new Baseball();
17.       s.play();
18. } }
```

What is the result?

A. baseball sport sport play play

B. baseball sport play x play sport

C. `baseball sport play x play baseball`

D. Compilation fails due to a single error.

E. Compilation fails due to errors on more than one line.

5. Given:

```
2. public class Self extends Thread {
3.   public static void main(String[] args) {
4.     try {
5.       Thread t = new Thread(new Self());
6.       t.start();
7.       t.start();
8.     } catch (Exception e) { System.out.print("e "); }
9.   }
10.  public void run() {
11.    for(int i = 0; i < 2; i++)
12.      System.out.print(Thread.currentThread().getName() + " ");
13. } }
```

Which are true? (Choose all that apply.)

A. Compilation fails.

B. No output is produced.

C. The output could be `Thread-1 Thread-1 e`

D. The output could be `Thread-1 e Thread-1`

E. The output could be `Thread-1 Thread-1 Thread-2 Thread-2`

F. The output could be `Thread-1 Thread-2 Thread-1 Thread-2`

G. The output could be `Thread-1 Thread-1 Thread-1 Thread-1`

6. Given:

```
3. class Stereo { void makeNoise() { assert true; } }
4. public class BoomBox2 extends Stereo {
5.   public static void main(String[] args) {
6.     new BoomBox2().go(args);
7.   }
8.   void go(String[] args) {
9.     if(args.length > 0)  makeNoise();
10.    if(args[0].equals("x")) System.out.print("x ");
11.    if(args[0] == "x") System.out.println("x2 ");
12. } }
```

And (if the code compiles), the invocation:

```
java -ea Boombox2 x
```

What is the result?

A. x

B. x x2

C. An Error is thrown at runtime.

D. Compilation fails due to an error on line 3.

E. Compilation fails due to an error on line 8.

F. Compilation fails due to an error on line 9.

7. Given:

```
2. import java.util.*;
3. public class Olives {
4.    public static void main(String[] args) {
5.       Set<Integer> s = new TreeSet<Integer>();
6.       s.add(23); s.add(42); s.add(new Integer(5));
7.       Iterator i = s.iterator();
8.       // while(System.out.print(i.next())) { }
9.       // for(Integer i2: i) System.out.print(i2);
10.      // for(Integer i3: s) System.out.print(i3);
11.      // while(i.hasNext()) System.out.print(i.get());
12.      // while(i.hasNext()) System.out.print(i.next());
13. } }
```

If lines 8–12 are uncommented, independently, which are true? (Choose all that apply.)

A. Line 8 will compile.

B. Line 9 will compile.

C. Line 10 will compile.

D. Line 11 will compile.

E. Line 12 will compile.

F. Of those that compile, the output will be 23425

G. Of those that compile, the output will be 52342

8. Given the proper `import` statements and:

```
23.   try {
24.      File file = new File("myFile.txt");
25.      PrintWriter pw = new PrintWriter(file);
26.      pw.println("line 1");
27.      pw.close();
28.      PrintWriter pw2 = new PrintWriter("myFile.txt");
29.      pw2.println("line 2");
30.      pw2.close();
31.   } catch (IOException e) { }
```

What is the result? (Choose all that apply.)

A. No file is created.

B. A file named `"myFile.txt"` is created.

C. Compilation fails due to an error on line 24.

D. Compilation fails due to an error on line 28.

E. `"myFile.txt"` contains only one line of data, `"line 1"`

F. `"myFile.txt"` contains only one line of data, `"line 2"`

G. `"myFile.txt"` contains two lines of data, `"line 1"` then `"line 2"`

9. Given this code in a method:

```
3.        String s = "-";
4.        boolean b = false;
5.        int x = 7, y = 8;
6.        if((x < 8) ^ (b = true))        s += "^";
7.        if(!(x > 8) | ++y > 5)          s += "|";
8.        if(++y > 9 && b == true)        s += "&&";
9.        if(y % 8 > 1 || y / (x - 7) > 1)  s += "%";
10.       System.out.println(s);
```

What is the result?

A. `-`

B. `-|%`

C. `-^|%`

D. `-|&&%`

E. `-^|&&%`

F. Compilation fails.

G. An exception is thrown at runtime.

10. Given:

```
3. public class Limits {
4.     private int x = 2;
5.     protected int y = 3;
6.     private static int m1 = 4;
7.     protected static int m2 = 5;
8.     public static void main(String[] args) {
9.         int x = 6;   int y = 7;
10.        int m1 = 8;  int m2 = 9;
11.        new Limits().new Secret().go();
12.    }
13.    class Secret {
14.        void go() { System.out.println(x + " " + y + " " + m1 + " " + m2); }
15. } }
```

What is the result?

A. 2 3 4 5

B. 2 7 4 9

C. 6 3 8 4

D. 6 7 8 9

E. Compilation fails due to multiple errors.

F. Compilation fails due only to an error on line 11.

G. Compilation fails due only to an error on line 14.

11. Note: This question concerns Serialization. As of this writing, the Serialization topic was officially removed from the objectives, *BUT* we were still getting reports that some testing centers were using versions of the exam that included Serialization questions. If you choose to ignore the Serialization topic, give yourself a free "correct answer" for this question. (FWIW, your authors believe it's a good topic to understand.)

Given:

```
3. import java.io.*;
4. class ElectronicDevice { ElectronicDevice() { System.out.print("ed "); }}
5. class Mp3player extends ElectronicDevice implements Serializable {
6.   Mp3player() { System.out.print("mp "); }
7. }
8. class MiniPlayer extends Mp3player {
9.   MiniPlayer() { System.out.print("mini "); }
10.   public static void main(String[] args) {
11.     MiniPlayer m = new MiniPlayer();
12.     try {
13.       FileOutputStream fos = new FileOutputStream("dev.txt");
14.       ObjectOutputStream os = new ObjectOutputStream(fos);
15.       os.writeObject(m);  os.close();
16.       FileInputStream fis = new FileInputStream("dev.txt");
17.       ObjectInputStream is = new ObjectInputStream(fis);
18.       MiniPlayer m2 = (MiniPlayer) is.readObject();  is.close();
19.     } catch (Exception x) { System.out.print("x "); }
20. } }
```

What is the result?

A. ed mp mini

B. ed mp mini ed

C. ed mp mini ed mini

D. ed mp mini ed mp mini

E. Compilation fails.

F. "ed mp mini", followed by an exception.

12. Given:

```
2. abstract interface Pixie {
3.   abstract void sprinkle();
4.   static int dust = 3;
5. }
6. abstract class TinkerBell implements Pixie {
7.   String fly() { return "flying "; }
8. }
9. public class ForReal extends TinkerBell {
10.   public static void main(String[] args) {
11.     new ForReal().sprinkle();
12.   }
13.   public void sprinkle() { System.out.println(fly() + " " + dust); }
14. }
```

What is the result? (Choose all that apply.)

A. `flying   3`

B. Compilation fails because `TinkerBell` doesn't properly implement `Pixie`.

C. Compilation fails because `ForReal` doesn't properly extend `TinkerBell`.

D. Compilation fails because `Pixie` is not a legal interface.

E. Compilation fails because `ForReal` doesn't properly implement `Pixie`.

F. Compilation fails because `TinkerBell` is not a legal abstract class.

13. Given:

```
2. public class Errrrr {
3.   static String a = null;
4.   static String s = "";
5.   public static void main(String[] args) {
6.     try {
7.       a = args[0];
8.       System.out.print(a);
9.       s += "t1 ";
10.     }
11.     catch (RuntimeException re) { s += "c1 "; }
12.     finally { s += "f1 "; }
13.     System.out.println(" " + s);
14. } }
```

And two command-line invocations:

```
java Errrrr
java Errrrr x
```

What is the result?

A. First: f1, then: x t1

B. First: f1, then: x t1 f1

C. First: c1, then: x t1

D. First: c1, then: x t1 f1

E. First: c1 f1, then: x t1

F. First: c1 f1, then: x t1 f1

G. Compilation fails.

14. Given:

```
51.    String s = "4.5x4.a.3";
52.    String[] tokens = s.split("\\s");
53.    for(String o: tokens)
54.      System.out.print(o + " ");
55.
56.    System.out.print("   ");
57.    tokens = s.split("\\..");
58.    for(String o: tokens)
59.      System.out.print(o + " ");
```

What is the result?

A. 4 x4

B. 4 x4 .

C. 4 x4 3

D. 4 5x4 a 3   4 x4

E. 4.5x4.a.3   4 x4

F. 4.5x4.a.3   4 x4 .

15. Given:

```
2. abstract class Tool {
3.    int SKU;
4.    abstract void getSKU();
5. }
6. public class Hammer {
7.    // insert code here
8. }
```

Which line(s), inserted independently at line 7, will compile? (Choose all that apply.)

A. void getSKU() { ; }

B. private void getSKU() { ; }

C. protected void getSKU() { ; }

D. public void getSKU() { ; }

16. Given:

```
3. public class Stubborn implements Runnable {
4.    static Thread t1;
5.    static int x = 5;
6.    public void run() {
7.      if(Thread.currentThread().getId() == t1.getId()) shove();
8.      else push();
9.    }
10.   static synchronized void push() { shove(); }
11.   static void shove() {
12.     synchronized(Stubborn.class) {
13.       System.out.print(x-- + " ");
14.       try { Thread.sleep(2000); } catch (Exception e) { ; }
15.       if(x > 0) push();
16.   } }
17.   public static void main(String[] args) {
18.     t1 = new Thread(new Stubborn());
19.     t1.start();
20.     new Thread(new Stubborn()).start();
21. } }
```

Which are true? (Choose all that apply.)

A. Compilation fails.

B. The output is 5 4 3 2 1

C. The output is 5 4 3 2 1 0

D. The program could deadlock.

E. The output could be 5, followed by deadlock.

F. If the sleep() invocation was removed, the chance of deadlock would decrease.

G. As it stands, the program can't deadlock, but if shove() was changed to synchronized, then the program could deadlock.

17. Given:

```
2. class Super {
3.    static String os = "";
4.    void doStuff() { os += "super "; }
5. }
6. public class PolyTest extends Super {
7.    public static void main(String[] args) { new PolyTest().go(); }
8.    void go() {
9.      Super s = new PolyTest();
10.     PolyTest p = (PolyTest)s;
11.     p.doStuff();
12.     s.doStuff();
13.     p.doPoly();
```

```
14.        s.doPoly();
15.        System.out.println(os);
16.     }
17.     void doStuff() { os += "over "; }
18.     void doPoly() { os += "poly "; }
19. }
```

What is the result?

A. Compilation fails.

B. over over poly poly

C. over super poly poly

D. super super poly poly

E. An exception is thrown at runtime.

18. Given two files:

```
1. package com.wickedlysmart;
2. import com.wickedlysmart2.*;
3. public class Launcher {
4.    public static void main(String[] args) {
5.       Utils u = new Utils();
6.       u.do1();
7.       u.do2();
8.       u.do3();
9. } }
```

and the correctly compiled and located:

```
1. package com.wickedlysmart2;
2. class Utils {
3.    void do1() { System.out.print("do1 "); }
4.    protected void do2() { System.out.print("do2 "); }
5.    public void do3() { System.out.print("do3 "); }
6. }
```

What is the result for Launcher? (Choose all that apply.)

A. do1 do2 do3

B. "do1 ", followed by an exception

C. Compilation fails due to an error on line 5 of Launcher.

D. Compilation fails due to an error on line 6 of Launcher.

E. Compilation fails due to an error on line 7 of Launcher.

F. Compilation fails due to an error on line 8 of Launcher.

19. Given:

```
2. public class Wacky {
3.    public static void main(String[] args) {
4.       int x = 5;
5.       int y = (x < 6) ? 7 : 8;
6.       System.out.print(y + " ");
7.       boolean b = (x < 6) ? false : true;
8.       System.out.println(b + " ");
9.       assert(x < 6) : "bob";
10.       assert( ((x < 6) ? false : true) ) : "fred";
11. } }
```

And, if the code compiles, the invocation:

```
java -ea Wacky
```

Which will be contained in the output? (Choose all that apply.)

A. 7

B. 8

C. bob

D. fred

E. true

F. false

G. Compilation fails.

20. Given:

```
3. class MotorVehicle {
4.    protected int doStuff(int x) { return x * 2; }
5. }
6. class Bicycle {
7.    void go(MotorVehicle m) {
8.       System.out.print(m.doStuff(21) + " ");
9. } }
10. public class Beemer extends MotorVehicle {
11.    public static void main(String[] args) {
12.       System.out.print(new Beemer().doStuff(11) + " ");
13.       new Bicycle().go(new Beemer());
14.       new Bicycle().go(new MotorVehicle());
15.    }
16.    int doStuff(int x) { return x * 3; }
17. }
```

What is the result? (Choose all that apply.)

A. 22 42 42

B. 22 63 63

C. 33 42 42

D. 33 63 42

E. Compilation fails.

F. An exception is thrown at runtime.

21. Which are true? (Choose all that apply.)

A. A single JAR file can contain only files from a single package.

B. A JAR file can be used only on the machine on which it was created.

C. When javac is using files within a JAR file, it will unJAR the file during compilation.

D. The Java SDK installation directory tree on a Java developer's computer usually includes a subdirectory tree named jre/lib/ext.

E. A JAR file is structured so that all the files and directories that you've "JARed" will be subdirectory(ies) of the META-INF directory.

F. When javac is invoked with a classpath option, and you need to find files in a JAR file, the name of the JAR file must be included at the end of the path.

22. Given the proper import(s), and given:

```
13. class NameCompare implements Comparator<Stuff> {
14.   public int compare(Stuff a, Stuff b) {
15.     return b.name.compareTo(a.name);
16. } }
18. class ValueCompare implements Comparator<Stuff> {
19.   public int compare(Stuff a, Stuff b) {
20.     return (a.value - b.value);
21. } }
```

Which are true? (Choose all that apply.)

A. This code does not compile.

B. This code allows you to use instances of Stuff as keys in Maps.

C. These two classes properly implement the Comparator interface.

D. NameCompare allows you to sort a collection of Stuff instances alphabetically.

E. ValueCompare allows you to sort a collection of Stuff instances in ascending numeric order.

F. If you changed both occurrences of "compare()" to "compareTo()", the code would compile.

23. Given:

```
3. public class Chopper {
4.    String a = "12b";
5.    public static void main(String[] args) {
6.       System.out.println(new Chopper().chop(args[0]));
7.    }
8.    int chop(String a) {
9.       if(a == null) throw new IllegalArgumentException();
10.      return Integer.parseInt(a);
11. } }
```

And, if the code compiles, the invocation:

```
java Chopper
```

What is the result?

A. 12

B. 12b

C. Compilation fails.

D. A NullPointerException is thrown.

E. A NumberFormatException is thrown.

F. An IllegalArgumentException is thrown.

G. An ArrayIndexOutOfBoundsException is thrown.

24. Which, concerning command-line options, are true? (Choose all that apply.)

A. The -D flag is used in conjunction with a name-value pair.

B. The -D flag can be used with javac to set a system property.

C. The -d flag can be used with java to disable assertions.

D. The -d flag can be used with javac to specify where to place .class files.

E. The -d flag can be used with javac to document the locations of deprecated APIs in source files.

25. Given that "it, IT" is the locale code for Italy and that "pt, BR" is the locale code for Brazil, and given:

```
51.    Date d = new Date();
52.    DateFormat df = DateFormat.getDateInstance(DateFormat.FULL);
53.    Locale[] la = {new Locale("it", "IT"), new Locale("pt", "BR")};
54.    for(Locale l: la) {
55.      df.setLocale(l);
56.      System.out.println(df.format(d));
57.    }
```

Which are true? (Choose all that apply.)

A. An exception is thrown at runtime.

B. Compilation fails due to an error on line 53.

C. Compilation fails due to an error on line 55.

D. Compilation fails due to an error on line 56.

E. The output will contain only today's date for the Italian locale.

F. The output will contain today's date for both Italian and Brazilian locales.

26. Given this code in a method:

```
4.      Integer[][] la = {{1,2}, {3,4,5}};
5.      Number[] na = la[1];
6.      Number[] na2 = (Number[])la[0];
7.      Object o = na2;
8.      la[1] = (Number[])o;
9.      la[0] = (Integer[])o;
```

What is the result? (Choose all that apply.)

A. Compilation succeeds.

B. Compilation fails due to an error on line 4.

C. Compilation fails due to an error on line 5.

D. Compilation fails due to an error on line 6.

E. Compilation fails due to an error on line 7.

F. Compilation fails due to an error on line 8.

G. Compilation fails due to an error on line 9.

H. Compilation succeeds but an exception is thrown at runtime.

27. Given:

```
3. public class Ice {
4.    Long[] stockings = {new Long(3L), new Long(4L), new Long(5L)};
5.    static int count = 0;
6.    public static void main(String[] args) {
7.       new Ice().go();
8.       System.out.println(count);
9.    }
10.   void go() {
11.      for(short x = 0; x < 5; x++) {
12.         if(x == 2) return;
13.         for(long ell: stockings) {
14.            count++;
15.            if(ell == 4) break;
16. } } } }
```

What is the result? (Choose all that apply.)

A. 2

B. 4

C. 8

D. 12

E. Compilation fails due to an error on line 13.

F. Compilation fails due to an error on line 16.

28. Given the proper import statement(s) and:

```
4.        Console c = System.console();
5.        char[] pw;
6.        if(c == null) return;
7.        pw = c.readPassword("%s", "pw: ");
8.        System.out.println(c.readLine("%s", "input: "));
```

Which statements are true? (Choose all that apply.)

A. An exception will be thrown on line 8.

B. The variable pw must be a String, not a char[].

C. No import statements are necessary for the code to compile.

D. If the code compiles and is invoked, line 7 might never run.

E. Without a third argument, the readPassword() method will echo the password the user types.

F. If line 4 was replaced with the following code, the program would still compile: "Console c = new Console();".

29. Given that:

Exception is the superclass of IOException, and

IOException is the superclass of FileNotFoundException, and

```
3. import java.io.*;
4. class Physicist {
5.   void think() throws IOException { }
6. }
7. public class Feynman extends Physicist {
8.   public static void main(String[] args) {
9.     new Feynman().think();
10.   }
11.   // insert method here
12. }
```

Which of the following methods, inserted independently at line 11, compiles? (Choose all that apply.)

A. `void think() throws Exception { }`

B. `void think() throws FileNotFoundException { }`

C. `public void think() { }`

D. `protected void think() throws IOException { }`

E. `private void think() throws IOException { }`

F. `void think() { int x = 7/0; }`

30. Given:

```
4. public class Zingseng extends Thread {
5.    public static void main(String[] args) throws Exception {
6.       Thread t1 = new Thread(new Zingseng());
7.       t1.start();
8.       // insert code here
9.       for(int i = 0; i < 1000; i++)   // Loop #1
10.         System.out.print(Thread.currentThread().getName() + " ");
11.    }
12.    public void run() {
13.       for(int i = 0; i < 1000; i++)   // Loop #2
14.         System.out.print(Thread.currentThread().getName() + " ");
15. } }
```

Which code, inserted independently at line 8, will make most (or all) of Loop #2's iterations run before most (or all) of Loop #1's iterations? (Choose all that apply.)

A. `// just a comment`

B. `t1.join();`

C. `t1.yield();`

D. `t1.sleep(1000);`

31. Given:

```
2. public class Kant extends Philosopher {
3.    // insert code here
5.    public static void main(String[] args) {
6.       new Kant("Homer");
7.       new Kant();
8.    }
9. }
10. class Philosopher {
11.    Philosopher(String s) { System.out.print(s + " "); }
12. }
```

Which set(s) of code, inserted independently at line 3, produce the output `"Homer Bart"`? (Choose all that apply.)

A. `Kant() { this("Bart"); }`
   `Kant(String s) { super(s); }`

B. `Kant() { super("Bart"); }`
   `Kant(String s) { super(s); }`

C. `Kant() { super(); }`
   `Kant(String s) { super(s); }`

D. `Kant() { super("Bart"); }`
   `Kant(String s) { this(); }`

E. `Kant() { super("Bart"); }`
   `Kant(String s) { this("Homer"); }`

32. Given:

```
2. public class Epoch {
3.    static int jurassic = 0;
4.    public static void main(String[] args) {
5.       assert(doStuff(5));
6.    }
7.    static boolean doStuff(int x) {
8.       jurassic += x;
9.       return true;
10. } }
```

Which are true? (Choose all that apply.)

A. The code compiles using `javac -ea Epoch.java`

B. The assert statement on line 5 is used appropriately.

C. The code compiles using `javac -source 1.3 Epoch.java`

D. The code compiles using `javac -source 1.4 Epoch.java`

E. The code compiles using `javac -source 1.6 Epoch.java`

F. The code will not compile using any version of the `javac` compiler.

33. Given

```
1. public class Kaput {
2.    Kaput myK;
3.    String degree = "0";
4.    public static void main(String[] args) {
5.       Kaput k1 = new Kaput();
6.       go(k1);
7.       System.out.println(k1.degree);
8.    }
```

```
9.    static Kaput go(Kaput k) {
10.        final Kaput k1 = new Kaput();
11.        k.myK = k1;
12.        k.myK.degree = "7";
13.        return k.myK;
14. } }
```

What is the result?

A. 0

B. 7

C. null

D. Compilation fails.

E. An exception is thrown at runtime.

34. Given:

```
3. class Holder {
4.    enum Gas { ARGON, HELIUM };
5. }
6. public class Basket extends Holder {
7.    public static void main(String[] args) {
8.        short s = 7; long l = 9L; float f = 4.0f;
9.        int i = 3; char c = 'c'; byte b = 5;
10.        // insert code here
11.            default: System.out.println("howdy");
12. } } }
```

Which line(s) of code (if any), inserted independently at line 10, will compile? (Choose all that apply.)

A. switch (s) {

B. switch (l) {

C. switch (f) {

D. switch (i) {

E. switch (c) {

F. switch (b) {

G. switch (Gas.ARGON) {

H. The code will not compile due to additional error(s).

35. Given

```
2. class Horse {
3.    static String s = "";
4.    void beBrisk() { s += "trot "; }
5. }
```

```
6. public class Andi extends Horse {
7.    void beBrisk() { s += "tolt "; }
8.    public static void main(String[] args) {
9.       Horse x0 = new Horse();
10.      Horse x1 = new Andi();   x1.beBrisk();
11.      Andi x2 = (Andi)x1;      x2.beBrisk();
12.      Andi x3 = (Andi)x0;      x3.beBrisk();
13.      System.out.println(s);
14. } }
```

What is the result?

A. `tolt tolt tolt`

B. `trot tolt trot`

C. `trot tolt tolt`

D. Compilation fails.

E. An exception is thrown at runtime.

36. Given:

```
3. class Tire {
4.    private static int x = 6;
5.    public static class Wheel {
6.       void go() { System.out.print("roll " + x++); }
7. } }
8. public class Car {
9.    public static void main(String[] args) {
10.      // insert code here
11. } }
```

And the three code fragments:

I. `new Tire.Wheel().go();`

II. `Tire t = new Tire();    t.Wheel().go();`

III. `Tire.Wheel w = new Tire.Wheel();    w.go();`

Assuming we insert a single fragment at line 10, which are true? (Choose all that apply.)

A. Once compiled, the output will be `"roll 6"`

B. Once compiled, the output will be `"roll 7"`

C. Fragment I, inserted at line 10, will compile.

D. Fragment II, inserted at line 10, will compile.

E. Fragment III, inserted at line 10, will compile.

F. Taken separately, class `Tire` will not compile on its own.

37. Given:

```
3. public class Fortran {
4.    static int bump(int i) { return i + 2; }
5.    public static void main(String[] args) {
6.      for(int x = 0; x < 5; bump(x))
7.        System.out.print(x + " ");
8. } }
```

What is the result?

A. 2 4

B. 0 2 4

C. 2 4 6

D. 0 2 4 6

E. Compilation fails.

F. Some other result occurs.

38. You need the three classes and/or interfaces to work together to produce the output "Kara Charis". Fill in the blanks using the following fragments so the correct is-a and has-a relationships are established to produce this output. Note: You may not need to fill in every empty blank space, but a blank space can hold only one fragment. Also note that not all the fragments will be used, and that fragments CAN be used more than once.

Code to complete:

```
_____ Nameable {
  _____
}
class Animal _____ {
  _____
  _____
}
public class Buddies _____ {
  _____
  public static void main(String[] args) {
    Animal b1 = new Animal("Kara");
    _____
    System.out.println(b1.getName() + " " +  b2.getName());
} }
```

Fragments:

```
interface                    Animal() { name = "Charis"; }
String name;                 Animal(String n) { name = n; }
abstract class               Buddies(String s) { super(); }
```

```
extends Animal                  Buddies b2 = new Buddies();
extends Nameable                Buddies(String s) { super(s); }
name = "Charis";                String getName() { return name; }
implements Animal               Buddies b2 = new Buddies("Charis");
implements Nameable             void Animal(String n) { name = n; }
                                void Buddies(String s) { super(s); }
```

39. Given:

```
1. import java.util.*;
2. public class PirateTalk {
3.   public static void main(String... arrrrgs) {
4.     Properties p = System.getProperties();
5.     p.setProperty("pirate", "scurvy");
6.     String s = p.getProperty("argProp") + " ";
7.     s += p.getProperty("pirate");
8.     System.out.println(s);
9. } }
```

And the command-line invocation:

```
java PirateTalk -DargProp="dog,"
```

What is the result?

A. dog, scurvy

B. null scurvy

C. scurvy dog,

D. scurvy null

E. Compilation fails.

F. An exception is thrown at runtime.

G. An "unrecognized option" command-line error is thrown.

40. Given:

```
2. import java.util.*;
3. public class VLA implements Comparator<VLA> {
4.   int dishSize;
5.   public static void main(String[] args) {
6.     VLA[] va = {new VLA(40), new VLA(200), new VLA(60)};
7.
8.     for(VLA v: va) System.out.print(v.dishSize + " ");
9.     int index = Arrays.binarySearch(va, new VLA(60), va[0]);
10.    System.out.print(index + " ");
11.    Arrays.sort(va);
12.    for(VLA v: va) System.out.print(v.dishSize + " ");
```

```
13.       index = Arrays.binarySearch(va, new VLA(60), va[0]);
14.       System.out.println(index);
15.    }
16.    public int compare(VLA a, VLA b) {
17.       return a.dishSize - b.dishSize;
18.    }
19.    VLA(int d) { dishSize = d; }
20. }
```

Which result is most likely?

A. Compilation fails.

B. "40 200 60 2 40 60 200 1"

C. "40 200 60 -2 40 60 200 1"

D. "40 200 60", followed by an exception.

E. "40 200 60 -2", followed by an exception.

41. Given:

```
2. class RainCatcher {
3.    static StringBuffer s;
4.    public static void main(String[] args) {
5.       Integer i = new Integer(42);
6.       for(int j = 40; j < i; i--)
7.          switch(i) {
8.             case 41: s.append("41 ");
9.             default: s.append("def ");
10.            case 42: s.append("42 ");
11.         }
12.       System.out.println(s);
13. } }
```

What is the result?

A. 41 def

B. 41 def 42

C. 42 41 def 42

D. An exception is thrown at runtime.

E. Compilation fails due to an error on line 6.

F. Compilation fails due to an error on line 7.

42. Given:

```
2. import java.util.*;
3. class Snack {
4.    static List<String> s1 = new ArrayList<String>();
```

```
 5. }
 6. public class Chips extends Snack {
 7.    public static void main(String[] args) {
 8.       List c1 = new ArrayList();
 9.       s1.add("1"); s1.add("2");
10.       c1.add("3"); c1.add("4");
11.       getStuff(s1, c1);
12.    }
13.    static void getStuff(List<String> a1, List a2) {
14.       for(String s1: a1) System.out.print(s1 + " ");
15.       for(String s2: a2) System.out.print(s2 + " ");
16. } }
```

What is the result? (Choose all that apply.)

A. "1 2 3 4"

B. "1 2", followed by an exception

C. An exception is thrown with no other output.

D. Compilation fails due to an error on line 13.

E. Compilation fails due to an error on line 14.

F. Compilation fails due to an error on line 15.

43. Given that `Calendar.MONTH` starts with January `== 0`, and given:

```
 3. import java.util.*;
 4. public class Wise {
 5.    public static void main(String[] args) {
 6.       Calendar c = Calendar.getInstance();
 7.       c.set(1999,11,25);
 8.       c.roll(Calendar.MONTH, 3);
 9.       c.add(Calendar.DATE, 10);
10.       System.out.println(c.getTime());
11. } }
```

And, if the program compiles, what date is represented in the output?

A. March 4, 1999

B. April 4, 1999

C. March 4, 2000

D. April 4, 2000

E. Compilation fails.

F. An exception is thrown at runtime.

44. Given the following two files containing `Light.java` and `Dark.java`:

```
2. package ec.ram;
3. public class Light{}
4. class Burn{}
```

```
2. package ec.ram;
3. public class Dark{}
4. class Melt{}
```

And if those two files are located in the following directory structure:

```
$ROOT
    |-- Light.java
    |-- Dark.java
    |-- checker
            |-- dira
            |-- dirb
```

And the following commands are executed, in order, from the ROOT directory:

```
javac Light.java -cp checker/dira -d checker/dirb
javac Dark.java -cp checker/dirb -d checker/dira
jar -cf checker/dira/a.jar checker
```

A new JAR file is created after executing the above commands. Which of the following files will exist inside that JAR file? (Choose all that apply.)

A. [JAR] /dira/ec/ram/Melt.class

B. [JAR] /checker/dirb/ec/ram/Burn.class

C. [JAR] /dirb/ec/ram/Melt.class

D. [JAR] /checker/dira/ec/ram/Burn.class

E. [JAR] /dira/a.jar

F. [JAR] /checker/dira/a.jar

45. Given:

```
42.    String s1 = " ";
43.    StringBuffer s2 = new StringBuffer(" ");
44.    StringBuilder s3 = new StringBuilder(" ");
45.    for(int i = 0; i < 1000; i++) // Loop #1
46.      s1 = s1.concat("a");
47.    for(int i = 0; i < 1000; i++) // Loop #2
48.      s2.append("a");
49.    for(int i = 0; i < 1000; i++) // Loop #3
50.      s3.append("a");
```

Which statements will typically be true? (Choose all that apply.)

A. Compilation fails.

B. Loop #3 will tend to execute faster than Loop #2.

C. Loop #1 will tend to use less memory than the other two loops.

D. Loop #1 will tend to use more memory than the other two loops.

E. All three loops will tend to use about the same amount of memory.

F. In order for this code to compile, the `java.util` package is required.

G. If multiple threads need to use an object, the `s2` object should be safer than the `s3` object.

46. Given:

```
2. public class Payroll {
3.    int salary;
4.    int getSalary() { return salary; }
5.    void setSalary(int s) {
6.       assert(s > 30000);
7.       salary = s;
8. } }
```

Which are true? (Choose all that apply.)

A. Compilation fails.

B. The class is well encapsulated as it stands.

C. Removing line 6 would weaken the class's degree of cohesion.

D. Removing line 6 would weaken the class's degree of encapsulation.

E. If the `salary` variable was `private`, the class would be well encapsulated.

F. Removing line 6 would make the class's use of assertions more appropriate.

47. Given:

```
1. class GardenTool {
2.    static String s = "";
3.    String name = "Tool ";
4.    GardenTool(String arg) { this(); s += name; }
5.    GardenTool() { s += "gt "; }
6. }
7. public class Rake extends GardenTool {
8.    { name = "Rake "; }
9.    Rake(String arg) { s += name; }
10.   public static void main(String[] args) {
11.      new GardenTool("hey ");
12.      new Rake("hi ");
13.      System.out.println(s);
14.   }
15.   { name = "myRake "; }
16. }
```

What is the result?

A. `Tool Rake`

B. `Tool myRake`

C. `gt Tool Rake`

D. `gt Tool myRake`

E. `gt Tool gt Rake`

F. `gt Tool gt myRake`

G. `gt Tool gt Tool myRake`

H. Compilation fails.

48. Given:

```
3. public class Race {
4.    public static void main(String[] args) {
5.       Horse h = new Horse();
6.       Thread t1 = new Thread(h, "Andi");
7.       Thread t2 = new Thread(h, "Eyra");
8.       new Race().go(t2);
9.       t1.start();
10.       t2.start();
11.    }
12.    void go(Thread t) { t.start(); }
13. }
14. class Horse implements Runnable {
15.    public void run() {
16.       System.out.print(Thread.currentThread().getName() + " ");
17. } }
```

What is the result? (Choose all that apply.)

A. Compilation fails.

B. No output is produced.

C. The output could be: `"Andi Eyra "`

D. The output could be: `"Eyra Andi Eyra "`

E. The output could be: `"Eyra "`, followed by an exception.

F. The output could be: `"Eyra Andi "`, followed by an exception.

49. Given the proper import statement(s) and given:

```
4.       Map<String, String> h = new Hashtable<String, String>();
5.       String[] k = {"1", "2", "3", null};
6.       String[] v = {"a", "b", null, "d"};
7.
8.       for(int i=0; i<4; i++) {
```

```
9.        h.put(k[i], v[i]);
10.        System.out.print(h.get(k[i]) + " ");
11.      }
12.      System.out.print(h.size() + " " + h.values() + "\n");
```

What result is most likely?

A. Compilation fails.

B. `"a b d 3 [b, d, a]"`

C. `"a b null d 3 [b, d, a]"`

D. `"a b null d 4 [b, d, null, a]"`

E. `"a b"`, followed by an exception.

F. `"a b null"`, followed by an exception.

50. Given:

```
3. public class Fiji {
4.    static Fiji base;
5.    Fiji f;
6.    public static void main(String[] args) {
7.       new Fiji().go();
8.       // do more stuff
9.    }
10.   void go() {
11.      Fiji f1 = new Fiji();
12.      base = f1;
13.      Fiji f2 = new Fiji();
14.      f1.f = f2;
15.      Fiji f3 = f1.f;
16.      f2.f = f1;
17.      base = null; f1 = null; f2 = null;
18.      // do stuff
19. } }
```

Which are true? (Choose all that apply.)

A. At line 8, one object is eligible for garbage collection.

B. At line 8, two objects are eligible for garbage collection.

C. At line 8, three objects are eligible for garbage collection.

D. At line 18, 0 objects are eligible for garbage collection.

E. At line 18, two objects are eligible for garbage collection.

F. At line 18, three objects are eligible for garbage collection.

51. Your company makes compute-intensive, 3D rendering software for the movie industry. Your chief scientist has just discovered a new algorithm for several key methods in a commonly used utility class. The new algorithm will decrease processing time by 15 percent, without having to change any method signatures. After you change these key methods, and in the course of rigorous system testing, you discover that the changes have introduced no new bugs into the software.

In terms of your software's overall design, which are probably true? (Choose all that apply.)

- A. Your software is well encapsulated.
- B. Your software demonstrated low cohesion.
- C. Your software demonstrated high cohesion.
- D. Your software demonstrated loose coupling.
- E. Your software demonstrated tight coupling.

52. Which are true about the classes and interfaces in `java.util`? (Choose all that apply.)

- A. `LinkedHashSet` is-a `Collection`.
- B. `Vector` is-a `List`.
- C. `LinkedList` is-a `Queue`.
- D. `LinkedHashMap` is-a `Collection`.
- E. `TreeMap` is-a `SortedMap`.
- F. `Queue` is-a `Collection`.
- G. `Hashtable` is-a `Set`.

53. Given that `File.createNewFile()` throws `IOException`, and that `FileNotFoundException` extends `IOException`, use the following fragments to fill in the blanks so that the code compiles. You must use all the fragments, and each fragment can be used only once. Note: As in the real exam, some drag-and-drop style questions might have several correct answers. You will receive full credit for ANY one of the correct answers.

```
import java.io.*;
public class SticksMud {
  public static void main(String[] args) {
    try {
      File dir = new File("dir");
      dir.createNewFile();
    }
    catch _____
    catch _____
    catch _____
    catch (IOException io) { }
    catch _____
    catch _____
    catch _____
    catch _____
} }
```

Fragments:

```
(Throwable t) { }              (RuntimeException rt) { }
(Exception e) { }              (IllegalArgumentException arg) { }
(NullPointerException np) { }  (FileNotFoundException fnf) { }
(ClassCastException cc) { }
```

54. Given:

```
2.  class Grandfather {
3.    static String name = "gf ";
4.    String doStuff() { return "grandf "; }
5.  }
6.  class Father extends Grandfather {
7.    static String name = "fa ";
8.    String doStuff() { return "father "; }
9.  }
10. public class Child extends Father {
11.    static String name = "ch ";
12.    String doStuff() { return "child "; }
13.    public static void main(String[] args) {
14.      Father f = new Father();
15.      System.out.print(((Grandfather)f).name
                     + ((Grandfather)f).doStuff()) ;
16.      Child c = new Child();
17.      System.out.println(((Grandfather)c).name
                     + ((Grandfather)c).doStuff() + ((Father)c).doStuff());
18. } }
```

What is the result? (Choose all that apply.)

A. Compilation fails.

B. `fa father ch child child`

C. `gf father gf child child`

D. `fa grandf ch grandf father`

E. `gf grandf gf grandf father`

F. An exception is thrown at runtime.

55. Given:

```
1. class MyClass { }
```

And given that `MyClass2` has properly overridden `equals()` and `hashCode()`, objects from which classes make good hashing keys? (Choose all that apply.)

A. `MyClass`

B. `MyClass2`

C. `java.lang.String`

D. `java.lang.Integer`

E. `java.lang.StringBuilder`

56. Given:

```
2. public class Buffalo {
3.    static int x;
4.    int y;
5.    public static int getX() { return x; }
6.    public static void setX(int newX) { x = newX; }
7.    public int getY() { return y; }
8.    public void setY(int newY) { y = newY; }
9. }
```

Which lines of code need to be changed to make the class thread safe? (Choose all that apply.)

A. Line 2

B. Line 3

C. Line 4

D. Line 5

E. Line 6

F. Line 7

G. Line 8

57. Given:

```
2. class Animal { }
3. class Dog extends Animal { }
4. class Cat extends Animal { }
5. public class Mixer<A extends Animal> {
6.    public <C extends Cat> Mixer<? super Dog> useMe(A a, C c) {
7.       //Insert Code Here
8. } }
```

Which, inserted independently at line 7, compile? (Choose all that apply.)

A. `return null;`

B. `return new Mixer<Dog>();`

C. `return new Mixer<Animal>();`

D. `return new Mixer<A>();`

E. `return new Mixer<a>();`

F. `return new Mixer<c>();`

58. Given:

```
2. class Chilis {
3.    Chilis(String c, int h) { color = c; hotness = h; }
4.    String color;
5.    private int hotness;
6.    public boolean equals(Object o) {
7.       Chilis c = (Chilis)o;
8.       if(color.equals(c.color) && (hotness == c.hotness))  return true;
9.       return false;
10.    }
11.    // insert code here
12. }
```

Which, inserted independently at line 11, fulfill the `equals()` and `hashCode()` contract for Chilis? (Choose all that apply.)

A. `public int hashCode() { return 7; }`

B. `public int hashCode() { return hotness; }`

C. `public int hashCode() { return color.length(); }`

D. `public int hashCode() { return (int)(Math.random() * 200); }`

E. `public int hashCode() { return (color.length() + hotness); }`

59. Given the proper import(s), and this code in a method:

```
4.    List<String> x = new LinkedList<String>();
5.    Set<String> hs = new HashSet<String>();
6.    String[] v = {"a", "b", "c", "b", "a"};
7.    for(String s: v) {
8.       x.add(s);  hs.add(s);
9.    }
10.   System.out.print(hs.size() + " " + x.size() + " ");
11.   HashSet hs2 = new HashSet(x);
12.   LinkedList x2 = new LinkedList(hs);
13.   System.out.println(hs2.size() + " " + x2.size());
```

What is the result?

A. 3 3 3 3

B. 3 5 3 3

C. 3 5 3 5

D. 5 5 3 3

E. 5 5 5 5

F. Compilation fails.

G. An exception is thrown at runtime.

60. Given the proper import(s), and given:

```
4.    public static void main(String[] args) {
5.        List<Integer> x = new ArrayList<Integer>();
6.        x.add(new Integer(3));
7.        doStuff(x);
8.        for(Integer i: x)
9.            System.out.print(i + " ");
10.   }
11.   static void doStuff(List y) {
12.        y.add(new Integer(4));
13.        y.add(new Float(3.14f));
14.   }
```

What is the result? (Choose all that apply.)

A. Compilation fails.

B. The output will be "4 "

C. The output will be "3 4 "

D. The output will be "3 4 3.14 "

E. The output will be "3 3.14 4 "

F. The output will be "3 4 ", followed by an exception.

G. An exception will be thrown before any output is produced.

QUICK ANSWER KEY

1.	B, C	21.	D, F	41.	D
2.	F	22.	C, E	42.	F
3.	E	23.	G	43.	B
4.	D	24.	A, D	44.	B
5.	C, D	25.	C	45.	B, D, G
6.	C	26.	F	46.	E, F
7.	C, E, G	27.	B	47.	F
8.	B, F	28.	D	48.	E, F
9.	D	29.	B, C, D, F	49.	E
10.	A	30.	B, D	50.	C, D
11.	B	31.	A, B	51.	A, D
12.	A	32.	D, E	52.	A, B, C, E, F
13.	F	33.	A	53.	Drag and Drop
14.	E	34.	A, D, E, F, G	54.	C
15.	A, B, C, D	35.	E	55.	B, C, D
16.	C	36.	A, C, E	56.	B through G
17.	A	37.	F	57.	A, B, C
18.	C, D, E, F	38.	Drag and Drop	58.	A, B, C, E
19.	A, D, F	39.	B	59.	B
20.	E	40.	E	60.	F

PRACTICE EXAM 2: ANSWERS

1. Concerning Java's Garbage Collector (GC), which are true? (Choose all that apply.)

   A. If Object X has a reference to Object Y, then Object Y cannot be GCed.

   B. A Java program can request that the GC runs, but such a request does NOT guarantee that the GC will actually run.

   C. If the GC decides to delete an object, and if `finalize()` has never been invoked for that object, it is guaranteed that the GC will invoke `finalize()` for that object before the object is deleted.

   D. Once the GC invokes `finalize()` on an object, it is guaranteed that the GC will delete that object once `finalize()` has completed.

   E. When the GC runs, it decides whether to remove objects from the heap, the stack, or both.

   Answer (for Objective 7.4):

   ☑ **B** and **C** are correct.

   ☒ **A** is incorrect because if no Object has a reference to Object X, then both X and Y can be GCed. **D** is incorrect because it's possible for `finalize()` to send a reference to itself back to an object in a live thread, making the GC candidate "ineligible" for GC. **E** is incorrect because the GC never touches the stack.

2. Given:

```
1. public class BackHanded {
2.    int state = 0;
3.    BackHanded(int s) { state = s; }
4.    public static void main(String... hi) {
5.      BackHanded b1 = new BackHanded(1);
6.      BackHanded b2 = new BackHanded(2);
7.      System.out.println(b1.go(b1) + " " + b2.go(b2));
8.    }
9.    int go(BackHanded b) {
10.     if(this.state == 2) {
11.       b.state = 5;
12.       go(this);
13.     }
14.     return ++this.state;
15. } }
```

What is the result?

A. 1 2

B. 1 3

C. 1 6

D. 1 7

E. 2 6

F. 2 7

G. Compilation fails.

H. An exception is thrown at runtime.

Answer (for Objective 7.3):

☑ **F** is correct. There are only two `BackHanded` objects. The first call to `go()` is pretty straightforward, but don't get confused; `"b"` and `"this"` are referring to the same object. The second call to `go()` is a little trickier—the `"if"` test is `true`, so `go()` is invoked a third time. The result of the third invocation would be 6, but it's not kept. When control is returned to the second invocation of `go()`, `state` (from the same object) is incremented again, to 7.

☒ **A, B, C, D, E, G,** and **H** are incorrect based on the above.

3. Given:

```
42.    String s = "";
43.    if(011 == 9) s += 4;
44.    if(0x11 == 17) s += 5;
45.    Integer I = 12345;
46.    if(I.intValue() == Integer.valueOf("12345")) s += 6;
47.    System.out.println(s);
```

What is the result?

A. 5

B. 45

C. 46

D. 56

E. 456

F. Compilation fails.

G. An exception is thrown at runtime.

Answer (for Objective 3.1):

☑ **E** is correct. Line 43 is comparing an octal `int` to an `int`. Line 44 is comparing a hexadecimal `int` to an `int`. Line 46 is comparing an `int` to an `Integer`, which is unboxed before the comparison is made.

☒ **A, B, C, D, F,** and **G** are incorrect based on the above.

4. Given:

```
3. class Sport {
4.    Sport play() { System.out.print("play "); return new Sport(); }
5.    Sport play(int x) { System.out.print("play x "); return new Sport(); }
6. }
7. class Baseball extends Sport {
8.    Baseball play() { System.out.print("baseball "); return new Baseball(); }
9.    Sport play(int x) { System.out.print("sport "); return new Sport(); }
10.
11.    public static void main(String[] args) {
12.       new Baseball().play();
13.       new Baseball().play(7);
14.       super.play(7);
15.       new Sport().play();
16.       Sport s = new Baseball();
17.       s.play();
18. } }
```

What is the result?

A. `baseball sport sport play play`

B. `baseball sport play x play sport`

C. `baseball sport play x play baseball`

D. Compilation fails due to a single error.

E. Compilation fails due to errors on more than one line.

Answer (for Objective 1.4):

☑ **D** is correct. The only error is on line 14: A call to `super` cannot be made from a `static` context. The overridden `play()` method on line 8 is an example of a covariant return, which is a legal override as of Java 5.

☒ **A, B, C,** and **E** are incorrect based on the above.

5. Given:

```
2. public class Self extends Thread {
3.    public static void main(String[] args) {
4.       try {
5.          Thread t = new Thread(new Self());
6.          t.start();
7.          t.start();
8.       } catch (Exception e) { System.out.print("e "); }
9.    }
10.   public void run() {
11.      for(int i = 0; i < 2; i++)
12.         System.out.print(Thread.currentThread().getName() + " ");
13. } }
```

Which are true? (Choose all that apply.)

A. Compilation fails.

B. No output is produced.

C. The output could be `Thread-1 Thread-1 e`

D. The output could be `Thread-1 e Thread-1`

E. The output could be `Thread-1 Thread-1 Thread-2 Thread-2`

F. The output could be `Thread-1 Thread-2 Thread-1 Thread-2`

G. The output could be `Thread-1 Thread-1 Thread-1 Thread-1`

Answer (for Objective 4.1):

☑ **C** and **D** are correct. When you attempt to invoke `start()` on the same thread more than once, an exception is thrown and a second thread is NOT started. That exception doesn't keep the first thread from completing.

☒ **A, B, E, F,** and **G** are incorrect based on the above.

6. Given:

```
3. class Stereo { void makeNoise() { assert true; } }
4. public class BoomBox2 extends Stereo {
5.    public static void main(String[] args) {
6.       new BoomBox2().go(args);
7.    }
8.    void go(String[] args) {
9.       if(args.length > 0)  makeNoise();
10.      if(args[0].equals("x")) System.out.print("x ");
11.      if(args[0] == "x") System.out.println("x2 ");
12. } }
```

And (if the code compiles), the invocation:

```
java -ea Boombox2 x
```

What is the result?

A. x

B. x x2

C. An error is thrown at runtime.

D. Compilation fails due to an error on line 3.

E. Compilation fails due to an error on line 8.

F. Compilation fails due to an error on line 9.

Answer (for Objective 2.6):

☑ **C** is correct. A NoClassDefFoundError is thrown. It's lame, but you have to watch out for this kind of thing. The invocation should be java -ea BoomBox2 x (both B's are capitalized). If the invocation was correct, the answer would be **A**.

☒ **A, B, D, E,** and **F** are incorrect based on the above.

7. Given:

```
2. import java.util.*;
3. public class Olives {
4.   public static void main(String[] args) {
5.     Set<Integer> s = new TreeSet<Integer>();
6.     s.add(23); s.add(42); s.add(new Integer(5));
7.     Iterator i = s.iterator();
8.     // while(System.out.print(i.next())) { }
9.     // for(Integer i2: i) System.out.print(i2);
10.    // for(Integer i3: s) System.out.print(i3);
11.    // while(i.hasNext()) System.out.print(i.get());
12.    // while(i.hasNext()) System.out.print(i.next());
13. } }
```

If lines 8–12 are uncommented, independently, which are true? (Choose all that apply.)

A. Line 8 will compile.

B. Line 9 will compile.

C. Line 10 will compile.

D. Line 11 will compile.

E. Line 12 will compile.

F. Of those that compile, the output will be 23425

G. Of those that compile, the output will be 52342

Answer (for Objective 6.3):

☑ **C, E,** and **G** are correct. Line 10 is a legal for-each loop. Line 12 uses legal syntax to iterate over the Set. Because this is a TreeSet, the output will be sorted.

☒ **A, B, D,** and **F** are incorrect based on the above.

8. Given the proper import statements and:

```
23.  try {
24.    File file = new File("myFile.txt");
25.    PrintWriter pw = new PrintWriter(file);
26.    pw.println("line 1");
27.    pw.close();
28.    PrintWriter pw2 = new PrintWriter("myFile.txt");
29.    pw2.println("line 2");
30.    pw2.close();
31.  } catch (IOException e) { }
```

What is the result? (Choose all that apply.)

A. No file is created.

B. A file named "myFile.txt" is created.

C. Compilation fails due to an error on line 24.

D. Compilation fails due to an error on line 28.

E. "myFile.txt" contains only one line of data, "line 1"

F. "myFile.txt" contains only one line of data, "line 2"

G. "myFile.txt" contains two lines of data, "line 1" then "line 2"

Answer (for Objective 3.2):

☑ **B** and **F** are correct. Both PrintWriter constructors are valid. When the second constructor is called, it truncates the existing file to zero size, then "line 2" is added to the file by the second println().

☒ **A, C, D, E,** and **G** are incorrect based on the above.

9. Given this code in a method:

```
3.        String s = "-";
4.        boolean b = false;
5.        int x = 7, y = 8;
6.        if((x < 8)  ^  (b = true))      s += "^";
7.        if(!(x > 8) | ++y > 5)          s += "|";
8.        if(++y > 9 && b == true)        s += "&&";
9.        if(y % 8 > 1 || y / (x - 7) > 1) s += "%";
10.       System.out.println(s);
```

What is the result?

A. -

B. - | %

C. - ^ | %

D. - | && %

E. - ^ | && %

F. Compilation fails.

G. An exception is thrown at runtime.

> Answer (for Objective 7.6):
>
> ☑ **D** is correct. The first if test fails because both comparisons are true ("b = true" is an assignment, not a test!) and the ^ is XOR—only one condition can be true. In the second if test, y is incremented because even though the comparison on the left side of the " | " is true, " | " is NOT a short-circuit operator, so the right side will be evaluated. The third if test is true because y has been incremented twice, and b was set to true in the first if test. The fourth if test is true because the left-hand side is true, so the short-circuit operator never tests the right-hand side. If it did, a divide by zero exception would be thrown.
>
> ☒ A, B, C, E, F, and G are incorrect based on the above.

10. Given:

```
3. public class Limits {
4.     private int x = 2;
5.     protected int y = 3;
6.     private static int m1 = 4;
7.     protected static int m2 = 5;
```

```
8.    public static void main(String[] args) {
9.        int x = 6;    int y = 7;
10.       int m1 = 8;  int m2 = 9;
11.       new Limits().new Secret().go();
12.   }
13.   class Secret {
14.       void go() { System.out.println(x + " " + y + " " + m1 + " " + m2); }
15. } }
```

What is the result?

A. 2 3 4 5

B. 2 7 4 9

C. 6 3 8 4

D. 6 7 8 9

E. Compilation fails due to multiple errors.

F. Compilation fails due only to an error on line 11.

G. Compilation fails due only to an error on line 14.

Answer (for Objective 1.1):

☑ **A** is correct. All of the code is legal. The inner class has access to all of the outer class's variables (even the `private` ones), except for `main()`'s local variables. Remember that an inner class must have an instance of the outer class to be tied to, which is why line 11 starts by creating an instance of `Limits`.

☒ **B, C, D, E, F,** and **G** are incorrect based on the above.

11. Note: This question concerns Serialization. As of this writing, the Serialization topic was officially removed from the objectives, *BUT* we were still getting reports that some testing centers were using versions of the exam that included Serialization questions. If you choose to ignore the Serialization topic, give yourself a free "correct answer" for this question. (FWIW, your authors believe it's a good topic to understand.)

Given:

```
3. import java.io.*;
4. class ElectronicDevice { ElectronicDevice() { System.out.print("ed "); }}
5. class Mp3player extends ElectronicDevice implements Serializable {
6.   Mp3player() { System.out.print("mp "); }
7. }
```

```
8. class MiniPlayer extends Mp3player {
9.    MiniPlayer() { System.out.print("mini "); }
10.   public static void main(String[] args) {
11.      MiniPlayer m = new MiniPlayer();
12.      try {
13.        FileOutputStream fos = new FileOutputStream("dev.txt");
14.        ObjectOutputStream os = new ObjectOutputStream(fos);
15.        os.writeObject(m);  os.close();
16.        FileInputStream fis = new FileInputStream("dev.txt");
17.        ObjectInputStream is = new ObjectInputStream(fis);
18.        MiniPlayer m2 = (MiniPlayer) is.readObject();  is.close();
19.      } catch (Exception x) { System.out.print("x "); }
20. } }
```

What is the result?

A. ed mp mini

B. ed mp mini ed

C. ed mp mini ed mini

D. ed mp mini ed mp mini

E. Compilation fails.

F. "ed mp mini", followed by an exception.

Answer (for the now defunct Serialization Objective 3.X):

☑ **B** is correct. It's okay for Mp3player to implement Serializable even though ElectronicDevice does not. In addition, because Mp3player implements Serializable, its subclass (MiniPlayer) does too. When the MiniPlayer object is deserialized, the only constructor that runs is for the only class that doesn't implement Serializable or in other words ElectronicDevice.

☒ **A, C, D, E,** and **F** are incorrect based on the above.

12. Given:

```
2. abstract interface Pixie {
3.    abstract void sprinkle();
4.    static int dust = 3;
5. }
6. abstract class TinkerBell implements Pixie {
7.    String fly() { return "flying "; }
8. }
```

```
 9. public class ForReal extends TinkerBell {
10.    public static void main(String[] args) {
11.      new ForReal().sprinkle();
12.    }
13.    public void sprinkle() { System.out.println(fly() + " " + dust); }
14. }
```

What is the result? (Choose all that apply.)

A. `flying  3`

B. Compilation fails because `TinkerBell` doesn't properly implement `Pixie`.

C. Compilation fails because `ForReal` doesn't properly extend `TinkerBell`.

D. Compilation fails because `Pixie` is not a legal interface.

E. Compilation fails because `ForReal` doesn't properly implement `Pixie`.

F. Compilation fails because `TinkerBell` is not a legal `abstract` class.

Answer (for Objective 1.2):

☑ **A** is correct, all of the declaration, implementing, and extending rules are satisfied.

☒ **B, C, D, E,** and **F** are incorrect based on the above.

13. Given:

```
 2. public class Errrrr {
 3.    static String a = null;
 4.    static String s = "";
 5.    public static void main(String[] args) {
 6.      try {
 7.        a = args[0];
 8.        System.out.print(a);
 9.        s += "t1 ";
10.      }
11.      catch (RuntimeException re) { s += "c1 "; }
12.      finally { s += "f1 "; }
13.      System.out.println(" " + s);
14. } }
```

And two command-line invocations:

```
java Errrrr
java Errrrr x
```

What is the result?

A. First: f1, then: x t1

B. First: f1, then: x t1 f1

C. First: c1, then: x t1

D. First: c1, then: x t1 f1

E. First: c1 f1, then: x t1

F. First: c1 f1, then: x t1 f1

G. Compilation fails.

Answer (for Objective 2.4):

☑ **F** is correct. The first invocation throws an exception which is caught, then `finally` runs. The second invocation throws no exception, but `finally` still runs.

☒ **A, B, C, D, E,** and **G** are incorrect based on the above.

14. Given:

```
51.    String s = "4.5x4.a.3";
52.    String[] tokens = s.split("\\s");
53.    for(String o: tokens)
54.      System.out.print(o + " ");
55.
56.    System.out.print("  ");
57.    tokens = s.split("\\..");
58.    for(String o: tokens)
59.      System.out.print(o + " ");
```

What is the result?

A. 4 x4

B. 4 x4 .

C. 4 x4 3

D. 4 5x4 a 3   4 x4

E. 4.5x4.a.3   4 x4

F. 4.5x4.a.3   4 x4 .

Answer (for Objective 3.4):

☑ **E** is correct. The first invocation of `split()` uses the `"\s"` metacharacter, which splits on whitespace. Since there is no whitespace in `String s`, the entire string is placed into `tokens[0]`. The second invocation of `split()` combines `"\\."` (which means look for `"."`), with a standalone `"."`, which is the metacharacter for "find any character." So the second `split()` reads "split on a dot followed by any character." Note that the `split()` method does not change the `String` being split.

☒ **A, B, C, D,** and **F** are incorrect based on the above.

15. Given:

```
2. abstract class Tool {
3.    int SKU;
4.    abstract void getSKU();
5. }
6. public class Hammer {
7.    // insert code here
8. }
```

Which line(s), inserted independently at line 7, will compile? (Choose all that apply.)

A. `void getSKU() { ; }`

B. `private void getSKU() { ; }`

C. `protected void getSKU() { ; }`

D. `public void getSKU() { ; }`

Answer (for Objective 1.2):

☑ **A, B, C,** and **D** are ALL correct. It's a trick question—you might get something like this on the real exam. It's easy if you notice that on line 6 the code does NOT say `"extends Tool"`. If line 6 did say `"extends Tool"`, the correct answer would be **A, C,** and **D**.

☒ There are no incorrect answers.

16. Given:

```
3. public class Stubborn implements Runnable {
4.    static Thread t1;
5.    static int x = 5;
6.    public void run() {
7.       if(Thread.currentThread().getId() == t1.getId()) shove();
8.       else push();
9.    }
```

```
10.    static synchronized void push() { shove(); }
11.    static void shove() {
12.      synchronized(Stubborn.class) {
13.        System.out.print(x-- + " ");
14.        try { Thread.sleep(2000); } catch (Exception e) { ; }
15.        if(x > 0) push();
16.    } }
17.    public static void main(String[] args) {
18.      t1 = new Thread(new Stubborn());
19.      t1.start();
20.      new Thread(new Stubborn()).start();
21. } }
```

Which are true? (Choose all that apply.)

A.   Compilation fails.

B.   The output is 5 4 3 2 1

C.   The output is 5 4 3 2 1 0

D.   The program could deadlock.

E.   The output could be 5, followed by deadlock.

F.   If the `sleep()` invocation was removed, the chance of deadlock would decrease.

G.   As it stands, the program can't deadlock, but if shove() was changed to `synchronized`, then the program could deadlock.

Answer (for Objective 4.3):

☑   **C** is correct. It might look like this code could deadlock, but there is only one lock, so no deadlock can occur.

☒   **A, B, D, E, F,** and **G** are incorrect based on the above.

---

17. Given:

```
2. class Super {
3.    static String os = "";
4.    void doStuff() { os += "super "; }
5. }
6. public class PolyTest extends Super {
7.    public static void main(String[] args) { new PolyTest().go(); }
8.    void go() {
9.      Super s = new PolyTest();
10.     PolyTest p = (PolyTest)s;
```

```
11.        p.doStuff();
12.        s.doStuff();
13.        p.doPoly();
14.        s.doPoly();
15.        System.out.println(os);
16.      }
17.      void doStuff() { os += "over "; }
18.      void doPoly() { os += "poly "; }
19. }
```

What is the result?

A. Compilation fails.

B. `over over poly poly`

C. `over super poly poly`

D. `super super poly poly`

E. An exception is thrown at runtime.

Answer (for Objective 5.2):

☑ **A** is correct. Compilation fails at line 14 because the `Super` class reference variable doesn't know about the `doPoly()` method.

☒ **B, C, D,** and **E** are incorrect based on the above.

18. Given two files:

```
1. package com.wickedlysmart;
2. import com.wickedlysmart2.*;
3. public class Launcher {
4.    public static void main(String[] args) {
5.       Utils u = new Utils();
6.       u.do1();
7.       u.do2();
8.       u.do3();
9. } }
```

and the correctly compiled and located:

```
1. package com.wickedlysmart2;
2. class Utils {
3.    void do1() { System.out.print("do1 "); }
4.    protected void do2() { System.out.print("do2 "); }
5.    public void do3() { System.out.print("do3 "); }
6. }
```

What is the result for Launcher? (Choose all that apply.)

A. do1 do2 do3

B. "do1 ", followed by an exception

C. Compilation fails due to an error on line 5 of Launcher.

D. Compilation fails due to an error on line 6 of Launcher.

E. Compilation fails due to an error on line 7 of Launcher.

F. Compilation fails due to an error on line 8 of Launcher.

Answer (for Objective 7.1):

☑ **C, D, E,** and **F** are correct. class Utils is not public so it CANNOT be accessed from a different package.

☒ **A** and **B** are incorrect based on the above.

19. Given:

```
2. public class Wacky {
3.    public static void main(String[] args) {
4.       int x = 5;
5.       int y = (x < 6) ? 7 : 8;
6.       System.out.print(y + " ");
7.       boolean b = (x < 6) ? false : true;
8.       System.out.println(b + " ");
9.       assert(x < 6) : "bob";
10.      assert( ((x < 6) ? false : true) ) : "fred";
11. } }
```

And, if the code compiles, the invocation:

```
java -ea Wacky
```

Which will be contained in the output? (Choose all that apply.)

A. 7

B. 8

C. bob

D. fred

E. true

F. false

G. Compilation fails.

Answer (for Objective 7.6):

☑ **A, D,** and **F** are correct. The ternary operator assigns the first value when the expression is true, so y == 7, and b == false. The second assert statement has a ternary operator as an expression and since the result is false, fred is added to the AssertionError stack trace.

☒ **B, C, E,** and **G** are incorrect based on the above.

20. Given:

```
3. class MotorVehicle {
4.   protected int doStuff(int x) { return x * 2; }
5. }
6. class Bicycle {
7.   void go(MotorVehicle m) {
8.     System.out.print(m.doStuff(21) + " ");
9. } }
10. public class Beemer extends MotorVehicle {
11.   public static void main(String[] args) {
12.     System.out.print(new Beemer().doStuff(11) + " ");
13.     new Bicycle().go(new Beemer());
14.     new Bicycle().go(new MotorVehicle());
15.   }
16.   int doStuff(int x) { return x * 3; }
17. }
```

What is the result? (Choose all that apply.)

A. 22 42 42

B. 22 63 63

C. 33 42 42

D. 33 63 42

E. Compilation fails.

F. An exception is thrown at runtime.

Answer (for Objective 5.3):

☑ **E** is correct. Beemer.doStuff() will not compile because it's attempting to override using a weaker access modifier.

☒ **A, B, C, D,** and **F** are incorrect based on the above.

21. Which are true? (Choose all that apply.)

A. A single JAR file can contain only files from a single package.

B. A JAR file can be used only on the machine on which it was created.

C. When `javac` is using files within a JAR file, it will unJAR the file during compilation.

D. The Java SDK installation directory tree on a Java developer's computer usually includes a subdirectory tree named `jre/lib/ext`.

E. A JAR file is structured so that all the files and directories that you've "JARed" will be subdirectory(ies) of the `META-INF` directory.

F. When `javac` is invoked with a `classpath` option, and you need to find files in a JAR file, the name of the JAR file must be included at the end of the path.

Answer (for Objective 7.5):

☑ **D** and **F** are correct statements.

☒ **A** and **B** are incorrect because JARs can contain many packages, and of course can be used on many machines. **C** is not true. **E** is incorrect because your directory structure will be a peer to the `META-INF` directory.

22. Given the proper import(s), and given:

```
13. class NameCompare implements Comparator<Stuff> {
14.   public int compare(Stuff a, Stuff b) {
15.     return b.name.compareTo(a.name);
16. } }
18. class ValueCompare implements Comparator<Stuff> {
19.   public int compare(Stuff a, Stuff b) {
20.     return (a.value - b.value);
21. } }
```

Which are true? (Choose all that apply.)

A. This code does not compile.

B. This code allows you to use instances of `Stuff` as keys in Maps.

C. These two classes properly implement the `Comparator` interface.

D. `NameCompare` allows you to sort a collection of `Stuff` instances alphabetically.

E. `ValueCompare` allows you to sort a collection of `Stuff` instances in ascending numeric order.

F. If you changed both occurrences of `"compare()"` to `"compareTo()"`, the code would compile.

Answer (for Objective 6.3):

☑ **C** and **E** are correct. The code is legal and `Collections.sort()` can use the `ValueCompare.compare()` method to sort in ascending numeric order.

☒ **A** is incorrect based on the above. **B** is incorrect because this code doesn't show us whether `Stuff` has overridden `equals()` and `hashCode()`, which would allow `Stuff` to be used successfully for keys. **D** is incorrect because the `NameCompare.compare()` method would be used to create sorts in reverse-alphabetical order. **F** is incorrect based on the above.

23. Given:

```
3. public class Chopper {
4.    String a = "12b";
5.    public static void main(String[] args) {
6.       System.out.println(new Chopper().chop(args[0]));
7.    }
8.    int chop(String a) {
9.      if(a == null) throw new IllegalArgumentException();
10.      return Integer.parseInt(a);
11. } }
```

And, if the code compiles, the invocation:

```
java Chopper
```

What is the result?

A. `12`

B. `12b`

C. Compilation fails.

D. A `NullPointerException` is thrown.

E. A `NumberFormatException` is thrown.

F. An `IllegalArgumentException` is thrown.

G. An `ArrayIndexOutOfBoundsException` is thrown.

Answer (for Objective 2.6):

☑ **G** is correct. Working backwards, if somehow we passed `parseInt()` the `String` `"12b"`, it would throw a `NumberFormatException`. If somehow we passed a null to `chop()`, we would get an `IllegalArgumentException`. But before any of that can happen, we attempt to access `args[0]`, which throws an `ArrayIndexOutOfBoundsException`.

☒ **A**, **B**, **C**, **D**, **E**, and **F** are incorrect based on the above.

24. Which, concerning command-line options, are true? (Choose all that apply.)

A. The -D flag is used in conjunction with a name-value pair.

B. The -D flag can be used with `javac` to set a system property.

C. The -d flag can be used with `java` to disable assertions.

D. The -d flag can be used with `javac` to specify where to place `.class` files.

E. The -d flag can be used with `javac` to document the locations of deprecated APIs in source files.

> Answer (for Objective 7.2):
>
> ☑ **A** and **D** are correct.
>
> ☒ **B** is incorrect because -D is used with the `java` command to set a system property. **C** is incorrect because -da is used to disable assertions. **E** is incorrect because the deprecation-related option is -deprecation. Note: You don't need to memorize all the `java` and `javac` command-line options, but -d, -D, and assertion options WILL be on the exam.

25. Given that `"it, IT"` is the locale code for Italy and that `"pt, BR"` is the locale code for Brazil, and given:

```
51.  Date d = new Date();
52.  DateFormat df = DateFormat.getDateInstance(DateFormat.FULL);
53.  Locale[] la = {new Locale("it", "IT"), new Locale("pt", "BR")};
54.  for(Locale l: la) {
55.    df.setLocale(l);
56.    System.out.println(df.format(d));
57.  }
```

Which are true? (Choose all that apply.)

A. An exception is thrown at runtime.

B. Compilation fails due to an error on line 53.

C. Compilation fails due to an error on line 55.

D. Compilation fails due to an error on line 56.

E. The output will contain only today's date for the Italian locale.

F. The output will contain today's date for both Italian and Brazilian locales.

Answer (for Objective 3.3):

☑ **C** is correct. Any instance of `DateFormat` has an immutable `Locale`—in other words, there is no `setLocale()` method. The rest of the code is legal.

☒ **A, B, D, E,** and **F** are incorrect based on the above.

26. Given this code in a method:

```
4.      Integer[][] la = {{1,2}, {3,4,5}};
5.      Number[] na = la[1];
6.      Number[] na2 = (Number[])la[0];
7.      Object o = na2;
8.      la[1] = (Number[])o;
9.      la[0] = (Integer[])o;
```

What is the result? (Choose all that apply.)

A. Compilation succeeds.

B. Compilation fails due to an error on line 4.

C. Compilation fails due to an error on line 5.

D. Compilation fails due to an error on line 6.

E. Compilation fails due to an error on line 7.

F. Compilation fails due to an error on line 8.

G. Compilation fails due to an error on line 9.

H. Compilation succeeds but an exception is thrown at runtime.

Answer (for Objective 1.3):

☑ **F** is correct. `Integer` extends `Number`, so you can't refer an `Integer[]` reference to a `Number[]` (an `Integer` can do things a `Number` can't.)

☒ **A** and **H** are incorrect based on the above. **B, C, D, E,** and **G** are incorrect because those lines of code perform legal array manipulations.

27. Given:

```
3. public class Ice {
4.     Long[] stockings = {new Long(3L), new Long(4L), new Long(5L)};
5.     static int count = 0;
6.     public static void main(String[] args) {
7.        new Ice().go();
```

```
8.        System.out.println(count);
9.      }
10.   void go() {
11.     for(short x = 0; x < 5; x++) {
12.       if(x == 2) return;
13.       for(long ell: stockings) {
14.         count++;
15.         if(ell == 4) break;
16. } } } }
```

What is the result? (Choose all that apply.)

A. 2

B. 4

C. 8

D. 12

E. Compilation fails due to an error on line 13.

F. Compilation fails due to an error on line 16.

Answer (for Objective 2.2):

☑ **B** is correct. In `for` loops (any flavor), a `return` immediately returns execution to the calling method (in this case, `main()`). A `break` moves execution to the first statement after the `for` loop (in this case, the inner `for` loop).

☒ **A, C, D, E**, and **F** are incorrect. Line 13 is a so-called for-each loop that's using auto-unboxing. Line 16 is ugly but legal. Don't be surprised to see this kind of thing on the real exam where the number of lines of code is limited by the test engine.

28. Given the proper import statement(s) and:

```
4.        Console c = System.console();
5.        char[] pw;
6.        if(c == null) return;
7.        pw = c.readPassword("%s", "pw: ");
8.        System.out.println(c.readLine("%s", "input: "));
```

Which statements are true? (Choose all that apply.)

A. An exception will be thrown on line 8.

B. The variable pw must be a `String`, not a `char[]`.

C. No import statements are necessary for the code to compile.

D. If the code compiles and is invoked, line 7 might never run.

E. Without a third argument, the readPassword() method will echo the password the user types.

F. If line 4 was replaced with the following code, the program would still compile: "Console c = new Console();".

Answer (for Objective 3.2):

☑ **D** is correct. The code is all legal, but it's possible to invoke a Java program in an environment that doesn't have a Console object—therefore, the if test on line 6 can sometimes be true. The readPassword() method ALWAYS disables echoing. The Console object is ALWAYS constructed using System.console(), but the Console class is in java.io.

☒ **A, B, C, E**, and **F** are incorrect based on the above.

29. Given that:

Exception is the superclass of IOException, and

IOException is the superclass of FileNotFoundException, and

```
3. import java.io.*;
4. class Physicist {
5.    void think() throws IOException { }
6. }
7. public class Feynman extends Physicist {
8.    public static void main(String[] args) {
9.       new Feynman().think();
10.    }
11.    // insert method here
12. }
```

Which of the following methods, inserted independently at line 11, compiles? (Choose all that apply.)

A. void think() throws Exception { }

B. void think() throws FileNotFoundException { }

C. public void think() { }

D. protected void think() throws IOException { }

E. private void think() throws IOException { }

F. void think() { int x = 7/0; }

Answer (for Objective 1.4):

☑ **B, C, D,** and **F** are correct. It's legal for overridden methods to have less restrictive access modifiers, to have fewer or narrower checked exceptions, and to have unchecked exceptions. (Note: Of course, **F** would throw an exception at runtime.)

☒ **A** is incorrect because `Exception` is broader. **E** is incorrect because `private` is more restrictive.

30. Given:

```
4. public class Zingseng extends Thread {
5.    public static void main(String[] args) throws Exception {
6.       Thread t1 = new Thread(new Zingseng());
7.       t1.start();
8.       // insert code here
9.       for(int i = 0; i < 1000; i++)   // Loop #1
10.          System.out.print(Thread.currentThread().getName() + " ");
11.    }
12.    public void run() {
13.       for(int i = 0; i < 1000; i++)   // Loop #2
14.          System.out.print(Thread.currentThread().getName() + " ");
15. } }
```

Which code, inserted independently at line 8, will make most (or all) of Loop #2's iterations run before most (or all) of Loop #1's iterations? (Choose all that apply.)

A. `// just a comment`

B. `t1.join();`

C. `t1.yield();`

D. `t1.sleep(1000);`

Answer (for Objective 4.2):

☑ **B** and **D** are correct. The `join()` method will tack the main thread's execution to the end of `t1`'s execution. The `t1.sleep(1000)` method will put the `main` thread to sleep for one second (remember `sleep()` is `static`!!!).

☒ **A** is incorrect because the two threads' run order will be unpredictable. **C** is incorrect because `yield()` might cause a tiny interruption (where 1000 milliseconds would be a HUGE interruption), but it probably wouldn't significantly change the run order.

31. Given:

```
2. public class Kant extends Philosopher {
3.    // insert code here
5.    public static void main(String[] args) {
6.       new Kant("Homer");
7.       new Kant();
8.    }
9. }
10. class Philosopher {
11.    Philosopher(String s) { System.out.print(s + " "); }
12. }
```

Which set(s) of code, inserted independently at line 3, produce the output "Homer Bart "? (Choose all that apply.)

A. `Kant() { this("Bart"); }`
    `Kant(String s) { super(s); }`

B. `Kant() { super("Bart"); }`
    `Kant(String s) { super(s); }`

C. `Kant() { super(); }`
    `Kant(String s) { super(s); }`

D. `Kant() { super("Bart"); }`
    `Kant(String s) { this(); }`

E. `Kant() { super("Bart"); }`
    `Kant(String s) { this("Homer"); }`

Answer (for Objective 1.5):

☑ **A** and **B** are two correct ways for Kant's constructors to interact with Philosopher's constructor.

☒ **C** will not compile because Kant's constructors assume Philosopher has a no-arg constructor. **D** compiles but produces the output "Bart Bart ". **E** will not compile because the one-arg constructor is attempting to call itself recursively.

32. Given:

```
2. public class Epoch {
3.    static int jurassic = 0;
4.    public static void main(String[] args) {
5.       assert(doStuff(5));
6.    }
```

```
7.    static boolean doStuff(int x) {
8.       jurassic += x;
9.       return true;
10. } }
```

Which are true? (Choose all that apply.)

A. The code compiles using `javac -ea Epoch.java`

B. The assert statement on line 5 is used appropriately.

C. The code compiles using `javac -source 1.3 Epoch.java`

D. The code compiles using `javac -source 1.4 Epoch.java`

E. The code compiles using `javac -source 1.6 Epoch.java`

F. The code will not compile using any version of the `javac` compiler.

Answer (for Objective 2.3):

☑ **D** and **E** are correct (and **C** is incorrect) because `"assert"` was not a keyword until Java 1.4.

☒ **A** is incorrect because `-ea` is a `java` command, not `javac`. **B** is incorrect because an assertion should never cause a state change. **F** is incorrect based on the above.

33. Given

```
1. public class Kaput {
2.    Kaput myK;
3.    String degree = "0";
4.    public static void main(String[] args) {
5.       Kaput k1 = new Kaput();
6.       go(k1);
7.       System.out.println(k1.degree);
8.    }
9.    static Kaput go(Kaput k) {
10.      final Kaput k1 = new Kaput();
11.      k.myK = k1;
12.      k.myK.degree = "7";
13.      return k.myK;
14. } }
```

What is the result?

A. 0

B. 7

C. null

D. Compilation fails.

E. An exception is thrown at runtime.

Answer (for Objective 7.3):

☑ **A** is correct. The `Kaput` object referred to by `k1` has a `Kaput` object, and that object's `degree` variable is updated, but the original `Kaput` object's `degree` variable is not updated.

☒ **B, C, D,** and **E** are incorrect based on the above.

34. Given:

```
3. class Holder {
4.    enum Gas { ARGON, HELIUM };
5. }
6. public class Basket extends Holder {
7.    public static void main(String[] args) {
8.        short s = 7; long l = 9L; float f = 4.0f;
9.        int i = 3; char c = 'c'; byte b = 5;
10.       // insert code here
11.          default: System.out.println("howdy");
12. } } }
```

Which line(s) of code (if any), inserted independently at line 10, will compile? (Choose all that apply.)

A. `switch (s) {`

B. `switch (l) {`

C. `switch (f) {`

D. `switch (i) {`

E. `switch (c) {`

F. `switch (b) {`

G. `switch (Gas.ARGON) {`

H. The code will not compile due to additional error(s).

Answer (for Objective 2.1):

☑ **A, D, E, F,** and **G** are correct. It's legal to use an `enum` in a `switch`.

☒ **B** and **C** are incorrect, `long` and `float` primitives cannot be used in `switch` statements. **H** is incorrect because the rest of the code is valid.

35. Given

```
2. class Horse {
3.    static String s = "";
4.    void beBrisk() { s += "trot "; }
5. }
6. public class Andi extends Horse {
7.    void beBrisk() { s += "tolt "; }
8.    public static void main(String[] args) {
9.       Horse x0 = new Horse();
10.      Horse x1 = new Andi();   x1.beBrisk();
11.      Andi x2 = (Andi)x1;      x2.beBrisk();
12.      Andi x3 = (Andi)x0;      x3.beBrisk();
13.      System.out.println(s);
14. } }
```

What is the result?

A. tolt tolt tolt

B. trot tolt trot

C. trot tolt tolt

D. Compilation fails.

E. An exception is thrown at runtime.

> Answer (for Objective 5.2):
>
> ☑ **E** is correct. On line 12, the code attempts to cast a Horse reference (the superclass) to an Andi reference, causing a ClassCastException.
>
> ☒ **A, B, C,** and **D** are incorrect based on the above.

36. Given:

```
3. class Tire {
4.    private static int x = 6;
5.    public static class Wheel {
6.       void go() { System.out.print("roll " + x++); }
7. } }
8. public class Car {
9.    public static void main(String[] args) {
10.      // insert code here
11. } }
```

And the three code fragments:

I. `new Tire.Wheel().go();`

II. `Tire t = new Tire();   t.Wheel().go();`

III. `Tire.Wheel w = new Tire.Wheel();   w.go();`

Assuming we insert a single fragment at line 10, which are true? (Choose all that apply.)

A. Once compiled, the output will be `"roll 6"`

B. Once compiled, the output will be `"roll 7"`

C. Fragment I, inserted at line 10, will compile.

D. Fragment II, inserted at line 10, will compile.

E. Fragment III, inserted at line 10, will compile.

F. Taken separately, class `Tire` will not compile on its own.

Answer (for Objective 1.5):

☑ **A, C,** and **E** are correct. The weird, static-specific syntax to use so-called "static inner classes" from outside the enclosing class is demonstrated with fragments I and III.

☒ **B, D,** and **F** are incorrect based on the above.

37. Given:

```
3. public class Fortran {
4.    static int bump(int i) { return i + 2; }
5.    public static void main(String[] args) {
6.       for(int x = 0; x < 5; bump(x))
7.          System.out.print(x + " ");
8. } }
```

What is the result?

A. `2 4`

B. `0 2 4`

C. `2 4 6`

D. `0 2 4 6`

E. Compilation fails.

F. Some other result occurs.

Answer (for Objective 2.2):

☑ **F** is correct. In a `for` loop, the iteration expression can be most any code statement that you want, such as the `bump()` method call shown on line 6. In this case, the result of the addition is not captured, so x's value never changes, therefore the `for` loop runs infinitely. If the iteration expression read "`x = bump(x)`", then **B** would be the correct answer.

☒ **A, B, C, D,** and **E** are incorrect based on the above.

38. You need the three classes and/or interfaces to work together to produce the output "`Kara Charis`". Fill in the blanks using the following fragments so the correct is-a and has-a relationships are established to produce this output. Note: You may not need to fill in every empty blank space, but a blank space can hold only one fragment. Also note that not all the fragments will be used, and that fragments CAN be used more than once.

Code to complete:

```
_____ Nameable {
    _____
}
class Animal _____ {
    _____
    _____
}
public class Buddies _____ {
    _____
    public static void main(String[] args) {
        Animal b1 = new Animal("Kara");
        _____
        System.out.println(b1.getName() + " " + b2.getName());
} }
```

Fragments:

```
interface                          Animal() { name = "Charis"; }
String name;                       Animal(String n) { name = n; }
abstract class                     Buddies(String s) { super(); }
extends Animal                     Buddies b2 = new Buddies();
extends Nameable                   Buddies(String s) { super(s); }
name = "Charis";                   String getName() { return name; }
implements Animal                  Buddies b2 = new Buddies("Charis");
implements Nameable                void Animal(String n) { name = n; }
                                   void Buddies(String s) { super(s); }
```

Answer (for Objective 5.5):

```
abstract class Nameable {
  String name;
}
class Animal extends Nameable {
  Animal(String n) { name = n; }
  String getName() { return name; }
}
public class Buddies extends Animal {
  Buddies(String s) { super(s); }
  public static void main(String[] args) {
    Animal b1 = new Animal("Kara");
    Buddies b2 = new Buddies("Charis");
    System.out.println(b1.getName() + " " + b2.getName());
} }
```

39. Given:

```
1. import java.util.*;
2. public class PirateTalk {
3.   public static void main(String... arrrrgs) {
4.     Properties p = System.getProperties();
5.     p.setProperty("pirate", "scurvy");
6.     String s = p.getProperty("argProp") + " ";
7.     s += p.getProperty("pirate");
8.     System.out.println(s);
9. } }
```

And the command-line invocation:

```
java PirateTalk -DargProp="dog,"
```

What is the result?

A. dog, scurvy

B. null scurvy

C. scurvy dog,

D. scurvy null

E. Compilation fails.

F. An exception is thrown at runtime.

G. An "unrecognized option" command-line error is thrown.

Answer (for Objective 7.2):

☑ **B** is correct. While the declaration of `main()` could be considered a plank-walking offense, it's legal. In order to send a system property to the program from the command line, the `-D` option must come before the name of the class file. As invoked, the JVM will ignore the `-D` argument, and the call to `getProperty()` for `"argProp"` will return a `null`. If the invocation was:

`java -DargProp="dog," PirateTalk` then the result would be `"dog, scurvy"`

☒ **A, C, D, E, F,** and **G** are incorrect based on the above.

40. Given:

```
2. import java.util.*;
3. public class VLA implements Comparator<VLA> {
4.    int dishSize;
5.    public static void main(String[] args) {
6.       VLA[] va = {new VLA(40), new VLA(200), new VLA(60)};
7.
8.       for(VLA v: va) System.out.print(v.dishSize + " ");
9.       int index = Arrays.binarySearch(va, new VLA(60), va[0]);
10.      System.out.print(index + " ");
11.      Arrays.sort(va);
12.      for(VLA v: va) System.out.print(v.dishSize + " ");
13.      index = Arrays.binarySearch(va, new VLA(60), va[0]);
14.      System.out.println(index);
15.   }
16.   public int compare(VLA a, VLA b) {
17.      return a.dishSize - b.dishSize;
18.   }
19.   VLA(int d) { dishSize = d; }
20. }
```

Which result is most likely?

A. Compilation fails.

B. `"40 200 60 2 40 60 200 1"`

C. `"40 200 60 -2 40 60 200 1"`

D. `"40 200 60"`, followed by an exception.

E. `"40 200 60 -2"`, followed by an exception.

Answer (for Objective 6.5):

☑ **E** is correct. `Arrays.sort()` assumes that the elements of the array to be sorted implement `Comparable` unless you provide a `Comparator`. Note that `Arrays.binarySearch()` doesn't throw an exception when passed an unsorted array, it just returns an unpredictable (usually negative) result.

☒ **A, B, C,** and **D** are incorrect based on the above.

41. Given:

```
2. class RainCatcher {
3.    static StringBuffer s;
4.    public static void main(String[] args) {
5.       Integer i = new Integer(42);
6.       for(int j = 40; j < i; i--)
7.          switch(i) {
8.             case 41: s.append("41 ");
9.             default: s.append("def ");
10.            case 42: s.append("42 ");
11.         }
12.      System.out.println(s);
13. } }
```

What is the result?

A. `41 def`

B. `41 def 42`

C. `42 41 def 42`

D. An exception is thrown at runtime.

E. Compilation fails due to an error on line 6.

F. Compilation fails due to an error on line 7.

Answer (for Objective 2.6):

☑ **D** is correct. A `NullPointerException` is thrown because no instance of `StringBuffer` was ever created. If the `StringBuffer` had been created, autoboxing allows the `Integer` to be used in the `for` and the `switch`, and the `switch` logic would produce the output in answer **C**.

☒ **A, B, C, E,** and **F** are incorrect based on the above.

42. Given:

```
2. import java.util.*;
3. class Snack {
4.    static List<String> s1 = new ArrayList<String>();
5. }
6. public class Chips extends Snack {
7.    public static void main(String[] args) {
8.       List c1 = new ArrayList();
9.       s1.add("1"); s1.add("2");
10.      c1.add("3"); c1.add("4");
11.      getStuff(s1, c1);
12.   }
13.   static void getStuff(List<String> a1, List a2) {
14.      for(String s1: a1) System.out.print(s1 + " ");
15.      for(String s2: a2) System.out.print(s2 + " ");
16. } }
```

What is the result? (Choose all that apply.)

A. "1 2 3 4"

B. "1 2", followed by an exception

C. An exception is thrown with no other output.

D. Compilation fails due to an error on line 13.

E. Compilation fails due to an error on line 14.

F. Compilation fails due to an error on line 15.

Answer (for Objective 6.3):

☑ **F** is correct. When getting elements from a non-generic collection, a cast (from `Object`) is required. The rest of the code is legal.

☒ **A, B, C, D,** and **E** are incorrect based on the above.

43. Given that `Calendar.MONTH` starts with January == 0, and given:

```
3. import java.util.*;
4. public class Wise {
5.    public static void main(String[] args) {
6.       Calendar c = Calendar.getInstance();
7.       c.set(1999,11,25);
8.       c.roll(Calendar.MONTH, 3);
9.       c.add(Calendar.DATE, 10);
10.      System.out.println(c.getTime());
11. } }
```

And, if the program compiles, what date is represented in the output?

A. March 4, 1999

B. April 4, 1999

C. March 4, 2000

D. April 4, 2000

E. Compilation fails.

F. An exception is thrown at runtime.

Answer (for Objective 3.3):

☑ **B** is correct. It's important to remember that `roll()` changes the `Calendar` field specified WITHOUT incrementing a date's bigger time chunks. The `add()` method changes the field's value AND also increments the bigger time chunks (like adding a new day or month), when appropriate. Note that `Calendar` instances are created using a factory method.

☒ **A, C, D, E,** and **F** are incorrect based on the above.

44. Given the following two files containing `Light.java` and `Dark.java`:

```
2. package ec.ram;
3. public class Light{}
4. class Burn{}
```

```
2. package ec.ram;
3. public class Dark{}
4. class Melt{}
```

And if those files are located in the following directory structure:

```
$ROOT
    |-- Light.java
    |-- Dark.java
    |-- checker
            |-- dira
            |-- dirb
```

And the following commands are executed, in order, from the ROOT directory:

```
javac Light.java -cp checker/dira -d checker/dirb
javac Dark.java -cp checker/dirb -d checker/dira
jar -cf checker/dira/a.jar checker
```

A new JAR file is created after executing the above commands. Which of the following files will exist inside that JAR file? (Choose all that apply.)

A. [JAR]/dira/ec/ram/Melt.class

B. [JAR]/checker/dirb/ec/ram/Burn.class

C. [JAR]/dirb/ec/ram/Melt.class

D. [JAR]/checker/dira/ec/ram/Burn.class

E. [JAR]/dira/a.jar

F. [JAR]/checker/dira/a.jar

Answer (for Objective 7.5):

☑ **B** is correct. When using the `jar` command with `-cf` switches, the given source directory will be copied to the JAR file together with its subdirectories and files.

☒ **D** is incorrect because the `-d` switch is used to specify the destination directory, so there will be no impact on the `classpath` directory during compilation or JAR file creation. **F** is incorrect because there was NO such JAR file before the creation of the new JAR file. **A**, **C**, and **E** are incorrect based on the above.

---

45. Given:

```
42.   String s1 = " ";
43.   StringBuffer s2 = new StringBuffer(" ");
44.   StringBuilder s3 = new StringBuilder(" ");
45.   for(int i = 0; i < 1000; i++) // Loop #1
46.       s1 = s1.concat("a");
47.   for(int i = 0; i < 1000; i++) // Loop #2
48.       s2.append("a");
49.   for(int i = 0; i < 1000; i++) // Loop #3
50.       s3.append("a");
```

Which statements will typically be true? (Choose all that apply.)

A. Compilation fails.

B. Loop #3 will tend to execute faster than Loop #2.

C. Loop #1 will tend to use less memory than the other two loops.

D. Loop #1 will tend to use more memory than the other two loops.

E. All three loops will tend to use about the same amount of memory.

F. In order for this code to compile, the `java.util` package is required.

G. If multiple threads need to use an object, the `s2` object should be safer than the `s3` object.

Answer (for Objective 3.1):

☑ **B, D,** and **G** are correct. `StringBuffer` object's methods are `synchronized`, which makes them better for multiple threads, and typically a little slower. Because `String` objects are not mutable, Loop #1 is likely to create about 1000 different `String` objects in memory.

☒ **A, C, E,** and **F** are incorrect based on the above, and because all three classes live in `java.lang`.

46. Given:

```
2. public class Payroll {
3.    int salary;
4.    int getSalary() { return salary; }
5.    void setSalary(int s) {
6.       assert(s > 30000);
7.       salary = s;
8. } }
```

Which are true? (Choose all that apply.)

A. Compilation fails.

B. The class is well encapsulated as it stands.

C. Removing line 6 would weaken the class's degree of cohesion.

D. Removing line 6 would weaken the class's degree of encapsulation.

E. If the `salary` variable was `private`, the class would be well encapsulated.

F. Removing line 6 would make the class's use of assertions more appropriate.

Answer (for Objectives 5.1 and 2.3):

☑ **E** and **F** are correct. **F** is correct because line 6 currently uses the `assert` mechanism to validate a non-`private` method's argument, which is not considered appropriate.

☒ **A** is incorrect because the code is legal. **B** is incorrect because `salary` is not `private`. **C** and **D** are incorrect because the assert mechanism is mainly independent of the OO concepts of cohesion and encapsulation.

47. Given:

```
1. class GardenTool {
2.    static String s = "";
3.    String name = "Tool ";
```

```
 4.    GardenTool(String arg) { this(); s += name; }
 5.    GardenTool() { s += "gt "; }
 6. }
 7. public class Rake extends GardenTool {
 8.    { name = "Rake "; }
 9.    Rake(String arg) { s += name; }
10.    public static void main(String[] args) {
11.      new GardenTool("hey ");
12.      new Rake("hi ");
13.      System.out.println(s);
14.    }
15.    { name = "myRake "; }
16. }
```

What is the result?

A. Tool Rake

B. Tool myRake

C. gt Tool Rake

D. gt Tool myRake

E. gt Tool gt Rake

F. gt Tool gt myRake

G. gt Tool gt Tool myRake

H. Compilation fails.

Answer (for Objective 5.4):

☑ **F** is correct. The Rake class has two instance initialization blocks, they run in the order they are encountered in the class, and they run when a new instance is created. Now for the constructors; GardenTool's 1-arg constructor calls it's no-arg constructor with the "this();" invocation. Finally, when the Rake is created, there is a call to GardenTool's no-arg constructor because the compiler added a call to super().

☒ **A, B, C, D, E, G,** and **H** are incorrect based on the above.

48. Given:

```
3. public class Race {
4.   public static void main(String[] args) {
5.     Horse h = new Horse();
```

```
6.        Thread t1 = new Thread(h, "Andi");
7.        Thread t2 = new Thread(h, "Eyra");
8.        new Race().go(t2);
9.        t1.start();
10.       t2.start();
11.    }
12.    void go(Thread t) { t.start(); }
13. }
14. class Horse implements Runnable {
15.    public void run() {
16.       System.out.print(Thread.currentThread().getName() + " ");
17. } }
```

What is the result? (Choose all that apply.)

A. Compilation fails.

B. No output is produced.

C. The output could be: `"Andi Eyra"`

D. The output could be: `"Eyra Andi Eyra"`

E. The output could be: `"Eyra"`, followed by an exception.

F. The output could be: `"Eyra Andi"`, followed by an exception.

Answer (for Objective 4.1):

☑ **E** and **F** are correct. Line 10 will throw an exception because you can't start the same thread (in this case, t2) more than once.

☒ **A, B, C,** and **D** are incorrect based on the above.

49. Given the proper import statement(s) and given:

```
4.        Map<String, String> h = new Hashtable<String, String>();
5.        String[] k = {"1", "2", "3", null};
6.        String[] v = {"a", "b", null, "d"};
7.
8.        for(int i=0; i<4; i++) {
9.          h.put(k[i], v[i]);
10.         System.out.print(h.get(k[i]) + " ");
11.       }
12.       System.out.print(h.size() + " " + h.values() + "\n");
```

What result is most likely?

A. Compilation fails.

B. `"a b d 3 [b, d, a]"`

C. `"a b null d 3 [b, d, a]"`

D. `"a b null d 4 [b, d, null, a]"`

E. `"a b"`, followed by an exception.

F. `"a b null"`, followed by an exception.

Answer (for Objective 6.1):

☑   **E** is correct. A `Hashtable` does NOT allow any `null` keys OR `null` values.

☒   **A, B, C, D,** and **F** are incorrect based on the above.

50. Given:

```
3. public class Fiji {
4.    static Fiji base;
5.    Fiji f;
6.    public static void main(String[] args) {
7.      new Fiji().go();
8.      // do more stuff
9.    }
10.   void go() {
11.     Fiji f1 = new Fiji();
12.     base = f1;
13.     Fiji f2 = new Fiji();
14.     f1.f = f2;
15.     Fiji f3 = f1.f;
16.     f2.f = f1;
17.     base = null; f1 = null; f2 = null;
18.     // do stuff
19. } }
```

Which are true? (Choose all that apply.)

A. At line 8, one object is eligible for garbage collection.

B. At line 8, two objects are eligible for garbage collection.

C. At line 8, three objects are eligible for garbage collection.

D. At line 18, 0 objects are eligible for garbage collection.

E. At line 18, two objects are eligible for garbage collection.

F. At line 18, three objects are eligible for garbage collection.

Answer (for Objective 7.4):

☑ **C** and **D** are correct. A total of three `Fiji` objects are created. At line 18, the anonymous (`main()`'s), `Fiji` can still be accessed via `"this"`, and the other two `Fiji` objects can be accessed via `f3` (`f3` and `f3.f`). At line 8, none of the three `Fiji` objects are accessible.

☒ **A**, **B**, **E**, and **F** are incorrect based on the above.

51. Your company makes compute-intensive, 3D rendering software for the movie industry. Your chief scientist has just discovered a new algorithm for several key methods in a commonly used utility class. The new algorithm will decrease processing time by 15 percent, without having to change any method signatures. After you change these key methods, and in the course of rigorous system testing, you discover that the changes have introduced no new bugs into the software.

In terms of your software's overall design, which are probably true? (Choose all that apply.)

A. Your software is well encapsulated.

B. Your software demonstrated low cohesion.

C. Your software demonstrated high cohesion.

D. Your software demonstrated loose coupling.

E. Your software demonstrated tight coupling.

Answer (for Objective 5.1):

☑ **A** and **D** are correct. This kind of question can be subjective, so focus on words like "probably." **A** is correct. A hallmark of well-encapsulated code is that methods can be re-implemented without causing side effects. **D** is correct. A hallmark of loose coupling is when one class can change without adversely affecting the workings of classes that interact with it.

☒ **B** and **C** are incorrect because it's not possible to determine the degree of cohesion based on the facts in the scenario. **E** is incorrect based on the above.

52. Which are true about the classes and interfaces in `java.util`? (Choose all that apply.)

A. `LinkedHashSet` is-a `Collection`

B. `Vector` is-a `List`

C. `LinkedList` is-a `Queue`

D. `LinkedHashMap` is-a `Collection`

E. `TreeMap` is-a `SortedMap`

F. `Queue` is-a `Collection`

G. `Hashtable` is-a `Set`

Answer (for Objective 5.5):

☑ **A, B, C, E,** and **F** are correct statements about these classes and interfaces.

☒ **D** is incorrect. Remember that, in general, `Map` interfaces and classes do NOT have the `Collection` interface in their hierarchy. **G** is incorrect because `Hashtable` is-a type of `Map`.

53. Given that `File.createNewFile()` throws `IOException`, and that `FileNotFoundException` extends `IOException`, use the following fragments to fill in the blanks so that the code compiles. You must use all the fragments, and each fragment can be used only once. Note: As in the real exam, some drag-and-drop style questions might have several correct answers. You will receive full credit for ANY one of the correct answers.

```
import java.io.*;
public class SticksMud {
  public static void main(String[] args) {
    try {
      File dir = new File("dir");
      dir.createNewFile();
    }
    catch _____
    catch _____
    catch _____
    catch (IOException io) { }
    catch _____
    catch _____
    catch _____
    catch _____
} } }
```

Fragments:

```
(Throwable t) { }                (RuntimeException rt) { }
(Exception e) { }                (IllegalArgumentException arg) { }
(NullPointerException np) { }    (FileNotFoundException fnf) { }
(ClassCastException cc) { }
```

Answer ([for Objective 2.5] one of several possible answers):

```
catch (ClassCastException cc) { }          // flexible
catch (IllegalArgumentException arg) { }   // flexible
catch (FileNotFoundException fnf) { }      // flexible
catch (IOException io) { }
catch (NullPointerException np) { }        // can't be FileNotFound
catch (RuntimeException rt) { }            // must go here
catch (Exception e) { }                    // must go here
catch (Throwable t) { }                    // must go here
```

It's easiest to work this question from the bottom up, as the "must go here" comments indicate.

54. Given:

```
2. class Grandfather {
3.    static String name = "gf ";
4.    String doStuff() { return "grandf "; }
5. }
6. class Father extends Grandfather {
7.    static String name = "fa ";
8.    String doStuff() { return "father "; }
9. }
10. public class Child extends Father {
11.    static String name = "ch ";
12.    String doStuff() { return "child "; }
13.    public static void main(String[] args) {
14.       Father f = new Father();
15.       System.out.print(((Grandfather)f).name
                          + ((Grandfather)f).doStuff()) ;
16.       Child c = new Child();
17.       System.out.println(((Grandfather)c).name
                          + ((Grandfather)c).doStuff() + ((Father)c).doStuff());
18. } }
```

What is the result? (Choose all that apply.)

A. Compilation fails.

B. `fa father ch child child`

C. `gf father gf child child`

D. `fa grandf ch grandf father`

E. `gf grandf gf grandf father`

F. An exception is thrown at runtime.

Answer (for Objective 5.3):

☑ **C** is correct. Overriding applies only to instance methods, therefore the reference variables' type is used to access the `static Strings` called `"name"`. During overriding, the object's type is used to determine which overridden method is used.

☒ **A, B, D, E,** and **F** are incorrect based on the above.

55. Given:

```
1. class MyClass { }
```

And given that `MyClass2` has properly overridden `equals()` and `hashCode()`, objects from which classes make good hashing keys? (Choose all that apply.)

A. `MyClass`

B. `MyClass2`

C. `java.lang.String`

D. `java.lang.Integer`

E. `java.lang.StringBuilder`

Answer (for Objective 6.2):

☑ **B, C,** and **D** are correct. In order for a class's instances to make good hashing keys, the class must properly override `equals()` and `hashCode()`. The `String` class and wrapper classes override these methods; `MyClass` and `StringBuilder` do not.

☒ **A** and **E** are incorrect based on the above.

56. Given:

```
2. public class Buffalo {
3.     static int x;
4.     int y;
5.     public static int getX() { return x; }
6.     public static void setX(int newX) { x = newX; }
7.     public int getY() { return y; }
8.     public void setY(int newY) { y = newY; }
9. }
```

Which lines of code need to be changed to make the class thread safe? (Choose all that apply.)

A. Line 2

B. Line 3

C. Line 4

D. Line 5

E. Line 6

F. Line 7

G. Line 8

Answer (for Objective 4.3):

☑ **B–G** are correct. The variables need to be `private`, and even methods that don't change a variable's value need to be `synchronized` if they access the variable.

☒ **A** is incorrect. This `class` statement has no effect on thread safety-ness.

57. Given:

```
2. class Animal { }
3. class Dog extends Animal { }
4. class Cat extends Animal { }
5. public class Mixer<A extends Animal> {
6.     public <C extends Cat> Mixer<? super Dog> useMe(A a, C c) {
7.         //Insert Code Here
8. } }
```

Which, inserted independently at line 7, compile? (Choose all that apply.)

A. `return null;`

B. `return new Mixer<Dog>();`

C. `return new Mixer<Animal>();`

D. `return new Mixer<A>();`

E. `return new Mixer<a>();`

F. `return new Mixer<c>();`

Answer (for Objective 6.4):

☑ **A, B,** and **C** are correct. **B** and **C** are correct because the return type of the method is `Mixer<? super Dog>`, which means a `Mixer` object with a generic type that is either a `Dog` or a supertype of `Dog`. **A** is correct because `null` is acceptable despite the reference type.

☒ **D, E,** and **F** are incorrect because you must specify an exact generic class type when instantiating a generic class.

58. Given:

```
2. class Chilis {
3.    Chilis(String c, int h) { color = c; hotness = h; }
4.    String color;
5.    private int hotness;
6.    public boolean equals(Object o) {
7.       Chilis c = (Chilis)o;
8.       if(color.equals(c.color) && (hotness == c.hotness))  return true;
9.       return false;
10.    }
11.    // insert code here
12. }
```

Which, inserted independently at line 11, fulfill the `equals()` and `hashCode()` contract for `Chilis`? (Choose all that apply.)

A. `public int hashCode() { return 7; }`

B. `public int hashCode() { return hotness; }`

C. `public int hashCode() { return color.length(); }`

D. `public int hashCode() { return (int)(Math.random() * 200); }`

E. `public int hashCode() { return (color.length() + hotness); }`

Answer (for Objective 6.2):

☑ **A, B, C,** and **E** are correct. They all guarantee that two objects that equals() says are equal, will return the same integer from hashCode(). The fact that hotness is private has no bearing on the legality or effectiveness of the hashCode() method.

☒ **D** is incorrect because the random() method will usually return different integers for two objects that equals() says are equal.

Note to test takers... It would also be good for you to know the following: If a map ended up containing a large number of Chilis-based keys, which of the legal hashCode() methods (above) would provide the fastest retrievals?

Sub-answer: **E** is correct. Of all the legal hashCode() methods, this one will create the most hash buckets, which will lead to the fastest retrieval times.

59. Given the proper import(s), and this code in a method:

```
4.      List<String> x = new LinkedList<String>();
5.      Set<String> hs = new HashSet<String>();
6.      String[] v = {"a", "b", "c", "b", "a"};
7.      for(String s: v) {
8.         x.add(s);  hs.add(s);
9.      }
10.     System.out.print(hs.size() + " " + x.size() + " ");
11.     HashSet hs2 = new HashSet(x);
12.     LinkedList x2 = new LinkedList(hs);
13.     System.out.println(hs2.size() + " " + x2.size());
```

What is the result?

A. 3 3 3 3

B. 3 5 3 3

C. 3 5 3 5

D. 5 5 3 3

E. 5 5 5 5

F. Compilation fails.

G. An exception is thrown at runtime.

Answer (for Objective 6.1):

☑ **B** is correct. The code is all legal and runs without exception. Since Sets don't allow duplicates, line 10's output, "3 5 ", should be no surprise. When the Collection (LinkedList x) is passed into hs2's constructor, the Collection is trimmed so that no duplicates are created.

☒ **A, C, D, E, F** and **G** are incorrect based on the above.

60. Given the proper import(s), and given:

```
4.    public static void main(String[] args) {
5.      List<Integer> x = new ArrayList<Integer>();
6.      x.add(new Integer(3));
7.      doStuff(x);
8.      for(Integer i: x)
9.        System.out.print(i + " ");
10.   }
11.   static void doStuff(List y) {
12.     y.add(new Integer(4));
13.     y.add(new Float(3.14f));
14.   }
```

What is the result? (Choose all that apply.)

A. Compilation fails.

B. The output will be "4 "

C. The output will be "3 4 "

D. The output will be "3 4 3.14 "

E. The output will be "3 3.14 4 "

F. The output will be "3 4 ", followed by an exception.

G. An exception will be thrown before any output is produced.

Answer (for Objective 6.4):

☑ **F** is correct. The doStuff() method doesn't know that "y" is a generic collection, so it allows the Float to be added at compile time. Once doStuff() completes, the for loop will succeed until it encounters the Float, at which point a ClassCastException will be thrown.

☒ **A, B, C, D, E,** and **G** are incorrect based on the above.

Analyzing Your Results

Table 5-1 assumes a passing score on the OCP Java SE Programmer exam is 58.33 percent (35 out of 60 questions). If you got less than 45 questions correct on the first full exam, you should have done better on this exam than on the first. If your score didn't improve, we would advise you to do more studying before taking any more practice exams. Practice exams are a crucial part of preparing for the OCP Java SE Programmer exam, but they are only one component of a successful plan.

| **TABLE 5-1** | What Your Score Means |

Number of Correct Answers	Recommended Plan
0–28	You should do a LOT of studying before taking more of the exams in this book.
29–35	You should do some additional studying before taking more of the exams in this book.
36–44	You're right on the "passing" boundary. Keep studying.
45–60	You're doing well, but did you improve?

More Study Tips

We hope you're starting to see that each practice exam hits on different themes for each of the exam objectives. Did you make a log while taking this exam? It'll be good for your studies if you write down those topics that you're still having problems with and focus more effort there. So, before taking the next exam, spend some time working on those topics where your knowledge is still weak.

6

Practice Exam 3

How Close Are You to Ready?

The penultimate practice exam! If you've been scoring 75 percent or better so far, then feel free to rush into this one. If you haven't been scoring that well, we urge you to follow the study tips we've discussed so far in the book. Of course, each exam covers the same set of objectives, but every objective has its own range of topics. With every practice exam you take, expect to find that new aspects of the objectives will be explored. In other words, when you're studying a topic, ask yourself whether you feel you just barely know what's going on, or whether you feel like the questions are easy. If you're just barely squeaking by, go back and do some more studying. Experiment with the code in the previous exams. Revise your flashcards, and so on.

PRACTICE EXAM 3

This practice exam has 60 questions and you are given three hours to complete it. On the real exam, and on all of the exams in this book, give yourself credit only for those questions that you answer 100 percent correctly. For instance, if a question has three correct answers and you get two of the three correct, you get zero credit. There is no partial credit. Good luck!

1. Given:

```
3. class Bonds {
4.    Bonds force() { return new Bonds(); }
5. }
6. public class Covalent extends Bonds {
7.    Covalent force() { return new Covalent(); }
8.    public static void main(String[] args) {
9.      new Covalent().go(new Covalent());
10.    }
11.    void go(Covalent c) {
12.      go2(new Bonds().force(), c.force());
13.    }
14.    void go2(Bonds b, Covalent c) {
15.      Covalent c2 = (Covalent)b;
16.      Bonds b2 = (Bonds)c;
17. } }
```

What is the result? (Choose all that apply.)

A. A `ClassCastException` is thrown at line 15.

B. A `ClassCastException` is thrown at line 16.

C. Compilation fails due to an error on line 7.

D. Compilation fails due to an error on line 12.

E. Compilation fails due to an error on line 15.

F. Compilation fails due to an error on line 16.

2. Given:

```
1. import java.util.*;
2. public class Drawers {
3.    public static void main(String[] args) {
4.      List<String> desk = new ArrayList<String>();
5.      desk.add("pen"); desk.add("scissors"); desk.add("redStapler");
6.      System.out.print(desk.indexOf("redStapler"));
7.      Collection.reverse(desk);
8.      System.out.print(" " + desk.indexOf("redStapler"));
9.      Collection.sort(desk);
10.     System.out.println(" " + desk.indexOf("redStapler"));
11. } }
```

What is the result?

A. 1 1 1

B. 2 0 1

C. 2 0 2

D. 2 2 2

E. Compilation fails.

F. An exception is thrown at runtime.

3. Given:

```
1. import java.util.*;
2. class Radio {
3.    String getFreq() { return "97.3"; }
4.    static String getF() { return "97.3"; }
5. }
6. class Ham extends Radio {
7.    String getFreq() { return "50.1"; }
8.    static String getF() { return "50.1"; }
9.    public static void main(String[] args) {
10.      List<Radio> radios = new ArrayList<Radio>();
11.      radios.add(new Radio());
12.      radios.add(new Ham());
13.      for(Radio r: radios)
14.        System.out.print(r.getFreq() + " " + r.getF() + "   ");
15. } }
```

What is the result?

A. 50.1 50.1   50.1 50.1

B. 50.1 97.3   50.1 97.3

C. 97.3 50.1   50.1 50.1

D. 97.3 97.3   50.1 50.1

E. 97.3 97.3   50.1 97.3

F. 97.3 97.3   97.3 97.3

G. Compilation fails.

H. An exception is thrown at runtime.

4. Given two files:

```
1. package com;
2. public class MyClass {
3.    public static void howdy() { System.out.print("howdy "); }
4.    public static final int myConstant = 343;
```

```
5.   public static final MyClass mc = new MyClass();
6.   public int instVar = 42;
7. }

11. import static com.MyClass.*;
12. public class TestImports {
13.    public static void main(String[] args) {
14.       System.out.print(myConstant + " ");
15.       howdy();
16.       System.out.print(mc.instVar + " ");
17.       System.out.print(instVar + " ");
18. } }
```

What is the result? (Choose ALL that apply.)

A. 343 howdy 42 42

B. Compilation fails due to an error on line 11.

C. Compilation fails due to an error on line 14.

D. Compilation fails due to an error on line 15.

E. Compilation fails due to an error on line 16.

F. Compilation fails due to an error on line 17.

5. Given this code in a method:

```
4.       int x = 0;
5.       int[] primes = {1,2,3,5};
6.       for(int i: primes)
7.         switch(i) {
8.           case 1: x += i;
9.           case 5: x += i;
10.          default: x += i;
11.          case 2: x += i;
12.        }
13.      System.out.println(x);
```

What is the result?

A. 11

B. 13

C. 24

D. 27

E. Compilation fails due to an error on line 7.

F. Compilation fails due to an error on line 10.

G. Compilation fails due to an error on line 11.

6. Given:

```
1. import java.util.*;
2. public class Elway {
3.    public static void main(String[] args) {
4.       ArrayList[] ls = new ArrayList[3];
5.       for(int i = 0; i < 3; i++) {
6.          ls[i] = new ArrayList();
7.          ls[i].add("a" + i);
8.       }
9.       Object o = ls;
10.      do3(ls);
11.      for(int i = 0; i < 3; i++) {
12.         // insert code here
13.      }
14.   }
15.   static Object do3(ArrayList[] a) {
16.      for(int i = 0; i < 3; i++)  a[i].add("e");
17.      return a;
18. } }
```

And the following fragments:

I.   `System.out.print(o[i] + " ");`

II. `System.out.print((ArrayList[])[i] + " ");`

III. `System.out.print( ((Object[])o)[i] + " ");`

IV. `System.out.print(((ArrayList[])o)[i] + " ");`

If the fragments are added to line 12, independently, which are true? (Choose all that apply.)

A. Fragment I will compile.

B. Fragment II will compile.

C. Fragment III will compile.

D. Fragment IV will compile.

E. Compilation fails due to other errors.

F. Of those that compile, the output will be: [a0] [a1] [a2]

G. Of those that compile, the output will be: [a0, e] [a1, e] [a2, e]

7. Given:

```
1. enum MyEnum {HI, ALOHA, HOWDY};
2. public class PassEnum {
3.    public static void main(String[] args) {
4.       PassEnum p = new PassEnum();
5.       MyEnum[] v = MyEnum.values();
```

```
6.     v = MyEnum.getValues();
7.     for(MyEnum me: MyEnum.values())    p.getEnum(me);
8.     for(int x = 0; x < MyEnum.values().length; x++)    p.getEnum(v[x]);
9.     for(int x = 0; x < MyEnum.length; x++)    p.getEnum(v[x]);
10.    for(MyEnum me: v)    p.getEnum(me);
11.    }
12.    public void getEnum(MyEnum e) {
13.       System.out.print(e + " ");
14. } }
```

Which line(s) of code will cause a compiler error? (Choose all that apply.)

A. line 1

B. line 5

C. line 6

D. line 7

E. line 8

F. line 9

G. line 10

H. line 12

8. Given:

```
3. public class Drip extends Thread {
4.    public static void main(String[] args) {
5.       Thread t1 = new Thread(new Drip());
6.       t1.start();
7.       t1.join();
8.       for(int i = 0; i < 1000; i++)   // Loop #1
9.          System.out.print(Thread.currentThread().getName() + " ");
10.    }
11.    public void run() {
12.       for(int i = 0; i < 1000; i++)   // Loop #2
13.          System.out.print(Thread.currentThread().getName() + " ");
14. } }
```

Which are true? (Choose all that apply.)

A. Compilation fails.

B. An exception is thrown at runtime.

C. Loop #1 will run most of its iterations before Loop #2.

D. Loop #2 will run most of its iterations before Loop #1.

E. There is no way to predict which loop will mostly run first.

9. Given this code in a method:

```
5.        int x = 3;
6.        for(int i = 0; i < 3; i++) {
7.          if(i == 1) x = x++;
8.          if(i % 2 == 0 && x % 2 == 0) System.out.print(".");
9.          if(i % 2 == 0 && x % 2 == 1) System.out.print("-");
10.         if(i == 2 ^ x == 4) System.out.print(",");
11.       }
12.       System.out.println("<");
```

What is the result?

A.   - . , <

B.   - - , <

C.   - . , , <

D.   - - , , <

E.   - . - , , <

F.   Compilation fails.

10. Given:

```
2. public class Incomplete {
3.    public static void main(String[] args) {  // change code here ?
4.       // insert code here ?
5.         new Incomplete().doStuff();
6.       // insert code here ?
...
10.    }
11.    static void doStuff() throws Exception {
12.       throw new Exception();
13. } }
```

Which are true? (Choose all that apply.)

A.   Compilation succeeds with no code changes.

B.   Compilation succeeds if main() is changed to throw an Exception.

C.   Compilation succeeds if a try-catch is added, surrounding line 5.

D.   Compilation succeeds if a try-finally is added, surrounding line 5.

E.   Compilation succeeds only if BOTH main() declares an Exception AND a try-catch is added, surrounding line 5.

11. Given the proper imports, and given:

```
24.   Date d1 = new Date();
25.   Date d2 = d1;
```

```
26.  System.out.println(d1);
27.  d2.setTime(d1.getTime() + (7 * 24 * 60 * 60));
28.  System.out.println(d2);
```

Which are true? (Choose all that apply.)

A. Compilation fails.

B. An exception is thrown at runtime.

C. Some of the output will be today's date.

D. Some of the output will be next week's date.

E. Some of the output will represent the Java "epoch" (i.e., January 1, 1970).

12. Given:

```
2. interface Machine { }
3. interface Engine { }
4. abstract interface Tractor extends Machine, Engine {
5.   void pullStuff();
6. }
7. class Deere implements Tractor {
8.   public void pullStuff() { System.out.print("pulling "); }
9. }
10. class LT255 implements Tractor extends Deere  {
11.   public void pullStuff() { System.out.print("pulling harder "); }
12. }
13. public class LT155 extends Deere implements Tractor, Engine { }
```

What is the result? (Choose all that apply.)

A. Compilation succeeds.

B. Compilation fails because of error(s) in `Tractor`.

C. Compilation fails because of error(s) in `Deere`.

D. Compilation fails because of error(s) in LT255.

E. Compilation fails because of error(s) in LT155.

13. Given this code in a method:

```
5.     boolean[] ba = {true, false};
6.     short[][] gr = {{1,2}, {3,4}};
7.     int i = 0;
8.     for( ; i < 10; ) i++;
9.     for(short s: gr) ;
10.    for(int j = 0, k = 10; k > j; ++j, k--) ;
11.    for(int j = 0; j < 3; System.out.println(j++)) ;
12.    for(Boolean b: ba) ;
```

What is the result? (Choose all that apply.)

A. Compilation succeeds.

B. Compilation fails due to an error on line 8.

C. Compilation fails due to an error on line 9.

D. Compilation fails due to an error on line 10.

E. Compilation fails due to an error on line 11.

F. Compilation fails due to an error on line 12.

14. Given:

```
2. package w.x;
3. import w.y.Zoom;
4. public class Zip {
5.    public static void main(String[] args) {
6.       new Zoom().doStuff();
7. } }
```

And the following command to compile Zip.java: `javac -cp w.jar -d . Zip.java`

And another class w.y.Zoom (with a doStuff() method), which has been compiled and deployed into a JAR file w.jar:

Fill in the blanks using the following fragments to show the directory structure and the contents of any directory(s) necessary to compile successfully from $ROOT. Note: NOT all the blanks must be filled, NOT all the fragments will be used, and fragments CANNOT be used more than once.

Fragments:

```
Zoom.java      Zip.java      Zoom.class
Zip.class      [Zoom.jar]    [w.jar]
   w              x              y
```

15. Given:

```
2. class Pancake { }
3. class BlueberryPancake extends Pancake { }
4. public class SourdoughBlueberryPancake2 extends BlueberryPancake {
5.    public static void main(String[] args) {
6.       Pancake p4 = new SourdoughBlueberryPancake2();
7.       // insert code here
8. } }
```

And the following six declarations (which are to be inserted independently at line 7):

I. `Pancake p5 = p4;`

II. `Pancake p6 = (BlueberryPancake)p4;`

III. `BlueberryPancake b2 = (BlueberryPancake)p4;`

IV. `BlueberryPancake b3 = (SourdoughBlueberryPancake2)p4;`

V. `SourdoughBlueberryPancake2 s1 = (BlueberryPancake)p4;`

VI. `SourdoughBlueberryPancake2 s2 = (SourdoughBlueberryPancake2)p4;`

Which are true? (Choose all that apply.)

A. All six declarations will compile.

B. Exactly one declaration will not compile.

C. More than one of the declarations will not compile.

D. Of those declarations that compile, none will throw an exception.

E. Of those declarations that compile, exactly one will throw an exception.

F. Of those declarations that compile, more than one will throw an exception.

16. Given:

```
3. class IcelandicHorse {
4.    void tolt() { System.out.print("4-beat "); }
5. }
6. public class Vafi extends IcelandicHorse {
7.    public static void main(String[] args) {
8.       new Vafi().go();
9.       new IcelandicHorse().tolt();
10.   }
11.   void go() {
12.      IcelandicHorse h1 = new Vafi();
13.      h1.tolt();
14.      Vafi v = (Vafi) h1;
15.      v.tolt();
16.   }
17.   void tolt() { System.out.print("pacey "); }
18. }
```

What is the result? (Choose all that apply.)

A. `4-beat pacey pacey`

B. `pacey pacey 4-beat`

C. `4-beat 4-beat 4-beat`

D. `4-beat pacey 4-beat`

E. `pacey`, followed by an exception

F. `4-beat`, followed by an exception

17. Given:

```
1. class MyException extends RuntimeException { }
2. public class Houdini {
3.   public static void main(String[] args) throws Exception {
4.     throw new MyException();
5.     System.out.println("success");
6. } }
```

Which are true? (Choose all that apply.)

A. The code runs without output.

B. The output "success" is produced.

C. Compilation fails due to an error on line 1.

D. Compilation fails due to an error on line 3.

E. Compilation fails due to an error on line 4.

F. Compilation fails due to an error on line 5.

18. Given:

```
3. public class Avast {
4.   static public void main(String[] scurvy) {
5.     System.out.print(scurvy[1] + " ");
6.     main(scurvy[2]);
7.   }
8.   public static void main(String dogs) {
9.     assert(dogs == null);
10.    System.out.println(dogs);
11. } }
```

And, if the code compiles, the command-line invocation:

```
java Avast -ea 1 2 3
```

What is the result? (Choose all that apply.)

A. 1 2

B. 2 3

C. Compilation fails due to an error on line 4.

D. Compilation fails due to an error on line 6.

E. Compilation fails due to an error on line 8.

F. Compilation fails due to an error on line 9.

G. Some output is produced and then an AssertionError is thrown.

19. Given:

```
2. class Wheel {
3.    Wheel(int s) { size = s; }
4.    int size;
5.    void spin() { System.out.print(size + " inch wheel spinning, "); }
6. }
7. public class Bicycle {
8.    public static void main(String[] args) {
9.       Wheel[] wa = {new Wheel(15), new Wheel(17)};
10.       for(Wheel w: wa)
11.          w.spin();
12. } }
```

Which are true? (Choose all that apply.)

A. Compilation fails.

B. If size was private, the degree of coupling would change.

C. If size was private, the degree of cohesion would change.

D. The Bicycle class is tightly coupled with the Wheel class.

E. The Bicycle class is loosely coupled with the Wheel class.

F. If size was private, the degree of encapsulation would change.

20. Given:

```
2. public class Mouthwash {
3.    static int x = 1;
4.    public static void main(String[] args) {
5.       int x = 2;
6.       for(int i=0; i< 3; i++) {
7.          if(i==1) System.out.print(x + " ");
8.       }
9.       go();
10.       System.out.print(x + " " + i);
11.    }
12.    static void go() { int x = 3; }
13. }
```

What is the result?

A. 1 2 2

B. 2 2 2

C. 2 2 3

D. 2 3 2

E. Compilation fails.

F. An exception is thrown at runtime.

21. Given the proper imports, and given:

```
23.   String s = "123 888888 x 345 -45";
24.   Scanner sc = new Scanner(s);
25.   while(sc.hasNext())
26.     if(sc.hasNextShort())
27.       System.out.print(sc.nextShort() + " ");
```

What is the result?

A. The output is 123 345

B. The output is 123 345 -45

C. The output is 123 888888 345 -45

D. The output is 123 followed by an exception.

E. The output is 123 followed by an infinite loop.

22. Given:

```
1. interface Horse { public void nicker(); }
```

Which will compile? (Choose all that apply.)

A. `public class Eyra implements Horse { public void nicker() { } }`

B. `public class Eyra implements Horse { public void nicker(int x) { } }`

C. `public class Eyra implements Horse {`
      `public void nicker() { System.out.println("huhuhuhuh..."); }`
    `}`

D. `public abstract class Eyra implements Horse {`
      `public void nicker(int loud) { }`
    `}`

E. `public abstract class Eyra implements Horse {`
      `public void nicker(int loud) ;`
    `}`

23. Given:

```
2. public class LaoTzu extends Philosopher {
3.   public static void main(String[] args) {
4.     new LaoTzu();
5.     new LaoTzu("Tigger");
6.   }
7.   LaoTzu() { this("Pooh"); }
8.   LaoTzu(String s) { super(s); }
9. }
10. class Philosopher {
11.   Philosopher(String s) { System.out.print(s + " "); }
12. }
```

What is the result?

A. Pooh Pooh

B. Pooh Tigger

C. Tigger Pooh

D. Tigger Tigger

E. Compilation fails due to a single error in the code.

F. Compilation fails due to multiple errors in the code.

24. Which are capabilities of Java's assertion mechanism? (Choose all that apply.)

A. You can, at the command line, enable assertions for a specific class.

B. You can, at the command line, disable assertions for a specific package.

C. You can, at runtime, enable assertions for any version of Java.

D. It's considered appropriate to catch and handle an `AssertionError` programmatically.

E. You can programmatically test whether assertions have been enabled without throwing an `AssertionError`.

25. Given:

```
4. public class Stone implements Runnable {
5.     static int id = 1;
6.     public void run() {
7.        try {
8.           id = 1 - id;
9.           if(id == 0) { pick(); } else { release(); }
10.       } catch(Exception e) { }
11.    }
12.    private static synchronized void pick() throws Exception {
13.       System.out.print("P ");    System.out.print("Q ");
14.    }
15.    private synchronized void release() throws Exception {
16.       System.out.print("R ");    System.out.print("S ");
17.    }
18.    public static void main(String[] args) {
19.       Stone st = new Stone();
20.       new Thread(st).start();
21.       new Thread(st).start();
22. } }
```

Which are true? (Choose all that apply.)

A. The output could be P Q R S

B. The output could be P R S Q

C. The output could be P R Q S

D. The output could be P Q P Q

E. The program could cause a deadlock.

F. Compilation fails.

26. Given:

```
3. public class States {
4.    static String s;
5.    static Boolean b;
6.    static Boolean t1() { return new Boolean("howdy"); }
7.    static boolean t2() { return new Boolean(s); }
8.    public static void main(String[] args) {
9.      if(t1()) System.out.print("t1 ");
10.     if(!t2()) System.out.print("t2 ");
11.     if(t1() != t2()) System.out.print("!= ");
12.   }
13. }
```

Which are true? (Choose all that apply.)

A. Compilation fails.

B. No output is produced.

C. The output will contain "t1 "

D. The output will contain "t2 "

E. The output will contain "!= "

F. The output is "t1 ", followed by an exception.

27. Which are valid command-line switches when working with assertions? (Choose all that apply.)

A. -ea

B. -da

C. -dsa

D. -eva

E. -enableassertions

28. Given:

```
4. class Account { Long acctNum, password; }
5. public class Banker {
6.   public static void main(String[] args) {
7.     new Banker().go();
8.     // do more stuff
9.   }
```

```
10.    void go() {
11.       Account a1 = new Account();
12.       a1.acctNum = new Long("1024");
13.       Account a2 = a1;
14.       Account a3 = a2;
15.       a3.password = a1.acctNum.longValue();
16.       a2.password = 4455L;
17. } }
```

When line 8 is reached, which are true? (Choose all that apply.)

A. `a1.acctNum == a3.password`

B. `a1.password == a2.password`

C. Three objects are eligible for garbage collection.

D. Four objects are eligible for garbage collection.

E. Six objects are eligible for garbage collection.

F. Less than three objects are eligible for garbage collection.

G. More than six objects are eligible for garbage collection.

29. Given:

```
2. public class Coyote {
3.    public static void main(String[] args) {
4.       int x = 4;
5.       int y = 4;
6.       while((x = jump(x)) < 8)
7.          do {
8.             System.out.print(x + " ");
9.          } while ((y = jump(y)) < 6);
10.    }
11.    static int jump(int x) { return ++x; }
12. }
```

What is the result?

A. 5 5 6 6

B. 5 5 6 7

C. 5 5 6 6 7

D. 5 6 5 6 7

E. Compilation fails due to a single error.

F. Compilation fails due to multiple errors.

30. Given:

```
2. class Engine {
3.    public class Piston {
4.       static int count = 0;
5.       void go() { System.out.print(" pump " + ++count); }
6.    }
7.    public Piston getPiston() { return new Piston(); }
8. }
9. public class Auto {
10.    public static void main(String[] args) {
11.       Engine e = new Engine();
12.       // Engine.Piston p = e.getPiston();
13.       e.Piston p = e.getPiston();
14.       p.go();   p.go();
15. } }
```

In order for the code to compile and produce the output " pump 1 pump 2", which are true? (Choose all that apply.)

A. The code is correct as it stands.

B. Line 4 must be changed. count can't be declared "static".

C. Line 12 must be un-commented, and line 13 must be removed.

D. Somewhere in the code, a second instance of Piston must be instantiated.

E. There are errors in the code that must be fixed, outside of lines 4, 12, and 13.

31. Given:

```
2. public class Juggler extends Thread {
3.    public static void main(String[] args) {
4.       try {
5.          Thread t = new Thread(new Juggler());
6.          Thread t2 = new Thread(new Juggler());
7.       } catch (Exception e) { System.out.print("e "); }
8.    }
9.    public void run() {
10.       for(int i = 0; i < 2; i++)   {
11.          try { Thread.sleep(500); }
12.          catch (Exception e) { System.out.print("e2 "); }
13.          System.out.print(Thread.currentThread().getName() + " ");
14. } } }
```

Which are true? (Choose all that apply.)

A. Compilation fails.

B. No output is produced.

C. The output could be Thread-1 Thread-1 e

D. The output could be Thread-1 Thread-1 Thread-3 Thread-3

E. The output could be Thread-1 Thread-3 Thread-1 Thread-3

F. The output could be Thread-1 Thread-1 Thread-3 Thread-2

32. Given:

```
3. class Department {
4.   Department getDeptName() { return new Department(); }
5. }
6. class Accounting extends Department {
7.   Accounting getDeptName() { return new Accounting(); }
8.   // insert code here
13. }
```

And the following four code fragments:

I. `String getDeptName(int x) { return "mktg"; }`

II. `void getDeptName(Department d) { ; }`

III. ```
void getDeptName(long x) throws NullPointerException {
    throw new NullPointerException();
}
```

IV. ```
Department getDeptName() throws NullPointerException {
    throw new NullPointerException();
    return new Department();
}
```

Which are true? (Choose all that apply.)

A. If fragment I is inserted at line 8, the code compiles.

B. If fragment II is inserted at line 8, the code compiles.

C. If fragment III is inserted at line 8, the code compiles.

D. If fragment IV is inserted at line 8, the code compiles.

E. If none of the fragments are inserted at line 8, the code compiles.

33. Given:

```
2. import java.util.*;
3. interface Canine { }
4. class Dog implements Canine { }
5. public class Collie extends Dog {
6.   public static void main(String[] args) {
7.     List<Dog> d = new ArrayList<Dog>();
8.     List<Collie> c = new ArrayList<Collie>();
9.     d.add(new Collie());
10.     c.add(new Collie());
```

```
11.      do1(d);    do1(c);
12.      do2(d);    do2(c);
13.    }
14.    static void do1(List<? extends Dog> d2) {
15.        d2.add(new Collie());
16.        System.out.print(d2.size());
17.    }
18.    static void do2(List<? extends Canine> c2) {  }
19. }
```

Which are true? (Choose all that apply.)

A. Compilation succeeds.

B. Compilation fails due to an error on line 9.

C. Compilation fails due to an error on line 14.

D. Compilation fails due to an error on line 15.

E. Compilation fails due to an error on line 16.

F. Compilation fails due to an error on line 18.

G. Compilation fails due to errors on lines 11 and 12.

34. Given:

```
42. void go() {
43.    int cows = 0;
44.    int[] twisters = {1,2,3};
45.    for(int i = 0; i < 4; i++)
46.        switch(twisters[i]) {
47.            case 2: cows++;
48.            case 1: cows += 10;
49.            case 0: go();
50.        }
51.    System.out.println(cows);
52. }
```

What is the result?

A. 11

B. 21

C. 22

D. Compilation fails.

E. A StackOverflowError is thrown at runtime.

F. An ArrayIndexOutOfBoundsException is thrown at runtime.

35. Given:

```
2. class Robot { }
3. interface Animal { }
4. class Feline implements Animal { }
5. public class BarnCat extends Feline {
6.    public static void main(String[] args) {
7.       Animal af = new Feline();
8.       Feline ff = new Feline();
9.       BarnCat b = new BarnCat();
10.      Robot r = new Robot();
11.      if(af instanceof Animal) System.out.print("1 ");
12.      if(af instanceof BarnCat) System.out.print("2 ");
13.      if(b instanceof Animal) System.out.print("3 ");
14.      if(ff instanceof BarnCat) System.out.print("4 ");
15.      if(r instanceof Animal) System.out.print("5 ");
16.   }
17. }
```

What is the result?

A. 1

B. 1 3

C. 1 2 3

D. 1 3 4

E. 1 2 3 4

F. Compilation fails.

G. An exception is thrown at runtime.

36. Given:

```
2. public class Sunny extends Weather {
3.    public static void main(String[] args) {
4.       try {
5.          new Sunny().do1();
6.          new Sunny().do2();
7.          new Sunny().do3();
8.       }
9.       catch(Throwable t) { System.out.print("exc "); }
10. } }
11. class Weather {
12.    void do1() { System.out.print("do1 "); }
13.    private void do2() { System.out.print("do2 "); }
14.    protected void do3() { System.out.print("do3 "); }
15. }
```

What is the result?

A. do1 exc

B. do1 do2 exc

C. do1 do2 do3

D. Compilation fails.

E. An exception is thrown at runtime.

37. Given that `FileNotFoundException` extends `IOException` and given:

```
2.  import java.io.*;
3.  public class Changeup {
4.     public static void main(String[] args) throws IOException {
5.        new Changeup().go();
6.        new Changeup().go2();
7.        new Changeup().go3();
8.     }
9.     void go() { throw new IllegalArgumentException(); }
10.
11.    void go2() throws FileNotFoundException { }
12.
13.    void go3() {
14.       try { throw new Exception(); }
15.       catch (Throwable th) { throw new NullPointerException(); }
16. } }
```

What is the result? (Choose all that apply.)

A. An `IOException` is thrown at runtime.

B. A `NullPointerException` is thrown at runtime.

C. An `IllegalArgumentException` is thrown at runtime.

D. Compilation fails due to an error at line 4.

E. Compilation fails due to an error at line 9.

F. Compilation fails due to an error at line 11.

G. Compilation fails due to an error at line 15.

38. Which are true? (Choose all that apply.)

A. If class A is-a class B, then class A cannot be considered well encapsulated.

B. If class A has-a class B, then class A cannot be considered well encapsulated.

C. If class A is-a class B, then the two classes are said to be cohesive.

D. If class A has-a class B, then the two classes are said to be cohesive.

E. If class A is-a class B, it's possible for them to still be loosely coupled.

F. If class A has-a class B, it's possible for them to still be loosely coupled.

39. Given:

```
2. import java.util.*;
3. public class Volleyball {
4.    public static void main(String[] args) {
5.       TreeSet<String> s = new TreeSet<String>();
6.       s.add("a");  s.add("f");  s.add("b");
7.       System.out.print(s + " ");
8.       Collections.reverse(s);
9.       System.out.println(s);
10. } }
```

What is the result?

A. Compilation fails.

B. `[a, b, f]  [a, b, f]`

C. `[a, b, f]  [f, b, a]`

D. `[a, f, b]  [b, f, a]`

E. `[a, b, f]`, followed by an exception.

F. `[a, f, b]`, followed by an exception.

40. Given:

```
2. public class Boggy {
3.    final static int mine = 7;
4.    final static Integer i = 57;
5.    public static void main(String[] args) {
6.       int x = go(mine);
7.       System.out.print(mine + " " + x + " ");
8.       x += mine;
9.       Integer i2 = i;
10.      i2 = go(i);
11.      System.out.println(x + " " + i2);
12.      i2 = new Integer(60);
13.    }
14.    static int go(int x) { return ++x; }
15. }
```

What is the result?

A. `7 7 14 57`

B. `7 8 14 57`

C. `7 8 15 57`

D. `7 8 15 58`

E. `7 8 16 58`

F. Compilation fails.

G. An exception is thrown at runtime.

41. Given:

```
3. import java.io.*;
4. public class Kesey {
5.    public static void main(String[] args) throws Exception {
6.       File file = new File("bigData.txt");
7.       FileWriter w = new FileWriter(file);
8.       w.println("lots o' data");
9.       w.flush();
10.      w.close();
11. } }
```

What is the result? (Choose all that apply.)

A. An empty file named `"bigData.txt"` is created.

B. Compilation fails due only to an error on line 5.

C. Compilation fails due only to an error on line 6.

D. Compilation fails due only to an error on line 7.

E. Compilation fails due only to an error on line 8.

F. Compilation fails due to errors on multiple lines.

G. A file named `"bigData.txt"` is created, containing one line of data.

42. Given:

```
3. class Wanderer implements Runnable {
4.    public void run() {
5.       for(int i = 0; i < 2; i++)
6.          System.out.print(Thread.currentThread().getName() + " ");
7. } }
8. public class Wander {
9.    public static void main(String[] args) {
10.      Wanderer w = new Wanderer();
11.      Thread t1 = new Thread();
12.      Thread t2 = new Thread(w);
13.      Thread t3 = new Thread(w, "fred");
14.      t1.start();   t2.start();   t3.start();
15. } }
```

Which are true? (Choose all that apply.)

A. Compilation fails.

B. No output is produced.

C. The output could be `Thread-1 fred fred Thread-1`

D. The output could be `Thread-1 Thread-1 Thread-2 Thread-2`

E. The output could be `Thread-1 fred Thread-1 Thread-2 Thread-2 fred`

F. The output could be `Thread-1 Thread-1 Thread-2 Thread-3 fred fred`

43. Given:

```
2. import java.util.*;
3. public class MyFriends {
4.    String name;
5.    MyFriends(String s) { name = s; }
6.    public static void main(String[] args) {
7.      Set<MyFriends> ms = new HashSet<MyFriends>();
8.      ms.add(new MyFriends("Bob"));
9.      System.out.print(ms + " ");
10.     ms.add(new MyFriends("Bob"));
11.     System.out.print(ms + " ");
12.     ms.add(new MyFriends("Eden"));
13.     System.out.print(ms + " ");
14.   }
15.   public String toString() { return name; }
16. }
```

What is the most likely result?

A. Compilation fails.

B. [Bob] [Bob] [Eden, Bob]

C. [Bob] [Bob] [Eden, Bob, Bob]

D. [Bob], followed by an exception.

E. [Bob] [Bob, Bob] [Eden, Bob, Bob]

44. Given the proper imports, and given:

```
17.  public void go() {
18.    NumberFormat nf, nf2;
19.    Number n;
20.    Locale[] la = NumberFormat.getAvailableLocales();
21.    for(int x=0; x < 10; x++) {
22.      nf = NumberFormat.getCurrencyInstance(la[x]);
23.      System.out.println(nf.format(123.456f));
24.    }
25.    nf2 = NumberFormat.getInstance();
26.    n = nf2.parse("123.456f");
27.    System.out.println(n);
28. }
```

Given that line 20 is legal, which are true? (Choose all that apply.)

A. Compilation fails.

B. An exception is thrown at runtime.

C. The output could contain "123.46"

D. The output could contain "123.456"

E. The output could contain "$123.46"

45. Given:

```
59.  Integer i1 = 2001;  // set 1
60.  Integer i2 = 2001;
61.  System.out.println((i1 == i2) + " " + i1.equals(i2));  // output 1
62.  Integer i3 = 21;   // set 2
63.  Integer i4 = new Integer(21);
64.  System.out.println((i3 == i4) + " " + i3.equals(i4));  // output 2
65.  Integer i5 = 21;   // set 3
66.  Integer i6 = 21;
67.  System.out.println((i5 == i6) + " " + i5.equals(i6));  // output 3
```

What is the result? (Choose all that apply.)

A. Compilation fails.

B. An exception is thrown at runtime.

C. All three sets of output will be the same.

D. The last two sets of output will be the same.

E. The first two sets of output will be the same.

F. The first and last sets of output will be the same.

46. Given:

```
2. public class Skip {
3.   public static void main(String[] args) throws Exception {
4.     Thread t1 = new Thread(new Jump());
5.     Thread t2 = new Thread(new Jump());
6.     t1.start(); t2.start();
7.     t1.join(500);
8.     new Jump().run();
9. } }
10. class Jump implements Runnable {
11.   public void run() {
12.     for(int i = 0; i < 5; i++) {
13.       try { Thread.sleep(200); }
14.       catch (Exception e) { System.out.print("e "); }
15.       System.out.print(Thread.currentThread().getId() + "-" + i + " ");
16. } } }
```

What is the result?

A. Compilation fails.

B. The main thread will run mostly before t1 runs.

C. The main thread will run after t1, but together with t2.

D. The main thread will run after t2, but together with t1.

E. The main thread will run after both t1 and t2 are mostly done.

F. The main thread's execution will overlap with t1 and t2's execution.

47. Given:

```
1. import java.util.*;
2. public class Piles {
3.   public static void main(String[] args) {
4.     TreeMap<String, String> tm = new TreeMap<String, String>();
5.     TreeSet<String> ts = new TreeSet<String>();
6.     String[] k = {"1", "b", "4", "3"};
7.     String[] v = {"a", "d", "3", "b"};
8.     for(int i=0; i<4; i++) {
9.       tm.put(k[i], v[i]);
10.      ts.add(v[i]);
11.    }
12.    System.out.print(tm.values() + " ");
13.    Iterator it2 = ts.iterator();
14.    while(it2.hasNext()) System.out.print(it2.next() + "-");
15. } }
```

Which of the following could be a part of the output? (Choose two.)

A. [a, b, 3, d]

B. [d, a, b, 3]

C. [3, a, b, d]

D. [a, b, d, 3]

E. [1, 3, 4, b]

F. [b, 1, 3, 4]

G. 3-a-b-d-

H. a-b-d-3-

I. a-d-3-b-

48. Given this code in a method:

```
5.     String s = "dogs. with words.";
6.     // insert code here
7.     for(String o: output)
8.       System.out.print(o + " ");
```

Which of the following, inserted independently at line 6, will produce output that contains the String "dogs"? (Choose all that apply.)

A. String[] output = s.split("s");

B. String[] output = s.split("d");

C. String[] output = s.split("\\d");

D. String[] output = s.split("\\s");

E. String[] output = s.split("\\w");

F. String[] output = s.split("\\.");

49. Given the design implied by this partially implemented class:

```
2. public class RobotDog {
3.     int size;
4.     void bark() { /* do barking */ }
5.     int getSize() { return size; }
6.     { size = 16; }
7.     int getNetworkPrinterID() {
8.        /* do lookup */
9.        return 37;
10.    }
11.    void printRobotDogStuff(int printerID) { /* print RobotDog stuff */ }
12. }
```

Which are true? (Choose all that apply.)

A. Compilation fails.

B. To improve cohesion, the `size` variable should be declared `private`.

C. To improve cohesion, the initialization block should be placed inside a constructor.

D. To improve cohesion, `printRobotDogStuff()` should be moved to a different class.

E. To improve cohesion, `getNetworkPrinterID()` should be moved to a different class.

50. Given:

```
2. import java.util.*;
3. public class Foggy extends Murky {
4.    public static void main(String[] args) {
5.       final List<String> s = new ArrayList<String>();
6.       s.add("a");  s.add("f");  s.add("a");
7.       new Foggy().mutate(s);
8.       System.out.println(s);
9.    }
10.   List<String> mutate(List<String> s) {
11.      List<String> ms = s;
12.      ms.add("c");
13.      return s;
14.   }
15. }
16. class Murky {
17.    final void mutate(Set s) { }
18. }
```

What is the most likely result?

A. `[a, f]`

B. `[a, f, a]`

C. `[a, f, c]`

D. [a, f, a, c]

E. Compilation fails.

F. An exception is thrown at runtime.

51. Given:

```
1. import java.util.*;
2. enum Heroes { GANDALF, HANS, ENDER }
3. public class MyStuff {
4.    public static void main(String[] args) {
5.      List<String> stuff = new ArrayList<String>();
6.      stuff.add("Bob"); stuff.add("Fred");
7.      new MyStuff().go();
8.    }
9.    Heroes myH = Heroes.ENDER;
10.   void go() {
11.     for(Heroes h: Heroes.values())
12.       if(h == myH) System.out.println(myH);
13. } }
```

Which are true? (Choose all that apply.)

A. Compilation fails.

B. main() has-a List

C. MyStuff has-a List

D. MyStuff has-a Heroes

E. The output is "ENDER"

F. The output is "Heroes.ENDER"

G. An exception is thrown at runtime.

52. Given:

```
2. public class Pregnant extends Thread {
3.    int x = 0;
4.    public static void main(String[] args) {
5.      Runnable r1 = new Pregnant();
6.      new Thread(r1).start();
7.      new Thread(r1).start();
8.    }
9.    public void run() {
10.     for(int j = 0; j < 3; j++) {
11.       x = x + 1;
12.       x = x + 10;
13.       System.out.println(x + " ");
14.       x = x + 100;
15. } } }
```

If the code compiles, which value(s) could appear in the output? (Choose all that apply.)

A. 12

B. 22

C. 122

D. 233

E. 244

F. 566

G. Compilation fails.

53. Fill in the blanks using the following fragments, so that the code compiles and the invocation "java Enchilada green 4" produces the output "wow". Note: You might not need to fill in all of the blanks, you won't use all of the fragments, and each fragment can be used more than once.

Code:

```
import java.util.*;
public class Enchilada {
    public static void main(String[] args) {
        Map<Chilis, String> m = new HashMap<Chilis, String>();
        Chilis myC = new Chilis("green", 4);
        _____(new Chilis("red", 4), "4 alarm");
        _____(new Chilis("green", 2), "mild");
        _____(myC, "wow");
        Chilis c = new Chilis(_____, _____(_____));
        System.out.println(_____);
    } }
class Chilis {
    Chilis(String c, int h) { color = c; hotness = h; }
    String color;
    private int hotness;
    public _____ equals(_____) {
        _____
        if(_____ __ _____) return ____;
        return _____;
    }
    public _____ hashCode() { return _____; }
}
```

Fragments:

/* empty */	Chilis c	1
m.put	m.add	true
args[2]	Integer.parseInt	false
args[1]	m.get(c)	(hotness == c.hotness)
boolean	int	Chilis c = (Chilis)o;

```
-1                  hotness              args[0]
color               m.contains(c)        Integer.intValue
(this == c)         void                 color.equals(c.color)
Object o            String               0
&&                  ||
```

54. Given:

```
2.  public class Toolbox {
3.    static Toolbox st;
4.    public static void main(String[] args) {
5.      new Toolbox().go();
6.      // what's eligible?
7.    }
8.    void go() {
9.      MyInner in = new MyInner();
10.      Integer i3 = in.doInner();
11.      Toolbox t = new Toolbox();
12.      st = t;
13.      System.out.println(i3);
14.    }
15.    class MyInner {
16.      public Integer doInner() { return new Integer(34); }
17.    }
18. }
```

When the code reaches line 6, which are eligible for garbage collection? (Choose all that apply.)

A. st

B. in

C. i3

D. The object created on line 5.

E. The object created on line 9.

F. The object created on line 10.

G. The object created on line 11.

55. Given:

```
2. class Ball {
3.    static String s = "";
4.    void doStuff() { s += "bounce "; }
5. }
6. class Basketball extends Ball {
7.    void doStuff() { s += "swish "; }
8. }
9. public class Golfball extends Ball {
```

```
10.   public static void main(String[] args) {
11.      Ball b = new Golfball();
12.      Basketball bb = (Basketball)b;
13.      b.doStuff();
14.      bb.doStuff();
15.      System.out.println(s);
16.   }
17.   void doStuff() { s += "fore "; }
18. }
```

What is the result?

A. fore fore

B. fore swish

C. bounce swish

D. bounce bounce

E. Compilation fails.

F. An exception is thrown at runtime.

56. Given the following three files:

```
2. package apollo;
3. import apollo.modules.Lunar;
4. public class Saturn {
5.   public static void main(String[] args){
6.      Lunar lunarModule = new Lunar();
7.      System.out.println(lunarModule);
8. } }
```

```
2. package apollo.modules;
3. public interface Module { /* more code  */ }
```

```
2. package apollo.modules;
3. public class Lunar implements Module { /* more code */ }
```

And given that Module.java and Lunar.java were successfully compiled and the directory structure is shown below:

```
$ROOT
  |-- apollo
  |      |-- modules
  |             |-- Lunar.class
  |-- controls.jar
  |             |-- apollo
  |                    |-- modules
  |                           |-- Module.class
  |-- Saturn.java
```

Which are correct about compiling and running the Saturn class from the $ROOT directory? (Choose all that apply.)

A. The command for compiling is `javac -d . -cp . Saturn.java`

B. The command for compiling is `javac -d . -cp controls.jar Saturn.java`

C. The command for compiling is `javac -d . -cp .:controls.jar Saturn.java`

D. The command for running is `java -cp . apollo.Saturn`

E. The command for running is `java -cp controls.jar apollo.Saturn`

F. The command for running is `java -cp .:controls.jar apollo.Saturn`

G. The command for running is `java -cp controls.jar -cp . apollo.Saturn`

57. Given:

```
5. class OOthing { void doStuff() { System.out.print("oo "); } }
6. class GuiThing extends OOthing {
7.   void doStuff() { System.out.print("gui "); }
8. }
9. public class Button extends GuiThing {
10.   void doStuff() { System.out.print("button "); }
11.   public static void main(String[] args) { new Button().go(); }
12.   void go() {
13.     GuiThing g = new GuiThing();
14.     // this.doStuff();
15.     // super.doStuff();
16.     // g.super.doStuff();
17.     // super.g.doStuff();
18.     // super.super.doStuff();
19. } }
```

If the commented lines are uncommented independently, which are true? (Choose all that apply.)

A. If line 14 is uncommented, "button" will be in the output.

B. If line 15 is uncommented, "gui" will be in the output.

C. If line 16 is uncommented, "oo" will be in the output.

D. If line 17 is uncommented, "oo" will be in the output.

E. If line 18 is uncommented, "oo" will be in the output.

58. Given:

```
2. import java.util.*;
3. public class Salt {
4.   public static void main(String[] args) {
5.     Set s1 = new HashSet();
6.     s1.add(0);
```

```
7.        s1.add("1");
8.        doStuff(s1);
9.     }
10.    static void doStuff(Set<Number> s) {
11.       do2(s);
12.       Iterator i = s.iterator();
13.       while(i.hasNext())  System.out.print(i.next() + " ");
14.       Object[] oa = s.toArray();
15.       for(int x = 0; x < oa.length; x++)
16.         System.out.print(oa[x] + " ");
17.       System.out.println(s.contains(1));
18.    }
19.    static void do2(Set s2) { System.out.print(s2.size() + " "); }
20. }
```

What is the most likely result?

A. 2 0 1 0 1 true

B. 2 0 1 0 1 false

C. Compilation fails.

D. An exception is thrown at line 8.

E. An exception is thrown at line 13.

F. An exception is thrown at line 14.

G. An exception is thrown at line 19.

59. Given:

```
1. public class Begin {
2.    static int x;
3.    { int[] ia2 = {4,5,6}; }
4.    static {
5.       int[] ia = {1,2,3};
6.       for(int i = 0; i < 3; i++)
7.         System.out.print(ia[i] + " ");
8.       x = 7;
9.       System.out.print(x + " ");
10. } }
```

And, if the code compiles, the invocation:

```
java Begin
```

What is the result?

A. Compilation fails.

B. "1 2 3 7", with no exception thrown.

C. "1 2 3 7", followed by an exception.

D. "1 2 3", followed by an `ExceptionInInitializerError`.

E. `ExceptionInInitializerError` is thrown before any output.

F. Some other exception is thrown before any other output.

60. Given:

```
2. public class Alamo {
3.   public static void main(String[] args) {
4.     try {
5.       assert(!args[0].equals("x")): "kate";
6.     } catch(Error e) { System.out.print("ae "); }
7.     finally {
8.       try {
9.         assert(!args[0].equals("y")): "jane";
10.       } catch(Exception e2) { System.out.print("ae2 "); }
11.       finally {
12.         throw new IllegalArgumentException();
13. } } } }
```

And, if the code compiles, the invocation:

```
java -ea Alamo y
```

Which will be included in the output? (Choose all that apply.)

A. ae

B. ae2

C. kate

D. jane

E. `AssertionError`

F. `IllegalArgumentException`

G. There is no output because compilation fails.

QUICK ANSWER KEY

1. A	21. E	41. E
2. E	22. A, C, D	42. C
3. E	23. B	43. E
4. F	24. A, B, E	44. A
5. D	25. A, B, C	45. E
6. C, D, G	26. D	46. F
7. C, F	27. A, B, C, E	47. A, G
8. A	28. B, D	48. C, D, F
9. B	29. B	49. E
10. B, C	30. B, C	50. D
11. C	31. B	51. D, E
12. D	32. A, B, C, E	52. A, B, C, D, E, F
13. C	33. D	53. Drag and Drop
14. Drag and Drop	34. E	54. D, E, F
15. B, D	35. B	55. F
16. B	36. D	56. A, C, F
17. F	37. C	57. A, B
18. A	38. E, F	58. B
19. E, F	39. A	59. C
20. E	40. D	60. F

PRACTICE EXAM 3: ANSWERS

1. Given:

```
3. class Bonds {
4.   Bonds force() { return new Bonds(); }
5. }
6. public class Covalent extends Bonds {
7.   Covalent force() { return new Covalent(); }
8.   public static void main(String[] args) {
9.     new Covalent().go(new Covalent());
10.   }
11.   void go(Covalent c) {
12.     go2(new Bonds().force(), c.force());
13.   }
14.   void go2(Bonds b, Covalent c) {
15.     Covalent c2 = (Covalent)b;
16.     Bonds b2 = (Bonds)c;
17. } }
```

What is the result? (Choose all that apply.)

A. A `ClassCastException` is thrown at line 15.

B. A `ClassCastException` is thrown at line 16.

C. Compilation fails due to an error on line 7.

D. Compilation fails due to an error on line 12.

E. Compilation fails due to an error on line 15.

F. Compilation fails due to an error on line 16.

Answer (for Objective 2.6):

☑ **A** is correct. The override on line 7 is a legal covariant return. The attempted cast at line 15 is incorrect because Covalent instances might do more than Bonds instances.

☒ **B, C, D, E**, and **F** are incorrect based on the above.

2. Given:

```
1. import java.util.*;
2. public class Drawers {
3.   public static void main(String[] args) {
4.     List<String> desk = new ArrayList<String>();
5.     desk.add("pen"); desk.add("scissors"); desk.add("redStapler");
```

```
6.      System.out.print(desk.indexOf("redStapler"));
7.      Collection.reverse(desk);
8.      System.out.print(" " + desk.indexOf("redStapler"));
9.      Collection.sort(desk);
10.     System.out.println(" " + desk.indexOf("redStapler"));
11. } }
```

What is the result?

A. 1 1 1

B. 2 0 1

C. 2 0 2

D. 2 2 2

E. Compilation fails.

F. An exception is thrown at runtime.

Answer (for Objective 6.1):

☑ **E** is correct. We had to throw at least one of these in here, sorry. The reverse() and sort() methods are in the Collections class, not the Collection class—*ouch*. Again, look for this kind of misdirection in the real exam! If the invocations had been Collections.reverse(desk) and Collections.sort(desk), the result would have been 2 0 1—remember, indexes are zero-based.

☒ **A, B, C, D,** and **F** are incorrect based on the above.

3. Given:

```
1. import java.util.*;
2. class Radio {
3.    String getFreq() { return "97.3"; }
4.    static String getF() { return "97.3"; }
5. }
6. class Ham extends Radio {
7.    String getFreq() { return "50.1"; }
8.    static String getF() { return "50.1"; }
9.    public static void main(String[] args) {
10.     List<Radio> radios = new ArrayList<Radio>();
11.     radios.add(new Radio());
12.     radios.add(new Ham());
13.     for(Radio r: radios)
14.       System.out.print(r.getFreq() + " " + r.getF() + "    ");
15. } }
```

What is the result?

A. 50.1 50.1   50.1 50.1

B. 50.1 97.3   50.1 97.3

C. 97.3 50.1   50.1 50.1

D. 97.3 97.3   50.1 50.1

E. 97.3 97.3   50.1 97.3

F. 97.3 97.3   97.3 97.3

G. Compilation fails.

H. An exception is thrown at runtime.

Answer (for Objective 5.3):

☑ **E** is correct. The important point is that the getF() methods are static. static methods CANNOT be overridden, but they can be redefined, as is the case in this code.

☒ **A, B, C, D, F, G**, and **H** are incorrect based on the above.

4. Given two files:

```
1. package com;
2. public class MyClass {
3.    public static void howdy() { System.out.print("howdy "); }
4.    public static final int myConstant = 343;
5.    public static final MyClass mc = new MyClass();
6.    public int instVar = 42;
7. }
```

```
11. import static com.MyClass.*;
12. public class TestImports {
13.    public static void main(String[] args) {
14.       System.out.print(myConstant + " ");
15.       howdy();
16.       System.out.print(mc.instVar + " ");
17.       System.out.print(instVar + " ");
18. } }
```

What is the result? (Choose ALL that apply.)

A. 343 howdy 42 42

B. Compilation fails due to an error on line 11.

C. Compilation fails due to an error on line 14.

D. Compilation fails due to an error on line 15.

E. Compilation fails due to an error on line 16.

F. Compilation fails due to an error on line 17.

Answer (for Objective 1.1):

☑ **F** is correct. Line 17 is incorrect syntax to access `instVar`. All of the remaining code is legal. It's legal to use static imports to access `static` methods, constants (which are `static` and `final`), and `static` object references.

☒ **A, B, C, D**, and **E** are incorrect based on the above.

5. Given this code in a method:

```
4.      int x = 0;
5.      int[] primes = {1,2,3,5};
6.      for(int i: primes)
7.        switch(i) {
8.          case 1: x += i;
9.          case 5: x += i;
10.         default: x += i;
11.         case 2: x += i;
12.        }
13.     System.out.println(x);
```

What is the result?

A. 11

B. 13

C. 24

D. 27

E. Compilation fails due to an error on line 7.

F. Compilation fails due to an error on line 10.

G. Compilation fails due to an error on line 11.

Answer (for Objective 2.1):

☑ **D** is correct. The code is all legal. A `switch`'s cases don't have to be in any particular order. Also remember that when a `case` is matched, its code, and all the subsequent cases' code, will run unless a `break` is encountered.

☒ **A, B, C, E, F**, and **G** are incorrect based on the above.

6. Given:

```
1.  import java.util.*;
2.  public class Elway {
3.    public static void main(String[] args) {
4.      ArrayList[] ls = new ArrayList[3];
5.      for(int i = 0; i < 3; i++) {
6.        ls[i] = new ArrayList();
7.        ls[i].add("a" + i);
8.      }
9.      Object o = ls;
10.     do3(ls);
11.     for(int i = 0; i < 3; i++) {
12.       // insert code here
13.     }
14.   }
15.   static Object do3(ArrayList[] a) {
16.     for(int i = 0; i < 3; i++)  a[i].add("e");
17.     return a;
18. } }
```

And the following fragments:

I.   `System.out.print(o[i] + " ");`

II. `System.out.print((ArrayList[])[i] + " ");`

III. `System.out.print( ((Object[])o)[i] + " ");`

IV. `System.out.print(((ArrayList[])o)[i] + " ");`

If the fragments are added to line 12, independently, which are true? (Choose all that apply.)

A. Fragment I will compile.

B. Fragment II will compile.

C. Fragment III will compile.

D. Fragment IV will compile.

E. Compilation fails due to other errors.

F. Of those that compile, the output will be `[a0]  [a1]  [a2]`

G. Of those that compile, the output will be `[a0, e]  [a1, e]  [a2, e]`

Answer (for Objective 7.3):

☑ **C**, **D**, and **G** are correct. Fragments III and IV are the correct syntax to cast the `Object` back to an array of objects. The references `"o"` and `"ls"` refer to the same object, so the changes made to `"ls"` in do3() are accessible via `"o"`.

☒ **A** and **B** are incorrect syntax. **E** and **F** are incorrect based on the above.

7. Given:

```
1. enum MyEnum {HI, ALOHA, HOWDY};
2. public class PassEnum {
3.   public static void main(String[] args) {
4.     PassEnum p = new PassEnum();
5.     MyEnum[] v = MyEnum.values();
6.     v = MyEnum.getValues();
7.     for(MyEnum me: MyEnum.values())   p.getEnum(me);
8.     for(int x = 0; x < MyEnum.values().length; x++)   p.getEnum(v[x]);
9.     for(int x = 0; x < MyEnum.length; x++)   p.getEnum(v[x]);
10.    for(MyEnum me: v)   p.getEnum(me);
11.   }
12.   public void getEnum(MyEnum e) {
13.     System.out.print(e + " ");
14. } }
```

Which line(s) of code will cause a compiler error? (Choose all that apply.)

A. line 1

B. line 5

C. line 6

D. line 7

E. line 8

F. line 9

G. line 10

H. line 12

Answer (for Objective 1.3):

☑ **C** and **F** are correct. At line 6, compilation will fail because the method getValues() is not defined. At line 9, the compilation will fail because enums don't have a length attribute.

☒ **A, B, D, E, G,** and **H** are incorrect. There are no compilation problems with the code described on these lines, although line 7 is probably most common because it doesn't need line 5.

8. Given:

```
3. public class Drip extends Thread {
4.   public static void main(String[] args) {
5.     Thread t1 = new Thread(new Drip());
6.     t1.start();
7.     t1.join();
```

```
8.      for(int i = 0; i < 1000; i++)  // Loop #1
9.         System.out.print(Thread.currentThread().getName() + " ");
10.   }
11.   public void run() {
12.      for(int i = 0; i < 1000; i++)  // Loop #2
13.         System.out.print(Thread.currentThread().getName() + " ");
14. } }
```

Which are true? (Choose all that apply.)

A.   Compilation fails.

B.   An exception is thrown at runtime.

C.   Loop #1 will run most of its iterations before Loop #2.

D.   Loop #2 will run most of its iterations before Loop #1.

E.   There is no way to predict which loop will mostly run first.

Answer (for Objective 4.2):

☑   **A** is correct. The `join()` method throws an exception, so it must be handled or declared; if it was, then **D** would be correct.

☒   **B, C, D,** and **E** are incorrect based on the above.

9. Given this code in a method:

```
5.      int x = 3;
6.      for(int i = 0; i < 3; i++) {
7.         if(i == 1) x = x++;
8.         if(i % 2 == 0 && x % 2 == 0) System.out.print(".");
9.         if(i % 2 == 0 && x % 2 == 1) System.out.print("-");
10.        if(i == 2 ^ x == 4) System.out.print(",");
11.     }
12.     System.out.println("<");
```

What is the result?

A.   - . , <

B.   - - , <

C.   - . , , <

D.   - - , , <

E.   - . - , , <

F.   Compilation fails.

Answer (for Objective 7.6):

☑ **B** is correct. The `%` operator returns the remainder of a division. The `^` (XOR) operator returns `true` only if exactly one of the expressions is `true`. The `x = x++;` line doesn't leave `x == 4` because the `++` is applied after the assignment has occurred.

☒ **A, C, D, E,** and **F** are incorrect based on the above.

10. Given:

```
2. public class Incomplete {
3.    public static void main(String[] args) {   // change code here ?
4.        // insert code here ?
5.          new Incomplete().doStuff();
6.        // insert code here ?
...
10.   }
11.    static void doStuff() throws Exception {
12.        throw new Exception();
13. } }
```

Which are true? (Choose all that apply.)

A. Compilation succeeds with no code changes.

B. Compilation succeeds if `main()` is changed to throw an `Exception`.

C. Compilation succeeds if a `try-catch` is added, surrounding line 5.

D. Compilation succeeds if a `try-finally` is added, surrounding line 5.

E. Compilation succeeds only if BOTH `main()` declares an `Exception` AND a `try-catch` is added, surrounding line 5.

Answer (for Objective 2.4):

☑ **B** and **C** are correct. Invoking `doStuff()` will cause an `Exception` that must either be handled (option C) or declared (option B). (Remember, you can compile a program in which `main()` throws an `Exception`.)

☒ **A** is incorrect based on the above. **D** is incorrect because a `try-finally` will not handle the `Exception`. **E** is incorrect because EITHER handling or declaring the exception is sufficient.

11. Given the proper imports, and given:

```
24.    Date d1 = new Date();
25.    Date d2 = d1;
```

```
26.  System.out.println(d1);
27.  d2.setTime(d1.getTime() + (7 * 24 * 60 * 60));
28.  System.out.println(d2);
```

Which are true? (Choose all that apply.)

A. Compilation fails.

B. An exception is thrown at runtime.

C. Some of the output will be today's date.

D. Some of the output will be next week's date.

E. Some of the output will represent the Java "epoch" (i.e., January 1, 1970).

Answer (for Objective 3.3):

☑ **C** is correct. When a `Date` is constructed with no arguments, the system's current time is used, not the Java "epoch." The code is correct, and the second date displayed is about 10 minutes after the first date because `Date` objects and `setTime()` both use millisecond precision. In order to add a week, we would have also had to multiply by 1000 in line 27.

☒ **A, B, D,** and **E** are incorrect based on the above.

12. Given:

```
2. interface Machine { }
3. interface Engine { }
4. abstract interface Tractor extends Machine, Engine {
5.    void pullStuff();
6. }
7. class Deere implements Tractor {
8.    public void pullStuff() { System.out.print("pulling "); }
9. }
10. class LT255 implements Tractor extends Deere  {
11.    public void pullStuff() { System.out.print("pulling harder "); }
12. }
13. public class LT155 extends Deere implements Tractor, Engine { }
```

What is the result? (Choose all that apply.)

A. Compilation succeeds.

B. Compilation fails because of error(s) in `Tractor`.

C. Compilation fails because of error(s) in `Deere`.

D. Compilation fails because of error(s) in `LT255`.

E. Compilation fails because of error(s) in `LT155`.

Answer (for Objective 1.2):

☑ **D** is correct. When a class `implements` and `extends`, the `extends` declaration comes first.

☒ **A, B, C,** and **E** are incorrect because all of the other code is legal. It is legal to "re-extend" an interface, and it's legal to implement several interfaces.

13. Given this code in a method:

```
5.      boolean[] ba = {true, false};
6.      short[][] gr = {{1,2}, {3,4}};
7.      int i = 0;
8.      for( ; i < 10; ) i++;
9.      for(short s: gr) ;
10.     for(int j = 0, k = 10; k > j; ++j, k--) ;
11.     for(int j = 0; j < 3; System.out.println(j++)) ;
12.     for(Boolean b: ba) ;
```

What is the result? (Choose all that apply.)

A. Compilation succeeds.

B. Compilation fails due to an error on line 8.

C. Compilation fails due to an error on line 9.

D. Compilation fails due to an error on line 10.

E. Compilation fails due to an error on line 11.

F. Compilation fails due to an error on line 12.

Answer (for Objective 2.2):

☑ **C** is correct. `"gr"` is a two-dimensional array, you can't stuff one of its dimensions (a one-dimensional array) into a primitive.

☒ **A, B, D, E,** and **F** are incorrect because all of the other `"for"` loop syntaxes are legal.

14. Given:

```
2. package w.x;
3. import w.y.Zoom;
4. public class Zip {
5.   public static void main(String[] args) {
6.     new Zoom().doStuff();
7. } }
```

And the following command to compile `Zip.java`: `javac -cp w.jar -d . Zip.java`

And another class `w.y.Zoom` (with a `doStuff()` method), which has been compiled and deployed into a JAR file `w.jar`:

Fill in the blanks using the following fragments to show the directory structure and the contents of any directory(s) necessary to compile successfully from $ROOT. Note: NOT all the blanks must be filled, NOT all the fragments will be used, and fragments CANNOT be used more than once.

```
$ROOT
  |-- _____
  |-- _____
  |-- _____
        |-- _____
            |-- _____
                |-- _____
                    |-- _____
```

Fragments:

Zoom.java	Zip.java	Zoom.class
Zip.class	[Zoom.jar]	[w.jar]
w	x	y

Answer (for Objective 7.5):

```
$ROOT
  |-- Zip.java
  |-- [w.jar]
        |-- w
            |-- y
                |-- Zoom.class
```

15. Given:

```
2. class Pancake { }
3. class BlueberryPancake extends Pancake { }
4. public class SourdoughBlueberryPancake2 extends BlueberryPancake {
5.   public static void main(String[] args) {
6.     Pancake p4 = new SourdoughBlueberryPancake2();
7.     // insert code here
8. } }
```

And the following six declarations (which are to be inserted independently at line 7):

I.   `Pancake p5 = p4;`

II. `Pancake p6 = (BlueberryPancake)p4;`

III. `BlueberryPancake b2 = (BlueberryPancake)p4;`

IV. `BlueberryPancake b3 = (SourdoughBlueberryPancake2)p4;`

V.   `SourdoughBlueberryPancake2 s1 = (BlueberryPancake)p4;`

VI. `SourdoughBlueberryPancake2 s2 = (SourdoughBlueberryPancake2)p4;`

Which are true? (Choose all that apply.)

A. All six declarations will compile.

B. Exactly one declaration will not compile.

C. More than one of the declarations will not compile.

D. Of those declarations that compile, none will throw an exception.

E. Of those declarations that compile, exactly one will throw an exception.

F. Of those declarations that compile, more than one will throw an exception.

Answer (for Objective 5.2):

☑ **B** and **D** are correct. Declaration V will not compile because
`SourdoughBlueberryPancake2` might have methods that `BlueberryPancake`
doesn't have. The other five declarations run without an exception.

☒ **A, C, E**, and **F** are incorrect based on the above.

16. Given:

```
3. class IcelandicHorse {
4.   void tolt() { System.out.print("4-beat "); }
5. }
6. public class Vafi extends IcelandicHorse {
7.   public static void main(String[] args) {
8.     new Vafi().go();
9.     new IcelandicHorse().tolt();
10.  }
11.  void go() {
12.    IcelandicHorse h1 = new Vafi();
13.    h1.tolt();
14.    Vafi v = (Vafi) h1;
15.    v.tolt();
16.  }
17.  void tolt() { System.out.print("pacey "); }
18. }
```

What is the result? (Choose all that apply.)

A. `4-beat pacey pacey`

B. `pacey pacey 4-beat`

C. `4-beat 4-beat 4-beat`

D. `4-beat pacey 4-beat`

E. `pacey`, followed by an exception

F. `4-beat`, followed by an exception

Answer (for Objective 1.4):

☑ **B** is correct. The `tolt()` method's first two invocations come from the `go()` method, and the object type determines which (overridden) method is used at runtime.

☒ **A**, **C**, and **D** are incorrect based on the above. **E** and **F** are incorrect. The casts are legal.

17. Given:

```
1. class MyException extends RuntimeException { }
2. public class Houdini {
3.   public static void main(String[] args) throws Exception {
4.     throw new MyException();
5.     System.out.println("success");
6. } }
```

Which are true? (Choose all that apply.)

A. The code runs without output.

B. The output `"success"` is produced.

C. Compilation fails due to an error on line 1.

D. Compilation fails due to an error on line 3.

E. Compilation fails due to an error on line 4.

F. Compilation fails due to an error on line 5.

Answer (for Objective 2.5):

☑ **F** is correct. The compiler sees that line 4 will always run, and therefore line 5 is unreachable. If line 5 was removed, the rest of the code would be legal, and **A** would be correct.

☒ **A**, **B**, **C**, **D**, and **E** are incorrect based on the above.

18. Given:

```
3. public class Avast {
4.    static public void main(String[] scurvy) {
5.       System.out.print(scurvy[1] + " ");
6.       main(scurvy[2]);
7.    }
8.    public static void main(String dogs) {
9.       assert(dogs == null);
10.      System.out.println(dogs);
11. } }
```

And, if the code compiles, the command-line invocation:

```
java Avast -ea 1 2 3
```

What is the result? (Choose all that apply.)

A. 1 2

B. 2 3

C. Compilation fails due to an error on line 4.

D. Compilation fails due to an error on line 6.

E. Compilation fails due to an error on line 8.

F. Compilation fails due to an error on line 9.

G. Some output is produced and then an `AssertionError` is thrown.

Answer (for Objective 7.2):

☑ A is correct. The code is legal. Traditionally, `main()`'s `String[]` argument is named `"args"`, but it's not required. The second `main()` is an overload. In order to enable assertions, the `-ea` flag must come before the name of the `.class` file to be run, so in this case `-ea` is treated as the first of the arguments, which are of course loaded into a zero-based array.

☒ B, C, D, E, F, and G are incorrect based on the above.

19. Given:

```
2. class Wheel {
3.    Wheel(int s) { size = s; }
4.    int size;
5.    void spin() { System.out.print(size + " inch wheel spinning, "); }
6. }
```

```
 7. public class Bicycle {
 8.    public static void main(String[] args) {
 9.      Wheel[] wa = {new Wheel(15), new Wheel(17)};
10.      for(Wheel w: wa)
11.        w.spin();
12. } }
```

Which are true? (Choose all that apply.)

A. Compilation fails.

B. If size was private, the degree of coupling would change.

C. If size was private, the degree of cohesion would change.

D. The Bicycle class is tightly coupled with the Wheel class.

E. The Bicycle class is loosely coupled with the Wheel class.

F. If size was private, the degree of encapsulation would change.

Answer (for Objective 5.1):

☑ **E** and **F** are correct. **E** is correct because, as it stands, Bicycle accesses Wheel only through its informal API, the method and the constructor. **F** is correct because Wheel is not well encapsulated, and making size private would make Wheel well encapsulated.

☒ **A** is incorrect because the code is legal. **B** and **C** are incorrect because, in general, encapsulation is mostly independent of cohesion, and Bicycle is already treating Wheel in a loosely coupled way. **D** is incorrect based on the above.

20. Given:

```
 2. public class Mouthwash {
 3.    static int x = 1;
 4.    public static void main(String[] args) {
 5.      int x = 2;
 6.      for(int i=0; i< 3; i++) {
 7.        if(i==1) System.out.print(x + " ");
 8.      }
 9.      go();
10.      System.out.print(x + " " + i);
11.    }
12.    static void go() { int x = 3; }
13. }
```

What is the result?

A.   1 2 2

B.   2 2 2

C.   2 2 3

D.   2 3 2

E.   Compilation fails.

F.   An exception is thrown at runtime.

Answer (for Objective 1.3):

☑   **E** is correct. When the code reaches line 10, the variable `"i"` is out of scope.

☒   **A, B, C, D,** and **F** are incorrect based on the above. If `"i"` was not mentioned on line 10, scoping and shadowing rules would create the output: `"2 2"`.

21.   Given the proper imports, and given:

```
23.   String s = "123 888888 x 345 -45";
24.   Scanner sc = new Scanner(s);
25.   while(sc.hasNext())
26.     if(sc.hasNextShort())
27.       System.out.print(sc.nextShort() + " ");
```

What is the result?

A.   The output is `123 345`

B.   The output is `123 345 -45`

C.   The output is `123 888888 345 -45`

D.   The output is `123` followed by an exception.

E.   The output is `123` followed by an infinite loop.

Answer (for Objective 3.4):

☑   **E** is correct. In the first `while` loop iteration a `short` is found, printed, AND the `nextShort()` method moves the scanner to the next token. When the second (through nth) iteration of the `while` executes, the token `888888` is found, which is not a `short`, so the program never moves to the third token. If line 28 read `"else sc.next();"`, then non-short tokens would be "consumed" and the scanning would proceed to produce answer **B**.

☒   **A, B, C,** and **D** are incorrect based on the above.

22. Given:

```
1. interface Horse { public void nicker(); }
```

Which will compile? (Choose all that apply.)

A. `public class Eyra implements Horse { public void nicker() { } }`

B. `public class Eyra implements Horse { public void nicker(int x) { } }`

C.
```
public class Eyra implements Horse {
   public void nicker() { System.out.println("huhuhuhuh..."); }
}
```

D.
```
public abstract class Eyra implements Horse {
   public void nicker(int loud) { }
}
```

E.
```
public abstract class Eyra implements Horse {
   public void nicker(int loud) ;
}
```

Answer (for Objective 1.1):

☑ **A, C,** and **D** correctly implement the Horse interface.

☒ **B** is incorrect because Horse's no-arg `nicker()` method is not implemented. **E** is incorrect because the overloaded `nicker()` method is not marked `abstract`, AND is not implemented.

23. Given:

```
2. public class LaoTzu extends Philosopher {
3.    public static void main(String[] args) {
4.      new LaoTzu();
5.      new LaoTzu("Tigger");
6.    }
7.    LaoTzu() { this("Pooh"); }
8.    LaoTzu(String s) { super(s); }
9. }
10. class Philosopher {
11.    Philosopher(String s) { System.out.print(s + " "); }
12. }
```

What is the result?

A. `Pooh Pooh`

B. `Pooh Tigger`

C. `Tigger Pooh`

D. `Tigger Tigger`

E. Compilation fails due to a single error in the code.

F. Compilation fails due to multiple errors in the code.

Answer (for Objective 1.5):

☑ **B** is correct. The no-arg `LaoTzu` constructor invokes the other `LaoTzu` constructor (via `"this"`), and the second `LaoTzu` constructor chains to the `Philosopher`'s constructor (via `"super"`).

☒ **A, C, D, E,** and **F** are incorrect based on the above.

24. Which are capabilities of Java's assertion mechanism? (Choose all that apply.)

A. You can, at the command line, enable assertions for a specific class.

B. You can, at the command line, disable assertions for a specific package.

C. You can, at runtime, enable assertions for any version of Java.

D. It's considered appropriate to catch and handle an `AssertionError` programmatically.

E. You can programmatically test whether assertions have been enabled without throwing an `AssertionError`.

Answer (for Objective 2.3):

☑ **A, B,** and **E** are correct. E is true because the `assert` statement's first expression must result in a `boolean` value, which could be a `boolean` assignment.

☒ **C** is incorrect because assertions are not available in versions of Java before version 1.4. **D** is incorrect because catching an `AssertionError` is considered inappropriate.

25. Given:

```
4. public class Stone implements Runnable {
5.    static int id = 1;
6.    public void run() {
7.       try {
8.          id = 1 - id;
9.          if(id == 0) { pick(); } else { release(); }
```

```
10.       } catch(Exception e) { }
11.     }
12.     private static synchronized void pick() throws Exception {
13.        System.out.print("P ");    System.out.print("Q ");
14.     }
15.     private synchronized void release() throws Exception {
16.        System.out.print("R ");    System.out.print("S ");
17.     }
18.     public static void main(String[] args) {
19.        Stone st = new Stone();
20.        new Thread(st).start();
21.        new Thread(st).start();
22.   } }
```

Which are true? (Choose all that apply.)

A. The output could be P Q R S

B. The output could be P R S Q

C. The output could be P R Q S

D. The output could be P Q P Q

E. The program could cause a deadlock.

F. Compilation fails.

Answer (for Objective 4.3):

☑ **A, B**, and **C** are correct. Since pick() is static and release() is non-static, there are two locks. If pick() was non-static, only **A** would be correct.

☒ **D** is incorrect because line 6 swaps the value of id between 0 and 1. There is no chance for the same method to be executed twice. **E** and **F** are incorrect based on the above.

26. Given:

```
3. public class States {
4.    static String s;
5.    static Boolean b;
6.    static Boolean t1() { return new Boolean("howdy"); }
7.    static boolean t2() { return new Boolean(s); }
8.    public static void main(String[] args) {
9.      if(t1()) System.out.print("t1 ");
10.      if(!t2()) System.out.print("t2 ");
11.      if(t1() != t2()) System.out.print("!= ");
12.    }
13. }
```

Which are true? (Choose all that apply.)

A. Compilation fails.

B. No output is produced.

C. The output will contain `"t1 "`

D. The output will contain `"t2 "`

E. The output will contain `" != "`

F. The output is `"t1 "`, followed by an exception.

Answer (for Objective 2.1):

☑   **D** is correct. Unboxing automatically converts the `Boolean` objects to `boolean` primitives. The `Boolean(String)` constructor views `null Strings` AND `Strings` that don't have the value of `"true"` (case-insensitive) to be `false`. It's legal for `"if"` tests to be based on method calls that return a `boolean`. Finally, when `"=="` or `"!="` is used to compare a wrapper object with a primitive, the wrapper is unwrapped before the comparison.

☒   **A, B, C, E**, and **F** are incorrect based on the above.

27. Which are valid command-line switches when working with assertions? (Choose all that apply.)

A. `-ea`

B. `-da`

C. `-dsa`

D. `-eva`

E. `-enableassertions`

Answer (for Objective 2.3):

☑   **A, B, C**, and **E** are valid command-line switches.

☒   **D** is incorrect because `-eva` does not exist.

28. Given:

```
4. class Account { Long acctNum, password; }
5. public class Banker {
6.   public static void main(String[] args) {
7.     new Banker().go();
```

```
8.       // do more stuff
9.     }
10.    void go() {
11.      Account a1 = new Account();
12.      a1.acctNum = new Long("1024");
13.      Account a2 = a1;
14.      Account a3 = a2;
15.      a3.password = a1.acctNum.longValue();
16.      a2.password = 4455L;
17.  } }
```

When line 8 is reached, which are true? (Choose all that apply.)

A. a1.acctNum == a3.password

B. a1.password == a2.password

C. Three objects are eligible for garbage collection.

D. Four objects are eligible for garbage collection.

E. Six objects are eligible for garbage collection.

F. Less than three objects are eligible for garbage collection.

G. More than six objects are eligible for garbage collection.

Answer (for Objective 7.4):

☑ **B** and **D** are correct. **B** is correct, although when line 8 is reached, the references are lost. **D** is correct because only one Account object is created, and a1, a2, and a3 all refer to it. The Account object has two Long objects associated with it, and finally the anonymous Banker object is also eligible.

☒ **A, C, E, F,** and **G** are incorrect based on the above.

29. Given:

```
2. public class Coyote {
3.   public static void main(String[] args) {
4.      int x = 4;
5.      int y = 4;
6.      while((x = jump(x)) < 8)
7.        do {
8.           System.out.print(x + " ");
9.        } while ((y = jump(y)) < 6);
10.   }
11.   static int jump(int x) { return ++x; }
12. }
```

What is the result?

A. 5 5 6 6

B. 5 5 6 7

C. 5 5 6 6 7

D. 5 6 5 6 7

E. Compilation fails due to a single error.

F. Compilation fails due to multiple errors.

Answer (for Objective 2.2):

☑ **B** is correct. It's legal for `while` expressions to include method calls. The `do` loop is nested inside the `while` loop. In the first iteration of the `while` loop, the `do` loop is executed twice, and `"y"` is left with the value of 6. In subsequent `while` iterations, the `do` loop executes only once because `"y"` just keeps getting bigger and bigger.

☒ **A, C, D, E,** and **F** are incorrect based on the above.

30. Given:

```
2. class Engine {
3.   public class Piston {
4.     static int count = 0;
5.     void go() { System.out.print(" pump " + ++count); }
6.   }
7.   public Piston getPiston() { return new Piston(); }
8. }
9. public class Auto {
10.   public static void main(String[] args) {
11.     Engine e = new Engine();
12.     // Engine.Piston p = e.getPiston();
13.     e.Piston p = e.getPiston();
14.     p.go();  p.go();
15. } }
```

In order for the code to compile and produce the output " pump 1 pump 2", which are true? (Choose all that apply.)

A. The code is correct as it stands.

B. Line 4 must be changed. `count` can't be declared `"static"`

C. Line 12 must be un-commented, and line 13 must be removed.

D. Somewhere in the code, a second instance of `Piston` must be instantiated.

E. There are errors in the code that must be fixed, outside of lines 4, 12, and 13.

Answer (for Objective 1.5):

☑ **B** and **C** are correct. Regular inner classes cannot have `static` declarations, and line 12 (not line 13), uses the correct syntax to create an inner class instance from outside the enclosing class. The rest of the code is correct.

☒ **A, D,** and **E** are incorrect based on the above.

31. Given:

```
2. public class Juggler extends Thread {
3.    public static void main(String[] args) {
4.       try {
5.          Thread t = new Thread(new Juggler());
6.          Thread t2 = new Thread(new Juggler());
7.       } catch (Exception e) { System.out.print("e "); }
8.    }
9.    public void run() {
10.      for(int i = 0; i < 2; i++)  {
11.         try { Thread.sleep(500); }
12.         catch (Exception e) { System.out.print("e2 "); }
13.         System.out.print(Thread.currentThread().getName() + " ");
14. } } }
```

Which are true? (Choose all that apply.)

A. Compilation fails.

B. No output is produced.

C. The output could be `Thread-1 Thread-1 e`

D. The output could be `Thread-1 Thread-1 Thread-3 Thread-3`

E. The output could be `Thread-1 Thread-3 Thread-1 Thread-3`

F. The output could be `Thread-1 Thread-1 Thread-3 Thread-2`

Answer (for Objective 4.1):

☑ **B** is correct. In `main()`, the `start()` method was never called to start "`t`" and "`t2`", so `run()` never ran. If `start()` was invoked for "`t`" and "`t2`", then **D** and **E** would have been correct.

☒ **A, C, D, E,** and **F** are incorrect based on the above.

32. Given:

```
3. class Department {
4.   Department getDeptName() { return new Department(); }
5. }
6. class Accounting extends Department {
7.   Accounting getDeptName() { return new Accounting(); }
8.   // insert code here
13. }
```

And the following four code fragments:

I. `String getDeptName(int x) { return "mktg"; }`

II. `void getDeptName(Department d) { ; }`

III. `void getDeptName(long x) throws NullPointerException {`
    `throw new NullPointerException();`
`}`

IV. `Department getDeptName() throws NullPointerException {`
    `throw new NullPointerException();`
    `return new Department();`
`}`

Which are true? (Choose all that apply.)

A. If fragment I is inserted at line 8, the code compiles.

B. If fragment II is inserted at line 8, the code compiles.

C. If fragment III is inserted at line 8, the code compiles.

D. If fragment IV is inserted at line 8, the code compiles.

E. If none of the fragments are inserted at line 8, the code compiles.

Answer (for Objective 1.4):

☑ **A, B, C,** and **E** are correct. As it stands, the code demonstrates a legal covariant return. Fragments I, II, and III are legal overloads.

☒ **D** is incorrect because fragment IV does not correctly overload the `Accounting.getDeptName()` method.

33. Given:

```
2. import java.util.*;
3. interface Canine { }
4. class Dog implements Canine { }
5. public class Collie extends Dog {
6.   public static void main(String[] args) {
```

```
 7.      List<Dog> d = new ArrayList<Dog>();
 8.      List<Collie> c = new ArrayList<Collie>();
 9.      d.add(new Collie());
10.      c.add(new Collie());
11.      do1(d);   do1(c);
12.      do2(d);   do2(c);
13.    }
14.    static void do1(List<? extends Dog> d2) {
15.      d2.add(new Collie());
16.      System.out.print(d2.size());
17.    }
18.    static void do2(List<? extends Canine> c2) {  }
19.  }
```

Which are true? (Choose all that apply.)

A. Compilation succeeds.

B. Compilation fails due to an error on line 9.

C. Compilation fails due to an error on line 14.

D. Compilation fails due to an error on line 15.

E. Compilation fails due to an error on line 16.

F. Compilation fails due to an error on line 18.

G. Compilation fails due to errors on lines 11 and 12.

Answer (for Objective 6.4):

☑ **D** is correct. When a method takes a wildcard generic type, the collection can be accessed or modified, but not both. The rest of the code is legal. It's legal to add a subclass element to a typed collection. It's legal for a method's argument to be a typed wildcarded interface.

☒ **A, B, C, E, F,** and **G** are incorrect based on the above.

34. Given:

```
42. void go() {
43.   int cows = 0;
44.   int[] twisters = {1,2,3};
45.   for(int i = 0; i < 4; i++)
46.     switch(twisters[i]) {
47.         case 2: cows++;
48.         case 1: cows += 10;
49.         case 0: go();
50.     }
51.   System.out.println(cows);
52. }
```

What is the result?

A. 11

B. 21

C. 22

D. Compilation fails.

E. A `StackOverflowError` is thrown at runtime.

F. An `ArrayIndexOutOfBoundsException` is thrown at runtime.

> Answer (for Objective 2.6):
>
> ☑ **E** is correct. Because of `switch` fall-through logic, the `go()` method is called recursively until the stack "explodes" (that's the vulgate). The `for` loop would fail with option **F** if it ever got to run to completion.
>
> ☒ **A, B, C, D**, and **F** are incorrect based on the above.

35. Given:

```
2.  class Robot { }
3.  interface Animal { }
4.  class Feline implements Animal { }
5.  public class BarnCat extends Feline {
6.    public static void main(String[] args) {
7.      Animal af = new Feline();
8.      Feline ff = new Feline();
9.      BarnCat b = new BarnCat();
10.     Robot r = new Robot();
11.     if(af instanceof Animal) System.out.print("1 ");
12.     if(af instanceof BarnCat) System.out.print("2 ");
13.     if(b instanceof Animal) System.out.print("3 ");
14.     if(ff instanceof BarnCat) System.out.print("4 ");
15.     if(r instanceof Animal) System.out.print("5 ");
16.   }
17. }
```

What is the result?

A. 1

B. 1 3

C. 1 2 3

D. 1 3 4

E. 1 2 3 4

F. Compilation fails.

G. An exception is thrown at runtime.

Answer (for Objective 7.6):

☑ **B** is correct. Line 12 and line 14s' `instanceof` tests fail because `BarnCat` is not a superclass of either `af` or `ff`'s respective objects. Line 15 compiles because it's possible that `Robot` could, at some point, implement `Animal`.

☒ **A, C, D, E, F,** and **G** are incorrect based on the above.

36. Given:

```
2. public class Sunny extends Weather {
3.    public static void main(String[] args) {
4.       try {
5.          new Sunny().do1();
6.          new Sunny().do2();
7.          new Sunny().do3();
8.       }
9.       catch(Throwable t) { System.out.print("exc "); }
10. } }
11. class Weather {
12.    void do1() { System.out.print("do1 "); }
13.    private void do2() { System.out.print("do2 "); }
14.    protected void do3() { System.out.print("do3 "); }
15. }
```

What is the result?

A. do1 exc

B. do1 do2 exc

C. do1 do2 do3

D. Compilation fails.

E. An exception is thrown at runtime.

Answer (for Objective 7.1):

☑ **D** is correct. Even a subclass can't access a superclass's `private` method.

☒ **A, B, C,** and **E** are incorrect based on the above.

37. Given that `FileNotFoundException` extends `IOException` and given:

```
2.  import java.io.*;
3.  public class Changeup {
4.    public static void main(String[] args) throws IOException {
5.      new Changeup().go();
6.      new Changeup().go2();
7.      new Changeup().go3();
8.    }
9.    void go() { throw new IllegalArgumentException(); }
10.
11.   void go2() throws FileNotFoundException { }
12.
13.   void go3() {
14.     try { throw new Exception(); }
15.     catch (Throwable th) { throw new NullPointerException(); }
16. } }
```

What is the result? (Choose all that apply.)

A. An `IOException` is thrown at runtime.

B. A `NullPointerException` is thrown at runtime.

C. An `IllegalArgumentException` is thrown at runtime.

D. Compilation fails due to an error at line 4.

E. Compilation fails due to an error at line 9.

F. Compilation fails due to an error at line 11.

G. Compilation fails due to an error at line 15.

Answer (for Objective 2.5):

☑ **C** is correct. It's legal for `main()` to throw an exception, and it's legal to catch a checked exception and re-throw a runtime exception.

☒ **A, B, D, E, F,** and **G** are incorrect based on the above.

38. Which are true? (Choose all that apply.)

A. If class A is-a class B, then class A cannot be considered well encapsulated.

B. If class A has-a class B, then class A cannot be considered well encapsulated.

C. If class A is-a class B, then the two classes are said to be cohesive.

D. If class A has-a class B, then the two classes are said to be cohesive.

E. If class A is-a class B, it's possible for them to still be loosely coupled.

F. If class A has-a class B, it's possible for them to still be loosely coupled.

Answer (for Objective 5.5):

☑ **E** and **F** are correct. Classes are loosely coupled if they interact with each other only through each other's APIs. It's possible to create is-a and has-a relationships that interact solely through APIs.

☒ **A** and **B** are incorrect because the concepts (is-a/has-a versus encapsulation) are more or less independent of each other. **C** and **D** are incorrect because the concepts (is-a/has-a versus cohesion) are more or less independent of each other.

39. Given:

```
2. import java.util.*;
3. public class Volleyball {
4.    public static void main(String[] args) {
5.       TreeSet<String> s = new TreeSet<String>();
6.       s.add("a");  s.add("f");  s.add("b");
7.       System.out.print(s + " ");
8.       Collections.reverse(s);
9.       System.out.println(s);
10. } }
```

What is the result?

A. Compilation fails.

B. `[a, b, f] [a, b, f]`

C. `[a, b, f] [f, b, a]`

D. `[a, f, b] [b, f, a]`

E. `[a, b, f]`, followed by an exception.

F. `[a, f, b]`, followed by an exception.

Answer (for Objective 6.5):

☑ **A** is correct. The `Collections` methods `sort()`, `reverse()`, and `binarySearch()` do not work on Sets.

☒ **B, C, D, E,** and **F** are incorrect based on the above.

40. Given:

```
2. public class Boggy {
3.    final static int mine = 7;
4.    final static Integer i = 57;
5.    public static void main(String[] args) {
```

```
6.      int x = go(mine);
7.      System.out.print(mine + " " + x + " ");
8.      x += mine;
9.      Integer i2 = i;
10.     i2 = go(i);
11.     System.out.println(x + " " + i2);
12.     i2 = new Integer(60);
13.   }
14.   static int go(int x) { return ++x; }
15. }
```

What is the result?

A. 7 7 14 57

B. 7 8 14 57

C. 7 8 15 57

D. 7 8 15 58

E. 7 8 16 58

F. Compilation fails.

G. An exception is thrown at runtime.

Answer (for Objective 7.3):

☑ **D** is correct. None of the `final` variables are modified. The `"i2"` variable initially refers to the same object as the `final "i"` variable, but that object can be modified, and `"i2"` can be referred to a different object. Autoboxing allows an `Integer` to work with `go()`'s int argument.

☒ **A, B, C, E, F,** and **G** are incorrect based on the above.

41. Given:

```
3. import java.io.*;
4. public class Kesey {
5.   public static void main(String[] args) throws Exception {
6.     File file = new File("bigData.txt");
7.     FileWriter w = new FileWriter(file);
8.     w.println("lots o' data");
9.     w.flush();
10.    w.close();
11. } }
```

What is the result? (Choose all that apply.)

A. An empty file named `"bigData.txt"` is created.

B. Compilation fails due only to an error on line 5.

C. Compilation fails due only to an error on line 6.

D. Compilation fails due only to an error on line 7.

E. Compilation fails due only to an error on line 8.

F. Compilation fails due to errors on multiple lines.

G. A file named `"bigData.txt"` is created, containing one line of data.

> **Answer (for Objective 3.2):**
>
> ☑ **E** is correct. It's legal for `main()` to declare an exception and not handle it. Line 8 fails because the `println()` method is one of the easier-to-use methods included in the `PrintWriter` class but not in the more low-level `FileWriter` class.
>
> ☒ **A, B, C, D, F,** and **G** are incorrect based on the above.

42. Given:

```
3. class Wanderer implements Runnable {
4.   public void run() {
5.     for(int i = 0; i < 2; i++)
6.       System.out.print(Thread.currentThread().getName() + " ");
7. } }
8. public class Wander {
9.   public static void main(String[] args) {
10.     Wanderer w = new Wanderer();
11.     Thread t1 = new Thread();
12.     Thread t2 = new Thread(w);
13.     Thread t3 = new Thread(w, "fred");
14.     t1.start();   t2.start();   t3.start();
15. } }
```

Which are true? (Choose all that apply.)

A. Compilation fails.

B. No output is produced.

C. The output could be `Thread-1 fred fred Thread-1`

D. The output could be `Thread-1 Thread-1 Thread-2 Thread-2`

E. The output could be `Thread-1 fred Thread-1 Thread-2 Thread-2 fred`

F. The output could be `Thread-1 Thread-1 Thread-2 Thread-3 fred fred`

Answer (for Objective 4.1):

☑ **C** is correct. Only t2 and t3 have a runnable target, and t3's name will certainly be "fred", so option **D** can't be correct.

☒ **A, B,** and **D** are incorrect based on the above. **E** and **F** are wrong because that output would require more than two threads with targets.

43. Given:

```
2. import java.util.*;
3. public class MyFriends {
4.    String name;
5.    MyFriends(String s) { name = s; }
6.    public static void main(String[] args) {
7.       Set<MyFriends> ms = new HashSet<MyFriends>();
8.       ms.add(new MyFriends("Bob"));
9.       System.out.print(ms + " ");
10.      ms.add(new MyFriends("Bob"));
11.      System.out.print(ms + " ");
12.      ms.add(new MyFriends("Eden"));
13.      System.out.print(ms + " ");
14.   }
15.   public String toString() { return name; }
16. }
```

What is the most likely result?

A. Compilation fails.

B. [Bob] [Bob] [Eden, Bob]

C. [Bob] [Bob] [Eden, Bob, Bob]

D. [Bob], followed by an exception.

E. [Bob] [Bob, Bob] [Eden, Bob, Bob]

Answer (for Objective 6.2):

☑ **E** is correct. The MyFriends class doesn't override equals(), so the two "Bob" instances are NOT seen as equal when added to the HashSet.

☒ **A, B, C,** and **D** are incorrect based on the above.

44. Given the proper imports, and given:

```
17.   public void go() {
18.     NumberFormat nf, nf2;
19.     Number n;
20.     Locale[] la = NumberFormat.getAvailableLocales();
21.     for(int x=0; x < 10; x++) {
22.       nf = NumberFormat.getCurrencyInstance(la[x]);
23.       System.out.println(nf.format(123.456f));
24.     }
25.     nf2 = NumberFormat.getInstance();
26.     n = nf2.parse("123.456f");
27.     System.out.println(n);
28.   }
```

Given that line 20 is legal, which are true? (Choose all that apply.)

A. Compilation fails.

B. An exception is thrown at runtime.

C. The output could contain "123.46"

D. The output could contain "123.456"

E. The output could contain "$123.46"

Answer (for Objective 3.3):

☑ **A** is correct. The parse() method throws an Exception that must be handled or declared. If the exception was handled, **C**, **D**, and **E** would be correct. Remember that when you create a NumberFormat object, its Locale is immutable, but in this code we're creating a new NumberFormat object with each iteration of the loop.

☒ **B** is incorrect based on the above.

45. Given:

```
59.   Integer i1 = 2001;   // set 1
60.   Integer i2 = 2001;
61.   System.out.println((i1 == i2) + " " + i1.equals(i2));   // output 1
62.   Integer i3 = 21;     // set 2
63.   Integer i4 = new Integer(21);
64.   System.out.println((i3 == i4) + " " + i3.equals(i4));   // output 2
65.   Integer i5 = 21;     // set 3
66.   Integer i6 = 21;
67.   System.out.println((i5 == i6) + " " + i5.equals(i6));   // output 3
```

What is the result? (Choose all that apply.)

A. Compilation fails.

B. An exception is thrown at runtime.

C. All three sets of output will be the same.

D. The last two sets of output will be the same.

E. The first two sets of output will be the same.

F. The first and last sets of output will be the same.

Answer (for Objective 3.1):

☑ **E** is correct. Yes, this is a bit of memorization, but it's a fairly common construct. The rule is that, for small values, wrappers created through boxing will be pooled, so i5 and i6 actually point to the same pooled instance of `Integer`. In each of the first two sets, two meaningfully equivalent instances are created.

☒ **A, B, C, D,** and **F** are incorrect based on the above.

46. Given:

```
2. public class Skip {
3.    public static void main(String[] args) throws Exception {
4.       Thread t1 = new Thread(new Jump());
5.       Thread t2 = new Thread(new Jump());
6.       t1.start(); t2.start();
7.       t1.join(500);
8.       new Jump().run();
9. } }
10. class Jump implements Runnable {
11.    public void run() {
12.       for(int i = 0; i < 5; i++) {
13.          try { Thread.sleep(200); }
14.          catch (Exception e) { System.out.print("e "); }
15.          System.out.print(Thread.currentThread().getId() + "-" + i + " ");
16. } } }
```

What is the result?

A. Compilation fails.

B. The main thread will run mostly before t1 runs.

C. The main thread will run after t1, but together with t2.

D. The main thread will run after t2, but together with t1.

E. The main thread will run after both t1 and t2 are mostly done.

F. The main thread's execution will overlap with t1 and t2's execution.

Answer (for Objective 4.2):

☑ **F** is correct. The key to this question is join(500). This means that the main thread will try to join to the end of t1, but it will only wait 500 milliseconds for t1 to complete. If t1 doesn't complete (and it will take at least 1000 milliseconds for t1 to complete), the main thread will start after waiting 500 milliseconds.

☒ **A, B, C, D,** and **E** are incorrect based on the above.

47. Given:

```
1.  import java.util.*;
2.  public class Piles {
3.    public static void main(String[] args) {
4.      TreeMap<String, String> tm = new TreeMap<String, String>();
5.      TreeSet<String> ts = new TreeSet<String>();
6.      String[] k = {"1", "b", "4", "3"};
7.      String[] v = {"a", "d", "3", "b"};
8.      for(int i=0; i<4; i++) {
9.        tm.put(k[i], v[i]);
10.       ts.add(v[i]);
11.     }
12.     System.out.print(tm.values() + " ");
13.     Iterator it2 = ts.iterator();
14.     while(it2.hasNext()) System.out.print(it2.next() + "-");
15. } }
```

Which of the following could be a part of the output? (Choose two.)

A. [a, b, 3, d]

B. [d, a, b, 3]

C. [3, a, b, d]

D. [a, b, d, 3]

E. [1, 3, 4, b]

F. [b, 1, 3, 4]

G. 3-a-b-d-

H. a-b-d-3-

I. a-d-3-b-

Answer (for Objective 6.1):

☑ **A** and **G** are correct. TreeMap.values() returns the values associated with sorted keys (in this case, "naturally sorted" keys). TreeSet iterators use the sorting sequence defined by the instance of TreeSet being used. In this case, the TreeSet was built using "natural ordering."

☒ **B, C, D, E, F, H,** and **I** are incorrect based on the above.

48. Given this code in a method:

```
5.       String s = "dogs. with words.";
6.       // insert code here
7.       for(String o: output)
8.         System.out.print(o + " ");
```

Which of the following, inserted independently at line 6, will produce output that contains the String `"dogs"`? (Choose all that apply.)

A. `String[] output = s.split("s");`

B. `String[] output = s.split("d");`

C. `String[] output = s.split("\\d");`

D. `String[] output = s.split("\\s");`

E. `String[] output = s.split("\\w");`

F. `String[] output = s.split("\\.");`

Answer (for Objective 3.4):

☑ **C, D**, and **F** are correct. The `"\\d"` tells the `split()` method to split Strings whenever a digit is encountered. The `"\\s"` tells the `split()` method to split Strings whenever a whitespace character is encountered. Because a standalone `"."` (dot) is a predefined metacharacter (like \d or \s), the `"\\."` tells the split method to split Strings whenever the character `"."` is encountered.

☒ **A** is incorrect because `"s"` characters are viewed as splitting characters and are removed from the output. **B** is incorrect because `"d"` characters are viewed as splitting characters. **E** is incorrect because the `"\\w"` tells the `split()` method to use letters, digits, and the underscore character as splitting characters.

49. Given the design implied by this partially implemented class:

```
2. public class RobotDog {
3.    int size;
4.    void bark() { /* do barking */ }
5.    int getSize() { return size; }
6.    { size = 16; }
7.    int getNetworkPrinterID() {
8.      /* do lookup */
9.      return 37;
10.    }
11.    void printRobotDogStuff(int printerID) { /* print RobotDog stuff */ }
12. }
```

Which are true? (Choose all that apply.)

A. Compilation fails.

B. To improve cohesion, the `size` variable should be declared `private`.

C. To improve cohesion, the initialization block should be placed inside a constructor.

D. To improve cohesion, `printRobotDogStuff()` should be moved to a different class.

E. To improve cohesion, `getNetworkPrinterID()` should be moved to a different class.

Answer (for Objective 5.1):

☑ **E** is correct. The `getNetworkPrinterID()` method implies a functionality that could be used by many different classes, not just the `RobotDog` class.

☒ **A** is incorrect because the code is legal. **B**'s change would improve encapsulation, not cohesion. **C** and **D**'s changes would have no effect on cohesion (it's okay for a class to print its own state).

50. Given:

```
2. import java.util.*;
3. public class Foggy extends Murky {
4.    public static void main(String[] args) {
5.      final List<String> s = new ArrayList<String>();
6.      s.add("a");   s.add("f");   s.add("a");
7.      new Foggy().mutate(s);
8.      System.out.println(s);
9.    }
10.   List<String> mutate(List<String> s) {
11.     List<String> ms = s;
12.     ms.add("c");
13.     return s;
14.   }
15. }
16. class Murky {
17.   final void mutate(Set s) { }
18. }
```

What is the most likely result?

A. `[a, f]`

B. `[a, f, a]`

C. `[a, f, c]`

D. [a, f, a, c]

E. Compilation fails.

F. An exception is thrown at runtime.

Answer (for Objective 7.3):

☑ **D** is correct. The List is `"final"`, but that doesn't mean its contents can't change. Lists can contain duplicates, and `mutate()` gets a copy of the reference variable, so it's adding to the same List. Murky's `final mutate()` isn't being overridden, it's being overloaded.

☒ **A**, **B**, **C**, **E**, and **F** are incorrect based on the above.

51. Given:

```
1. import java.util.*;
2. enum Heroes { GANDALF, HANS, ENDER }
3. public class MyStuff {
4.   public static void main(String[] args) {
5.     List<String> stuff = new ArrayList<String>();
6.     stuff.add("Bob"); stuff.add("Fred");
7.     new MyStuff().go();
8.   }
9.   Heroes myH = Heroes.ENDER;
10.   void go() {
11.     for(Heroes h: Heroes.values())
12.       if(h == myH) System.out.println(myH);
13. } }
```

Which are true? (Choose all that apply.)

A. Compilation fails.

B. `main()` has-a List

C. MyStuff has-a List

D. MyStuff has-a Heroes

E. The output is `"ENDER"`

F. The output is `"Heroes.ENDER"`

G. An exception is thrown at runtime.

Answer (for Objective 5.5):

☑ D and E are correct. MyStuff has-a Heroes named myH.

☒ A, F, and G are incorrect based on the above. B is incorrect because methods aren't said to "have" classes in the OO "has-a" vernacular (i.e., terminology). C is incorrect because MyStuff's main() "uses" a List, but MyStuff doesn't "have" a List.

52. Given:

```
2. public class Pregnant extends Thread {
3.    int x = 0;
4.    public static void main(String[] args) {
5.       Runnable r1 = new Pregnant();
6.       new Thread(r1).start();
7.       new Thread(r1).start();
8.    }
9.    public void run() {
10.      for(int j = 0; j < 3; j++) {
11.         x = x + 1;
12.         x = x + 10;
13.         System.out.println(x + " ");
14.         x = x + 100;
15. } } }
```

If the code compiles, which value(s) could appear in the output? (Choose all that apply.)

A. 12

B. 22

C. 122

D. 233

E. 244

F. 566

G. Compilation fails.

Answer (for Objective 4.3):

☑ A, B, C, D, E, and F are all correct. The variable x is "shared" by both threads, and collectively the two threads will iterate through the for loop six times. Remember that either thread can pause any number of times, and at any point within the run() method.

☒ G is incorrect based on the above.

53. Fill in the blanks using the following fragments, so that the code compiles and the invocation "java Enchilada green 4" produces the output "wow". Note: You might not need to fill in all of the blanks, you won't use all of the fragments, and each fragment can be used more than once.

Code:

```
import java.util.*;
public class Enchilada {
  public static void main(String[] args) {
    Map<Chilis, String> m = new HashMap<Chilis, String>();
    Chilis myC = new Chilis("green", 4);
    _____(new Chilis("red", 4), "4 alarm");
    _____(new Chilis("green", 2), "mild");
    _____(myC, "wow");
    Chilis c = new Chilis(_____, _____(_____));
    System.out.println(_____);
} }
class Chilis {
  Chilis(String c, int h) { color = c; hotness = h; }
  String color;
  private int hotness;
  public _____ equals(_____) {
    _____
    if(_____ __ _____) return _____;
    return _____;
  }
  public _____ hashCode() { return _____; }
}
```

Fragments:

```
/* empty */        Chilis c              1
m.put              m.add                 true
args[2]            Integer.parseInt      false
args[1]            m.get(c)              (hotness == c.hotness)
boolean            int                   Chilis c = (Chilis)o;
-1                 hotness               args[0]
color              m.contains(c)         Integer.intValue
(this == c)        void                  color.equals(c.color)
Object o           String                0
&&                 ||
```

Answer (for Objective 6.2):

```
import java.util.*;
public class Enchilada {
  public static void main(String[] args) {
    Map<Chilis, String> m = new HashMap<Chilis, String>();
    Chilis myC = new Chilis("green", 4);
    m.put(new Chilis("red", 4), "4 alarm");
    m.put(new Chilis("green", 2), "mild");
    m.put(myC, "wow");
    Chilis c = new Chilis(args[0], Integer.parseInt(args[1]));
    System.out.println(m.get(c));
} }
class Chilis {
  Chilis(String c, int h) { color = c; hotness = h; }
  String color;
  private int hotness;
  public boolean equals(Object o) {
    Chilis c = (Chilis)o;
    if(color.equals(c.color) && (hotness == c.hotness))  return true;
    return false;
  }
  public int hashCode() { return hotness; }
}
```

54. Given:

```
2. public class Toolbox {
3.    static Toolbox st;
4.    public static void main(String[] args) {
5.       new Toolbox().go();
6.       // what's eligible?
7.    }
8.    void go() {
9.       MyInner in = new MyInner();
10.      Integer i3 = in.doInner();
11.      Toolbox t = new Toolbox();
12.      st = t;
13.      System.out.println(i3);
14.    }
15.    class MyInner {
16.       public Integer doInner() { return new Integer(34); }
17.    }
18. }
```

When the code reaches line 6, which are eligible for garbage collection? (Choose all that apply.)

A. st

B. in

C. i3

D. The object created on line 5.

E. The object created on line 9.

F. The object created on line 10.

G. The object created on line 11.

Answer (for Objective 7.4):

☑ D, E, and F are correct.

☒ A, B, and C are incorrect because only objects are considered by the GC. G is incorrect because main() could still access line 11's Toolbox object through st.

---

55. Given:

```
2. class Ball {
3.    static String s = "";
4.    void doStuff() { s += "bounce "; }
5. }
6. class Basketball extends Ball {
7.    void doStuff() { s += "swish "; }
8. }
9. public class Golfball extends Ball {
10.    public static void main(String[] args) {
11.       Ball b = new Golfball();
12.       Basketball bb = (Basketball)b;
13.       b.doStuff();
14.       bb.doStuff();
15.       System.out.println(s);
16.    }
17.    void doStuff() { s += "fore "; }
18. }
```

What is the result?

A. fore fore

B. fore swish

C. bounce swish

D. bounce bounce

E. Compilation fails.

F. An exception is thrown at runtime.

Answer (for Objective 5.2):

☑ **F** is correct. On line 12, a `ClassCastException` is thrown. Variable b refers to a subtype (`Golfball`), and it can be cast only to another `Golfball` reference variable.

☒ **A, B, C, D,** and **E** are incorrect based on the above.

56. Given the following three files:

```
2. package apollo;
3. import apollo.modules.Lunar;
4. public class Saturn {
5.    public static void main(String[] args){
6.      Lunar lunarModule = new Lunar();
7.      System.out.println(lunarModule);
8. } }
```

```
2. package apollo.modules;
3. public interface Module { /* more code  */ }
```

```
2. package apollo.modules;
3. public class Lunar implements Module { /* more code */ }
```

And given that `Module.java` and `Lunar.java` were successfully compiled and the directory structure is shown below:

```
$ROOT
  |-- apollo
  |      |-- modules
  |                |-- Lunar.class
  |-- controls.jar
  |          |-- apollo
  |                |-- modules
  |                      |-- Module.class
  |-- Saturn.java
```

Which are correct about compiling and running the `Saturn` class from the `$ROOT` directory? (Choose all that apply.)

A. The command for compiling is `javac -d . -cp . Saturn.java`

B. The command for compiling is `javac -d . -cp controls.jar Saturn.java`

C. The command for compiling is `javac -d . -cp .:controls.jar Saturn.java`

D. The command for running is `java -cp . apollo.Saturn`

E. The command for running is `java -cp controls.jar apollo.Saturn`

F. The command for running is `java -cp .:controls.jar apollo.Saturn`

G. The command for running is `java -cp controls.jar -cp . apollo.Saturn`

Answer (for Objective 7.5):

☑ **A, C,** and **F** are correct. In order to successfully compile the Saturn class, you ONLY need the Lunar class to be on the classpath, so **A** and **C** are correct.

☒ **F** is correct, because in order to successfully run the Saturn class, the classpath should include BOTH the JAR file and the base location of the Saturn and Lunar classes. Here, the JAR file is required because the Lunar class has to access the Module class at runtime. When specifying multiple locations for the classpath, each location should be separated with the `":"` symbol, although in real life that character depends on the platform. **B, D, E,** and **G** are incorrect based on the above.

---

57. Given:

```
5. class OOthing { void doStuff() { System.out.print("oo "); } }
6. class GuiThing extends OOthing {
7.   void doStuff() { System.out.print("gui "); }
8. }
9. public class Button extends GuiThing {
10.   void doStuff() { System.out.print("button "); }
11.   public static void main(String[] args) { new Button().go(); }
12.   void go() {
13.     GuiThing g = new GuiThing();
14.     // this.doStuff();
15.     // super.doStuff();
16.     // g.super.doStuff();
17.     // super.g.doStuff();
18.     // super.super.doStuff();
19. } }
```

If the commented lines are uncommented independently, which are true? (Choose all that apply.)

A. If line 14 is uncommented, `"button"` will be in the output.

B. If line 15 is uncommented, `"gui"` will be in the output.

C. If line 16 is uncommented, `"oo"` will be in the output.

D. If line 17 is uncommented, "oo" will be in the output.

E. If line 18 is uncommented, "oo" will be in the output.

Answer (for Objective 5.4):

☑ **A** and **B** use the correct syntax.

☒ **C, D,** and **E** are incorrect because none of them allow you to invoke OOThing .doStuff() (the super, super class of Button) from the Button class.

58. Given:

```
 2. import java.util.*;
 3. public class Salt {
 4.    public static void main(String[] args) {
 5.       Set s1 = new HashSet();
 6.       s1.add(0);
 7.       s1.add("1");
 8.       doStuff(s1);
 9.    }
10.    static void doStuff(Set<Number> s) {
11.       do2(s);
12.       Iterator i = s.iterator();
13.       while(i.hasNext())  System.out.print(i.next() + " ");
14.       Object[] oa = s.toArray();
15.       for(int x = 0; x < oa.length; x++)
16.          System.out.print(oa[x] + " ");
17.       System.out.println(s.contains(1));
18.    }
19.    static void do2(Set s2) { System.out.print(s2.size() + " "); }
20. }
```

What is the most likely result?

A. 2 0 1 0 1 true

B. 2 0 1 0 1 false

C. Compilation fails.

D. An exception is thrown at line 8.

E. An exception is thrown at line 13.

F. An exception is thrown at line 14.

G. An exception is thrown at line 19.

Answer (for Objective 6.3):

☑ **B** is correct. Set s1 (which contains a String and an Integer) can be iterated over, copied to an Object [], sized, and searched.

☒ **A** is incorrect because s1 doesn't contain an Integer with a value of 1. **C, D, E, F,** and **G** are incorrect because the code is all legal and runs without exception.

59. Given:

```
1. public class Begin {
2.    static int x;
3.    { int[] ia2 = {4,5,6}; }
4.    static {
5.       int[] ia = {1,2,3};
6.       for(int i = 0; i < 3; i++)
7.          System.out.print(ia[i] + " ");
8.       x = 7;
9.       System.out.print(x + " ");
10. } }
```

And, if the code compiles, the invocation:

```
java Begin
```

What is the result?

A. Compilation fails.

B. "1 2 3 7", with no exception thrown.

C. "1 2 3 7", followed by an exception.

D. "1 2 3", followed by an ExceptionInInitializerError

E. ExceptionInInitializerError is thrown before any output.

F. Some other exception is thrown before any other output.

Answer (for Objective 2.6):

☑ **C** is correct. If you invoke a .class file with no main(), the static init blocks will execute before throwing a NoSuchMethodError exception. (Note that you don't need to know the name of the NoSuchMethodError exception to get this question correct!)

☒ **A, B, D, E,** and **F** are incorrect based on the above.

60. Given:

```
2. public class Alamo {
3.    public static void main(String[] args) {
4.       try {
5.          assert(!args[0].equals("x")): "kate";
6.       } catch(Error e) { System.out.print("ae "); }
7.       finally {
8.          try {
9.             assert(!args[0].equals("y")): "jane";
10.         } catch(Exception e2) { System.out.print("ae2 "); }
11.         finally {
12.            throw new IllegalArgumentException();
13. } } } }
```

And, if the code compiles, the invocation:

```
java -ea Alamo y
```

Which will be included in the output? (Choose all that apply.)

A. ae

B. ae2

C. kate

D. jane

E. AssertionError

F. IllegalArgumentException

G. There is no output because compilation fails.

Answer (for Objectives 2.4 and 2.3):

☑ **F** is correct. Line 9 throws an `AssertionError` (which the second `catch` statement cannot catch). Before it can be reported, the second `finally` statement MUST run, which throws `IllegalArgumentException`, so the `AssertionError` never gets reported.

☒ **A, B, C, D, E,** and **G** are incorrect based on the above. (The code is legal.)

Analyzing Your Results

It's hard to know for sure, but our feeling is that the exam you just finished might be a bit easier than Exam 2. Because of that, the recommended plans listed in Table 6-1 might seem a little harsher. Again, a passing score on the OCP Java SE Programmer exam is 58.33 percent (35 out of 60 questions).

TABLE 6-1   What Your Score Means

Number of Correct Answers	Recommended Plan
0–28	First, do a LOT of studying. Then, return to the first full practice exam and retake the first three exams before attempting the next one.
29–35	Do some more studying, and retake a few exams before attempting the last one.
36–46	You're still on the boundary, and not quite ready for the last exam.
47–60	If this isn't your best score yet, you're not quite bombproof.

Revenge of the Study Tips

As we've mentioned, retaking these exams provides diminishing returns. Memory of the answers starts kicking in, rather than testing for knowledge of the topics. That said, if you're not getting at least 75 percent correct at this point, we'd advise you to do more studying, and then retake a couple of the previous exams before proceeding to the final exam in the book.

Review Your Exam Logs   Most candidates report that they have certain objectives where they are consistently weak. Study your exam logs. You should be able to determine areas where you can focus your studies.

Still Not Achieving 75 Percent?   The bottom line is that, one way or another, passing this exam takes a lot of work. Let's summarize our "Top Four Study Tips":

1. Write lots of code. By now you should have a library of at least 100 small programs you've written. Make more.

2. Use flashcards for memorization. Throw some out, add new ones, take them with you to the DMV, or wherever you have to stand in long lines.

3. Ask questions on JavaRanch.com, and then, ANSWER questions on JavaRanch.com.

4. Get a good Study Guide. If you're trying to study for the exam without a study guide, it might be time to get one. We understand that study guides can be expensive, but our feeling is that if you value your time at all, a good study guide is one of the best investments you can make.

7

Practice Exam 4

How Close Are You to Ready?

Our advice would be that if you're not getting at least 40 questions correct on the previous exams, do some more studying before you tackle this last one. If you are ready to take this exam, then remember that this is also one more opportunity to be honest with yourself.

Take a separate set of notes as you go along. Ask yourself how confident you are about your answers. Did you barely have enough knowledge about a certain topic, or did you find the questions well within your skill set? How about the time limit? Did you finish with lots of time left, or did you find that three hours was barely enough? When you're feeling good about your answers to all of these questions, go for it!

PRACTICE EXAM 4

The real exam has 60 questions and you are given three hours to complete it. On the real exam, and on all of the exams in this book, give yourself credit only for those questions that you answer 100 percent correctly. For instance, if a question has three correct answers and you get two of the three correct, you get zero credit. There is no partial credit. Good luck!

1. Given:

```
1. abstract class Vibrate {
2.    static String s = "-";
3.    Vibrate() {  s += "v"; }
4. }
5. public class Echo extends Vibrate {
6.    Echo() { this(7); s += "e"; }
7.    Echo(int x) { s += "e2"; }
8.    public static void main(String[] args) {
9.      System.out.print("made " + s + " ");
10.    }
11.    static {
12.      Echo e = new Echo();
13.      System.out.print("block " + s + " ");
14. } }
```

What is the result?

A. made -ve2e

B. block -ee2v

C. block -ve2e

D. made -eve2 block -eve2

E. made -ve2e block -ve2e

F. block -ve2e made -ve2e

G. block -ve2e made -ve2eve2e

H. Compilation fails.

2. Given:

```
3. public class KaChung {
4.    public static void main(String[] args) {
5.      String s = "";
6.      if(Integer.parseInt("011") == Integer.parseInt("9")) s += 1;
7.      if(021 == Integer.valueOf("17")) s += 2;
8.      if(1024 == new Integer(1024)) s += 3;
9.      System.out.println(s);
10. } }
```

What is the result?

A. 2

B. 3

C. 13

D. 23

E. 123

F. Compilation fails.

G. An exception is thrown at runtime.

3. Given the invocation "java GiveUp" and:

```
2. public class GiveUp {
3.    public static void main(String[] args) throws Exception {
4.       try {
5.          assert false;
6.          System.out.print("t ");
7.       }
8.       catch (Error e) {
9.          System.out.print("c ");
10.          throw new Exception();
11.       }
12.       finally { System.out.print("f "); }
13. } }
```

What is the result?

A. c

B. c f

C. t f

D. Compilation fails.

E. "c f " followed by an uncaught exception.

4. Given:

```
3. import java.util.*;
4. public class VC {
5.    public static void main(String[] args) {
6.       List<Integer> x = new ArrayList<Integer>();
7.       Integer[] a = {3, 1, 4, 1};
8.       x = Arrays.asList(a);
9.       a[3] = 2;
10.      x.set(0, 7);
11.      for(Integer i: x) System.out.print(i + " ");
12.      x.add(9);
13.      System.out.println(x);
14. } }
```

What is the result?

A. Compilation fails.

B. 3 1 4 2 [7, 1, 4, 1]

C. 3 1 4 2 [7, 1, 4, 2]

D. 7 1 4 2 [7, 1, 4, 2]

E. 3 1 4 2 [7, 1, 4, 1, 9]

F. 3 1 4 2 [7, 1, 4, 2, 9]

G. 7 1 4 2, followed by an exception.

H. 3 1 4 2, followed by an exception.

5. Given:

```
3. public class Honcho {
4.    static boolean b1 = false;
5.    static int z = 7;
6.    static Long y;
7.    public static void main(String[] args) {
8.      for(int i = 0; i < 4; i++)
9.        go(i);
10.   }
11.   static void go(int x) {
12.     try {
13.       if((x == 0) && (!b1 && z == 7)) System.out.print("0 ");
14.       if(x < 2 ^ x < 10) System.out.print("1 ");
15.       if((x == 2) &&
                (y == null | (y.longValue() == 0))) System.out.print("2 ");
16.       if(z <= (x + 4)) System.out.print("3 ");
17.     }
18.     catch(Exception e) { System.out.print("e "); }
19. } }
```

What is the result?

A. 0 1 2 3

B. 1 e 1 3

C. 0 1 e 1 3

D. 0 1 1 1 1 3

E. 1 1 1 2 1 3

F. 0 1 1 1 2 1 3

G. Compilation fails.

6. Given:

```
2. class Chilis {
3.    Chilis(String c, int h) { color = c; hotness = h; }
4.    String color;
5.    int hotness;
6.    public boolean equals(Object o) {
7.       Chilis c = (Chilis)o;
8.       if(this.color == c.color) return true;
9.       return false;
10.   }
11.   public int hashCode() { return (color.length() + hotness); }
12. }
```

If instances of class Chilis are to be used as keys in a Map, which are true? (Choose all that apply.)

A. The code will not compile.

B. The hashCode() and equals() contracts have been supported.

C. The equals() method is reflexive, symmetric, and transitive.

D. The Chilis class CANNOT be used to create keys to reliably add and retrieve entries in a Map.

E. If the hashCode() method is not considered, the equals() method could be an override that supports the equals() contract.

F. If the equals() method is not considered, the hashCode() method could be an override that supports the hashCode() contract.

7. Given:

```
2. package pack.clients;
3. import pack.banking.Bank;
4. public class Client{
5.    public static void main(String[] args){
6.       Bank bank = new Bank();
7.       System.out.println(bank.getMoney(2000L));
8. } }
```

And given that Client.java resides in the $ROOT directory and is not yet compiled. There is another class named pack.banking.Bank, which has a method called getMoney(long) that returns a value. Bank class is compiled and deployed into a JAR file called pack.jar, as shown in the following directory structure

```
$ROOT
    |-- Client.java
    |-- [pack.jar]
               |-- pack
                     |-- banking
                            |-- Bank.class
```

Which are correct about compiling or running the Client class from the $ROOT directory? (Choose all that apply.)

A. To compile, use `javac -cp pack.jar -d . Client.java`

B. To compile, use `javac -cp pack.jar#pack.banking.Bank -d . Client.java`

C. To compile, use `javac -cp * -d . Client.java`

D. To run, use `java -cp pack.jar pack.clients.Client`

E. To run, use `java -cp . -d pack.jar pack.clients.Client`

F. To run, use `java -cp . -cp pack.jar pack.clients.Client`

G. To run, use `java -cp .:pack.jar pack.clients.Client`

8. Given:

```
2. class Bird {
3.    public static String s = "";
4.    public static void fly() { s += "fly "; }
5. }
6. public class Hummingbird extends Bird {
7.    public static void fly() { s += "hover "; }
8.    public static void main(String[] args) {
9.       Bird b1 = new Bird();
10.      Bird b2 = new Hummingbird();
11.      Bird b3 = (Hummingbird)b2;
12.      Hummingbird b4 = (Hummingbird)b2;
13.
14.      b1.fly();  b2.fly();  b3.fly();  b4.fly();
15.      System.out.println(s);
16. } }
```

What is the result?

A. `fly fly fly fly`

B. `fly fly fly hover`

C. `fly fly hover hover`

D. `fly hover hover hover`

E. `hover hover hover hover`

F. Compilation fails.

G. An exception is thrown at runtime.

9. Given two files:

```
1. package com;
2. public class Extramuros {
3.    public static void howdy() { System.out.print("howdy "); }
4.    public static final Extramuros ex = new Extramuros();
```

```
5.    public int instVar = 42;
6.    public enum avout {OROLO, JAD};
7. }
```

```
1. // insert code here
   ...
6. public class Theorics {
7.    public static void main(String[] args) {
8.       Extramuros.howdy();
9.       System.out.print(Extramuros.avout.OROLO + " ");
10.      howdy();
11.      System.out.print(ex.instVar + " ");
12. } }
```

Which are the minimum line(s) of code to add at `"insert code here"` for the files to compile? (Choose all that apply.)

A. `import static com.*;`

B. `import com.Extramuros;`

C. `import com.Extramuros.*;`

D. `import static com.Extramuros;`

E. `import static com.Extramuros.*;`

F. Even with correct imports, the code will not compile due to other errors.

10. Given:

```
2. import java.text.*;
3. import java.util.*;
4. public class Vogue {
5.    public static void main(String[] args) {
6.       DateFormat df1 = DateFormat.getInstance();
7.       DateFormat df2 = DateFormat.getInstance(DateFormat.SHORT);
8.       DateFormat df3 = DateFormat.getDateInstance(DateFormat.FULL);
9.       DateFormat df4 = DateFormat.getDateInstance(DateFormat.EXTENDED);
10. } }
```

Which are true? (Choose all that apply.)

A. Line 2 is not necessary.

B. Line 3 is not necessary.

C. Compilation fails due to an error on line 6.

D. Compilation fails due to an error on line 7.

E. Compilation fails due to an error on line 8.

F. Compilation fails due to an error on line 9.

11. Given:

```
 2. public class Cult extends Thread {
 3.    static int count = 0;
 4.    public void run() {
 5.      for(int i = 0; i < 100; i++) {
 6.        if(i == 5 && count < 3) {
 7.          Thread t = new Cult(names[count++]);
 8.          t.start();
 9.          // insert code here
10.        }
11.        System.out.print(Thread.currentThread().getName() + " ");
12.      }
13.    }
14.    public static void main(String[] args) {
15.      new Cult("t0").start();
16.    }
17.    Cult(String s) { super(s); }
18.    String[] names = {"t1", "t2", "t3"};
19. }
```

And these two fragments:

I. `try { t.join(); }  catch(Exception e) { }`

II. `try { Thread.currentThread().join(); }  catch(Exception e) { }`

When each fragment is inserted independently at line 9, which are true? (Choose all that apply.)

A. With fragment I, t0 completes last.
B. With fragment I, t3 completes last.
C. With fragment II, t0 completes last.
D. With fragment II, t3 completes last.
E. With both fragments, compilation fails.
F. With fragment I, the code never completes.
G. With fragment II, the code never completes.

12. Which are true? (Choose all that apply.)

A. If a class's member's values can be retrieved, but not changed, without using the class's API, the class is not cohesive.
B. If a class's member's values can be retrieved, but not changed, without using the class's API, tight coupling could occur.

C. If a class's member's values can be retrieved, but not changed, without using the class's API, the class is not well encapsulated.

D. If a class's member's values can be updated only through the use of its API, or by an inner class, the class is well encapsulated.

E. If a class's member's values can be updated only through the use of its API, or by an inner class, the class is NOT well encapsulated.

13. Given:

```
3. public class BigData {
4.    static BigData bd;
5.    public static void main(String[] args) {
6.       new BigData().doStuff();
7.       // do lots of memory intensive stuff
...      // JVM finds an eligible BigData object for GC
...      // JVM invokes finalize()
...      // do more stuff
48.    }
49.    void doStuff() {  }
50.    // insert code here
51.       bd = this;
52.    }
53. }
54. class MyException extends Exception { }
```

and the following four fragments:

I. `protected void finalize() throws Throwable {`

II. `protected void finalize() {`

III. `protected void finalize() throws MyException {`

IV. `void finalize() {`

If the fragments are inserted, independently, at line 50, which are true? (Choose all that apply.)

A. Fragment I compiles.

B. Fragment II compiles.

C. Fragment III compiles.

D. Fragment IV compiles.

E. Of those that compile, the GC will collect any given object after the JVM has called `finalize()` on that object.

F. Because of the way `finalize()` has been overridden, the GC will never collect eligible objects of type `BigData`.

14. Given:

```
2. interface Clickable {  void click();  }
3. // insert code here
```

Which code, inserted independently at line 3, will compile? (Choose all that apply.)

A. `interface Keyboard extends Clickable { }`

B. `interface Keyboard extends Clickable { void click(); }`

C. `interface Keyboard extends Clickable { void doClick(); }`

D. `interface Keyboard extends Clickable { void click() { ; } }`

E. `interface Keyboard extends Clickable { protected void click(); }`

F. `interface Keyboard extends Clickable { void click(); void doClick(); }`

15. Given:

```
1. public class Argue {
2.    static boolean b;
3.    static int x = 0;
4.    public static void main(String[] args) {
5.       int guess = (int)(Math.random() * 5);
6.       if(guess < 0) assert false;
7.       assert b = true;
8.       assert x = 0;
9.       assert x == 0;
10. } }
```

Which are true? (Choose all that apply.)

A. The code compiles.

B. The `assert` on line 6 is appropriate.

C. Compilation fails due to an error on line 6.

D. Compilation fails due to an error on line 7.

E. Compilation fails due to an error on line 8.

F. Compilation fails due to an error on line 9.

16. Given two files:

```
1. package com.wickedlysmart2;
2. public class Utils {
3.    void do1() { System.out.print("do1 "); }
4.    protected void do2() { System.out.print("do2 "); }
5.    public void do3() { System.out.print("do3 "); }
6. }
```

```
1. import com.wickedlysmart2.*;
2. public class UPS extends Utils {
3.   public static void main(String[] args) {
4.     Utils u = new Utils();
5.     u.do1();
6.     u.do2();
7.     u.do3();
8. } }
```

What is the result? (Choose all that apply.)

A. do1 do2 do3

B. "do1 ", followed by an exception.

C. Compilation fails due to an error on line 4 of UPS.

D. Compilation fails due to an error on line 5 of UPS.

E. Compilation fails due to an error on line 6 of UPS.

F. Compilation fails due to an error on line 7 of UPS.

17. Given:

```
4. class Electricity { int getCharge() { return 24; } }
5. public class Voltage extends Electricity {
6.   enum volts {twelve, twentyfour, oneten};
7.   public static void main(String[] args) {
8.     volts v = volts.twentyfour;
9.     switch (v) {
10.      case twelve:
11.        System.out.print("12 ");
12.      default:
13.        System.out.print(getCharge() + " ");
14.      case oneten:
15.        System.out.print("110 ");
16. } } }
```

What is the result? (Choose all that apply.)

A. 24

B. 24 110

C. 24 110 12

D. Compilation fails due to a misuse of enums.

E. Compilation fails due to a non-enum issue.

18. Given:

```
2. import java.io.*;
3. public class Uboat {
4.   public static void main(String[] args) {
```

```
5.      try {
6.         File f1 = new File("sub1");
7.         f1.mkdir();
8.         File f2 = new File(f1,"sub2");
9.         File f3 = new File(f1,"sub3");
10.        PrintWriter pw = new PrintWriter(f3);
11.      } catch (Exception e) { System.out.println("ouch"); }
12. } }
```

And, if the code compiles, what is the result if "java Uboat" is invoked TWICE? (Choose all that apply.)

A. Compilation fails.

B. The second invocation produces the output "ouch"

C. The second invocation creates at least one new file as a peer to the new directory.

D. The first invocation creates a new directory and one new file in that directory.

E. The first invocation creates a new directory and two new files in that directory.

F. The first invocation creates a new directory and at least one new file as a peer to it.

19. Given:

```
2. class Car {
3.    private Car() { }
4.    protected Car(int x) { }
5. }
6. public class MG extends Car {
7.    // MG(int x) { }
8.    // MG(int x) { super(); }
9.    // MG(int x) { super(x); }
10.   // private MG(int x) { super(x); }
11.   // MG() { }
12.   // MG() { this(); }
13.   // MG() { this(6); }
14.   // MG() { super(7); }
15.   public static void main(String[] args) {
16.      new MG(7);
17.      new MG();
18. } }
```

Which sets of constructors can be uncommented for the code to compile? (Choose all that apply.)

A. Line 7 and line 11.

B. Line 7 and line 14.

C. Line 8 and line 12.

D. Line 8 and line 13.

E. Line 9 and line 12.

F. Line 9 and line 13.

G. Line 10 and line 11.

H. Line 10 and line 14.

20. Given:

```
2. interface Gadget {
3.    int patent = 12345;
4.    Gadget doStuff();
5. }
6. public class TimeMachine implements Gadget {
7.    int patent = 34567;
8.    public static void main(String[] args) {
9.       new TimeMachine().doStuff();
10.    }
11.    TimeMachine doStuff() {
12.       System.out.println( ++patent);
13.       return new TimeMachine();
14. } }
```

If javac is invoked twice:

```
javac -source 1.4 TimeMachine.java
javac TimeMachine.java
```

And, if "java TimeMachine" is invoked whenever TimeMachine compiles, what is the result?

A. First, compilation fails, then 12346

B. First, compilation fails, then 34568

C. First, 12346, then compilation fails.

D. First, 34568, then compilation fails.

E. First, 12346, then 34568

F. Compilation fails on both javac invocations.

21. Given:

```
1. import java.util.*;
2. public class LogSplitter {
3.    public static void main(String[] args) {
4.       for(int x = 1; x < args.length; x++)
5.          System.out.print(args[0].split(args[x]).length + " ");
6. } }
```

And the command-line invocation:

```
java LogSplitter "x1 23 y #" "\d" "\s" "\w"
```

What is the result?

A.   4 4 6

B.   3 3 6

C.   5 4 6

D.   4 6 4

E.   3 6 3

F.   5 6 4

G.   Compilation fails.

H.   An exception is thrown at runtime.

22.   Given this code in a method:

```
3.        int y, count = 0;
4.        for(int x = 3; x < 6; x++) {
5.          try {
6.            switch(x) {
7.              case 3: count++;
8.              case 4: count++;
9.              case 7: count++;
10.             case 9: { y = 7 / (x - 4); count += 10; }
11.           }
12.         } catch (Exception ex) { count++; }
13.       }
14.       System.out.println(count);
```

What is the result?

A.   2

B.   15

C.   16

D.   25

E.   26

F.   Compilation fails.

G.   An exception is thrown with no other output.

23.   Given:

```
5. abstract class Thing { static String s = ""; Thing() { s += "t "; } }
6. class Steel extends Thing {
7.    Steel() { s += "s "; }
8.    Steel(String s1) {
9.      s += s1;
10.     new Steel();
```

```
11.    }
12. }
13. public class Tungsten extends Steel {
14.    Tungsten(String s1) {
15.       s += s1;
16.       new Steel(s);
17.    }
18.    public static void main(String[] args) {
19.       new Tungsten("tu ");
20.       System.out.println(s);
21. } }
```

What is the result?

A. s tu s tu s

B. t s tu t s t s

C. t s tu t t s tu t s

D. t tu t s tu t t tu t s tu t s

E. Compilation fails.

F. An exception is thrown at runtime.

24. You want to add a capability to MyStuff so that collections of MyStuff objects can be sorted in a "natural" order. Use the fragments to fill in the blanks to create this capability. Note: Not all the fragments will be used, not all the blanks have to be filled (maybe), and you can use each fragment more than once

Second note: As in the real exam's Drag-and-Drop questions, there may be more than one correct answer. Here, give yourself bonus points if you create more than one correct answer. In the real exam, you'll get full credit for ANY correct answer.

```
import java.util.*;
class MyStuff _____  _____ {
   MyStuff(String n, int v) { name = n; value = v; }
   String name; int value;

   _____  _____  _____  _____ {
   return _____  _____ ;
   }
   public String toString() { return name + " " + value + " "; }
}
```

Fragments:

Comparable	Comparator	public
Comparable<MyStuff>	Comparator<MyStuff>	protected
implements	extends	boolean

(MyStuff m)	(MyStuff a, MyStuff b)	String
name.compareTo	compare	(b.name)
value - m.value	compares	(m.name)
m.value - value	sort	(name, n.name)
name.equals(m.name)	compareTo	(a.name, b.name)
a.name.compareTo	a.name.equals(b.name)	int

25. Given:

```
2. public class Swanky {
3.    Swanky s;
4.    public static void main(String[] args) {
5.      Swanky s1 = new Swanky();
6.      s1.s = new Swanky();
7.      go(s1.s);
8.      Swanky s2 = go(s1);
9.      if(s2.s.equals(s1)) System.out.print("1 ");
10.     if(s2.equals(s1)) System.out.print("2 ");
11.     if(s1.s.equals(s1)) System.out.print("3 ");
12.     if(s2.s.equals(s2)) System.out.print("4 ");
13.    }
14.   static Swanky go(Swanky s) {
15.     Swanky gs = new Swanky();
16.     gs.s = s;
17.     return gs;
18. } }
```

What is the result?

A. 1

B. 1 2

C. 1 2 4

D. Compilation fails.

E. "1 ", followed by an exception.

F. "1 2 ", followed by an exception.

26. Given:

```
2. import java.util.*;
3. public class AndOver {
4.   public static void main(String[] args) {
5.     List g = new ArrayList();
6.     g.add(new Gaited("Eyra"));
7.     g.add(new Gaited("Vafi"));
8.     g.add(new Gaited("Andi"));
9.     Iterator i2 = g.iterator();
```

```
10.      while(i2.hasNext()) {
11.         System.out.print(i2.next().name + " ");
12. } } }
13. class Gaited {
14.    public String name;
15.    Gaited(String n) { name = n; }
16. }
```

What is the result?

A. Vafi Andi

B. Andi Eyra Vafi

C. Andi Vafi Eyra

D. Eyra Vafi Andi

E. Compilation fails.

F. The output order is unpredictable.

27. Given:

```
2. interface Plant {
3.    int greenness = 7;
4.    void grow();
5. }
6. class Grass implements Plant {
7.    // static int greenness = 5;
8.    // int greenness = 5;
9.    public static void main(String[] args) {
10.      int greenness = 2;
11.      new Grass().grow();
12.    }
13.    public void grow() {
14.       System.out.println(++greenness);
15. } }
```

Which are true? (Choose all that apply.)

A. As the code stands, the output is 3.

B. As the code stands, the output is 8.

C. As the code stands, it will NOT compile.

D. If line 7 is un-commented, the output is 6.

E. If line 8 is un-commented, the output is 6.

F. If line 7 is un-commented, the output is 8.

G. If line 7 is un-commented, the code will NOT compile.

28. Given:

```
2. class Grab {
3.   static int x = 5;
4.   synchronized void adjust(Grab y) {
5.     System.out.print(x-- + " ");
6.     y.view(y);
7.   }
8.   synchronized void view(Grab z) { if(x > 0) z.adjust(z); }
9. }
10. public class Grapple implements Runnable {
11.   static Thread t1;
12.   static Grab g, g2;
13.   public void run() {
14.     if(Thread.currentThread().getId() == t1.getId()) g.adjust(g2);
15.     else g2.view(g);
16.   }
17.   public static void main(String[] args) {
18.     g = new Grab();
19.     g2 = new Grab();
20.     t1 = new Thread(new Grapple());
21.     t1.start();
22.     new Thread(new Grapple()).start();
23. } }
```

Which are true? (Choose all that apply.)

A. Compilation fails.

B. The output could be 5 4 3 2 1

C. The output could be 5 4 3 2 1 0

D. The program could produce thousands of lines of output.

E. The program could deadlock before producing any output.

F. The output could be "5 ", followed by the program deadlocking.

29. Given:

```
3. import java.util.*;
4. public class Corner {
5.   public static void main(String[] args) {
6.     TreeSet<String> t1 = new TreeSet<String>();
7.     TreeSet<String> t2 = new TreeSet<String>();
8.     t1.add("b");  t1.add("7");
9.     t2 = (TreeSet)t1.subSet("5", "c");
10.     try {
11.       t1.add("d");
12.       t2.add("6");
```

```
13.        t2.add("3");
14.      }
15.      catch (Exception e) { System.out.print("ex "); }
16.      System.out.println(t1 + " " + t2);
17. } }
```

What is the result?

A. `[6, 7, b] [6, 7, b]`

B. `[6, 7, b, d] [6, 7, b]`

C. `ex [6, 7, b] [6, 7, b]`

D. `ex [6, 7, b, d] [6, 7, b]`

E. `[3, 6, 7, b, d] [6, 7, b]`

F. `ex [6, 7, b, d] [6, 7, b, d]`

G. Compilation fails due to error(s) in the code.

30. Given the current directory is bigApp, and the directory structure:

```
bigApp
    |-- classes
              |-- Cloned.class
              |-- com
                     |-- Cloned.class
                     |-- wickedlysmart
                                   |-- Cloned.class
```

And the three files:

```
public class Cloned {
  public static void main(String[] args) { System.out.println("classes"); }
}
public class Cloned {
  public static void main(String[] args) { System.out.println("com"); }
}
public class Cloned {
  public static void main(String[] args) { System.out.println("ws"); }
}
```

Have been compiled into the classes, com, and wickedlysmart directories, respectively.

Which will produce the output `"ws"`? (Choose all that apply.)

A. `java -cp wickedlysmart:. Cloned`

B. `java -cp classes/com/wickedlysmart Cloned`

C. `java -cp classes/com/wickedlysmart:classes Cloned`

> D. `java -cp classes:classes/com/wickedlysmart Cloned`
> E. `java -cp .:classes/com/wickedlysmart:classes Cloned`
> F. `java -cp .:classes/com:classes/com/wickedlysmart Cloned`

31. Given:

```
1. import java.io.*;
2. public class Edgy {
3.    public static void main(String[] args) {
4.      try {
5.        wow();
6.        // throw new IOException();
7.      } finally {
8.        // throw new Error();
9.        // throw new IOException();
10.      }
11.    }
12.    static void wow() {
13.      // throw new IllegalArgumentException();
14.      // throw new IOException();
15. } }
```

And given that `IOException` is a direct subclass of `java.lang.Exception:` and that `IllegalArgumentException` is a runtime exception, which of the following, if uncommented independently, will compile? (Choose all that apply.)

A. Line 6

B. Line 8

C. Line 9

D. Line 13

E. Line 14

F. The code will NOT compile as is.

32. Given two files:

```
1. package com;
2. public class MyClass {
3.    public static void howdy() { System.out.print("howdy "); }
4.    public static final int myConstant = 343;
5.    public static final MyClass mc = new MyClass();
6.    public int instVar = 42;
7. }


11. import com.MyClass;
12. public class TestImports2 {
```

```
13.    public static void main(String[] args) {
14.       MyClass.howdy();
15.       System.out.print(MyClass.myConstant + " ");
16.       System.out.print(myConstant + " ");
17.       howdy();
18.       System.out.print(mc.instVar + " ");
19.       System.out.print(instVar + " ");
20.  } }
```

What is the result? (Choose all that apply.)

A. howdy 343 343 howdy 42 42

B. Compilation fails due to an error on line 14.

C. Compilation fails due to an error on line 15.

D. Compilation fails due to an error on line 16.

E. Compilation fails due to an error on line 17.

F. Compilation fails due to an error on line 18.

G. Compilation fails due to an error on line 19.

33. Given this code inside a method:

```
13.    int count = 0;
14.    outer:
15.    for(int x = 0; x < 5; x++) {
16.       middle:
17.       for(int y = 0; y < 5; y++) {
18.          if(y == 1) continue middle;
19.          if(y == 3) break middle;
20.          count++;
21.       }
22.       if(x > 2) continue outer;
23.          count = count + 10;
24.    }
25.    System.out.println("count: " + count);
```

What is the result?

A. count: 33

B. count: 40

C. count: 45

D. count: 65

E. Compilation fails.

F. The code runs in an endless loop.

34. Given:

```
2. public class Organic<E> {
3.    void react(E e) { }
4.    static void main(String[] args) {
5.       // Organic<? extends Organic> compound = new Aliphatic<Organic>();
6.       // Organic<? super Aliphatic> compound = new Aliphatic<Organic>();
7.       compound.react(new Organic());
8.       compound.react(new Aliphatic());
9.       compound.react(new Hexane());
10. } }
11. class Aliphatic<F> extends Organic<F> { }
12. class Hexane<G> extends Aliphatic<G> { }
```

Which, taken independently, are true? (Choose all that apply.)

A. If line 5 is uncommented, compilation fails due to an error at line 7.

B. If line 5 is uncommented, compilation fails due to an error at line 8.

C. If line 5 is uncommented, compilation fails due to an error at line 9.

D. If line 6 is uncommented, compilation fails due to an error at line 7.

E. If line 6 is uncommented, compilation fails due to an error at line 8.

F. If line 6 is uncommented, compilation fails due to an error at line 9.

35. Given:

```
4. public class Hemlock {
5.    static StringBuffer sb;
6.    StringBuffer sb2;
7.    public static void main(String[] args) {
8.       sb = sb.append(new Hemlock().go(new StringBuffer("hey")));
9.       System.out.println(sb);
10.   }
11.   { sb2 = new StringBuffer("hi "); }
12.   StringBuffer go(StringBuffer s) {
13.      System.out.print(s + " oh " + sb2);
14.      return new StringBuffer("ey");
15.   }
16.   static { sb = new StringBuffer("yo "); }
17. }
```

What is the result?

A. yo ey

B. hey oh hi

C. hey oh hi ey

D. oh hi hey

E. hey oh hi yo ey

F. yo hey oh hi ey

G. Compilation fails.

H. An exception is thrown at runtime.

36. Given:

```
1. class Hotel {
2.   static void doStuff(int x) {
3.     assert (x < 0) : "hotel";
4.   }
5. }
6. public class Motel13 extends Hotel {
7.   public static void main(String[] args) {
8.     doStuff(-5);
9.     int y = 0;
10.     assert (y < 0) : "motel";
11. } }
```

Which of the following invocations will run without exception? (Choose all that apply.)

A. java Motel13

B. java -ea Motel13

C. java -da:Hotel Motel13

D. java -da:Motel13 Motel13

E. java -ea -da:Hotel Motel13

F. java -ea -da:Motel13 Motel13

37. Given:

```
3. class One {
4.   void go1() { System.out.print("1 "); }
5.   final void go2() { System.out.print("2 "); }
6.   private void go3() { System.out.print("3 "); }
7. }
8. public class OneB extends One {
9.   void go1() { System.out.print("1b "); }
10.   void go3() { System.out.print("3b "); }
11.
12.   public static void main(String[] args) {
13.     new OneB().go1();
14.     new One().go1();
15.     new OneB().go2();
16.     new OneB().go3();
17.     new One().go3();
18. } }
```

What is the result?

A.   1 1 2 3 3

B.   1b 1 2 3b 3

C.   1b 1b 2 3b 3b

D.   Compilation fails due to a single error.

E.   Compilation fails due to errors on more than one line.

38.   Given:

```
3. public class Gauntlet {
4.    public static void main(String[] args) {
5.       String r = "0";
6.       int x = 3, y = 4;
7.       boolean test = false;
8.       if((x > 2) || (test = true))
9.       if((y > 5) || (++x == 4))
10.      if((test == true) || (++y == 4))
11.         r += "1";
12.      else if(y == 5) r += "2";
13.      else r += "3";
14.      else r += "4";
15.      // else r += "5";
16.      System.out.println(r);
17. } }
```

And given that, if necessary you can add line 15 to make the code compile, what is the result? (Choose all that apply.)

A.   At line 10, test will equal true

B.   At line 10, test will equal false

C.   The output will be 02

D.   The output will be 03

E.   The output will be 023

F.   The code will compile as is.

G.   The code will only compile if line 15 is added

39.   Given:

```
2. import rt.utils.Remote;
3. public class Controller{
4.    public static void main(String[] args){
5.       Remote remote = new Remote();
6. }  }
```

And rt.utils.Remote class is properly bundled into a JAR file called rtutils.jar.

And given the following steps:

P. Place rtutils.jar in the $ROOT directory

Q. Extract rtutils.jar and put rt directory with its subdirectories in the $ROOT directory

R. Extract rtutils.jar and place Remote.class in the $ROOT directory

S. Place rtutils.jar in the $JAVA_HOME/jre/lib/ext directory

X. Compile using: javac -cp rtutils.jar Controller.java

Y. Compile using: javac Controller.java

Z. Compile using: javac -cp . Controller.java

If Controller.java resides in the $ROOT directory, which set(s) of steps will compile the Controller class? (Choose all that apply.)

A. P -> X

B. Q -> Y

C. R -> Z

D. P -> Z

E. R -> Y

F. S -> X

G. S -> Z

40. Given:

```
2. public class Boot {
3.    static String s;
4.    static { s = ""; }
5.    { System.out.print("shinier "); }
6.    static { System.out.print(s.concat("better ")); }
7.    Boot() { System.out.print(s.concat("bigger ")); }
8.    public static void main(String[] args) {
9.       new Boot();
10.      System.out.println("boot");
11. } }
```

What is the result?

A. better bigger boot

B. better bigger shinier boot

C. better shinier bigger boot

D. bigger shinier better boot

E. shinier better bigger boot

F. A NullPointerException is thrown at runtime.

G. An ExceptionInInitializationError is thrown at runtime.

41. Fill in the blanks using the following fragments, so the code compiles and produces the output:
"0 4 "

Note: You might not need to fill in all of the blanks, you won't use all of the fragments, and each fragment can be used only once.

Code:

```
import _____
public class Latte {
  public static void main(String[] args) {
    Pattern p = _____
    Matcher m = p.matcher(_____);
    while(_____)
        System.out.print(_____ + " ");
} }
```

Fragments:

```
java.util.*;                 Pattern.getPattern("aba");
Pattern.compile("aba");      "ab aa ba"
new Pattern("aba");          " aba baabaa ba"
m.find()                     "abaababa"
m.next()                     "abababa"
m.hasNext()                  m.start()
java.regex.*;                m.match()
java.util.regex.*;
```

42. Given:

```
3. public static void main(String[] args) {
4.    try {
5.       throw new Error();
6.    }
7.    catch (Error e) {
8.       try { throw new RuntimeException(); }
9.       catch (Throwable t) { }
10.    }
11.    System.out.println("phew");
12. }
```

Which are true? (Choose all that apply.)

A. The output is phew

B. The code runs without output.

C. Compilation fails due to an error on line 5.

D. Compilation fails due to an error on line 7.

E. Compilation fails due to an error on line 8.

F. Compilation fails due to an error on line 9.

43. Given:

```
1. import java.util.*;
2. public class Analyzer {
3.    static List<Exception> me;
4.    Exception myEx;
5.    public static void main(String[] args) {
6.      Analyzer[] aa = {new Analyzer(), new Analyzer()};
7.      me = new ArrayList<Exception>();
8.      for(int i = 0; i < 2; i++) {
9.        try {
10.         if(i == 0) throw new Exception();
11.         if(i == 1) throw new MyException();
12.       }
13.       catch(Exception e) {
14.         me.add(e);
15.         aa[i].myEx = e;
16.       }
17.     }
18.     System.out.println(aa.length + " " + me.size());
19.     aa = null; me = null;
20.     // do more stuff
21. } }
22. class MyException extends Exception { }
```

When line 20 is reached, how many objects are eligible for garbage collection?

A. 2

B. 4

C. 5

D. 6

E. 7

F. 8

44. Given the following from the java.io.File API:

Field Summary: static String separator

Method Summary: static File[] listRoots()

And given:

```
2. // insert code here
3. // insert code here
4. public class Eieio {
5.   public static void main(String[] args) {
6.     try {
7.       String s = "subdir" + separator + "myFile.txt";
8.       java.io.File f = new java.io.File(s);
```

```
9.          java.io.FileReader fr = new java.io.FileReader(f);
10.         java.io.File[] r = listRoots();
11.         fr.close();
12.       }
13.     catch(Exception e) { }
14. } }
```

And the following four fragments:

I. `import java.io.*;`

II. `import static java.io.File.*;`

III. `import static java.io.File.separator;`

IV. `import static java.io.File.listRoots;`

Which set(s) of fragments, inserted independently on lines 2 and/or 3, will compile? (Choose all that apply.)

A. Fragment I

B. Fragment II

C. Fragments I and III

D. Fragments I and IV

E. Fragments II and IV

F. Fragments III and IV

45. Given:

```
1. import java.util.*;
2. public class Bucket {
3.    public static void main(String[] args) {
4.       Set<String> hs = new HashSet<String>();
5.       Set<String> lh = new LinkedHashSet<String>();
6.       Set<String> ts = new TreeSet<String>();
7.       List<String> al = new ArrayList<String>();
8.       String[] v = {"1", "3", "1", "2"};
9.       for(int i=0; i< v.length; i++) {
10.        hs.add(v[i]);  lh.add(v[i]);  ts.add(v[i]);  al.add(v[i]);
11.      }
12.      Iterator it = hs.iterator();
13.      while(it.hasNext()) System.out.print(it.next() + " ");
14.      Iterator it2 = lh.iterator();
15.      while(it2.hasNext()) System.out.print(it2.next() + " ");
16.      Iterator it3 = ts.iterator();
17.      while(it3.hasNext()) System.out.print(it3.next() + " ");
18.      Iterator it5 = al.iterator();
19.      while(it5.hasNext()) System.out.print(it5.next() + " ");
20. } }
```

Which statements are true? (Choose all that apply.)

A. An exception is thrown at runtime.

B. Compilation fails due to an error on line 18.

C. "1 3 2" is only guaranteed to be in the output once.

D. "1 2 3" is only guaranteed to be in the output once.

E. "1 3 2" is guaranteed to be in the output more than once.

F. "1 2 3" is guaranteed to be in the output more than once.

G. "1 3 1 2" is guaranteed to be in the output at least once.

H. Compilation fails due to error(s) on lines other than line 18.

46. Given:

```
 2. public class Maize {
 3.    public static void main(String[] args) {
 4.       String s = "12";
 5.       s.concat("ab");
 6.       s = go(s);
 7.       System.out.println(s);
 8.    }
 9.    static String go(String s) {
10.       s.concat("56");
11.       return s;
12. } }
```

What is the result?

A. ab

B. 12

C. ab56

D. 12ab

E. 1256

F. 12ab56

G. Compilation fails.

47. Given:

```
 4. class MySuper { protected MySuper() { System.out.print("ms "); } }
 5. public class MyTester extends MySuper {
 6.    private MyTester() { System.out.print("mt "); }
 7.    public static void main(String[] args) {
 8.       new MySuper();
```

```
 9.      class MyInner {
10.         private MyInner() { System.out.print("mi "); }
11.         { new MyTester(); }
12.         { new MySuper(); }
13.      }
14.      new MyInner();
15. } }
```

What is the result?

A. ms mi mt ms

B. ms mt ms mi

C. ms mi ms mt ms

D. ms ms mt ms mi

E. Compilation fails.

F. An exception is thrown at runtime.

48. Given:

```
 2. public class Tshirt extends Thread {
 3.    public static void main(String[] args) {
 4.       System.out.print(Thread.currentThread().getId() + " ");
 5.       Thread t1 = new Thread(new Tshirt());
 6.       Thread t2 = new Thread(new Tshirt());
 7.       t1.start();
 8.       t2.run();
 9.    }
10.    public void run() {
11.       for(int i = 0; i < 2; i++)
12.          System.out.print(Thread.currentThread().getId() + " ");
13. } }
```

Which are true? (Choose all that apply.)

A. No output is produced.

B. The output could be 1 1 9 9 1

C. The output could be 1 2 9 9 2

D. The output could be 1 9 9 9 9

E. An exception is thrown at runtime.

F. Compilation fails due to an error on line 4.

G. Compilation fails due to an error on line 8.

49. Given:

```
14.    FileWriter fw1 =
           new FileWriter(new File("f1.txt"));
15.    FileWriter fw2 =
           new FileWriter(new BufferedWriter(new PrintWriter("f2.txt")));
16.    PrintWriter pw1 =
           new PrintWriter(new BufferedWriter(new FileWriter("f3.txt")));
17.    PrintWriter pw2 =
           new PrintWriter(new FileWriter(new File("f4.txt")));
```

And given the proper imports and error handling, what is the result?

A. Compilation succeeds.

B. Compilation fails due to multiple errors.

C. Compilation fails due only to an error on line 14.

D. Compilation fails due only to an error on line 15.

E. Compilation fails due only to an error on line 16.

F. Compilation fails due only to an error on line 17.

50. Given:

```
2. import java.util.*;
3. public class GIS {
4.    public static void main(String[] args) {
5.       TreeMap<String, String> m1 = new TreeMap<String, String>();
6.       m1.put("a", "amy"); m1.put("f", "frank");
7.       NavigableMap<String, String> m2 = m1.descendingMap();
8.       try {
9.         m1.put("j", "john");
10.        m2.put("m", "mary");
11.      }
12.      catch (Exception e) { System.out.print("ex "); }
13.      m1.pollFirstEntry();
14.      System.out.println(m1 + " " + m2);
15. } }
```

What is the result?

A. {f=frank, j=john} {f=frank}

B. {f=frank, j=john} {m=mary, f=frank}

C. ex {f=frank, j=john} {f=frank}

D. {f=frank, j=john, m=mary} {m=mary, j=john, f=frank}

E. ex {f=frank, j=john, m=mary} {f=frank}

F. ex {f=frank, j=john, m=mary} {f=frank, a=amy}

G. {a=amy, f=frank, j=john, m=mary} {f=frank, a=amy}

H. Compilation fails due to error(s) in the code.

51. Given:

```
2. public class Clover extends Harrier {
3.    String bark() { return "feed me "; }
4.    public static void main(String[] args) {
5.       Dog[] dogs = new Dog[3];
6.       dogs[0] = new Harrier();
7.       dogs[1] = (Dog)new Clover();
8.       dogs[2] = (Dog)new Harrier();
9.       for(Dog d: dogs)  System.out.print(d.bark());
10. } }
11. class Dog { String bark() { return "bark "; } }
12. class Harrier extends Dog { String bark() { return "woof "; } }
```

What is the result? (Choose all that apply.)

A. bark bark bark

B. woof bark bark

C. woof feed me woof

D. Compilation fails due to an error on line 6.

E. Compilation fails due to an error on line 7.

F. Compilation fails due to an error on line 8.

G. Compilation fails due to an error on line 9.

52. Given:

```
1. public class Egg<E extends Object> {
2.    E egg;
3.    public Egg(E egg) {
4.       this.egg=egg;
5.    }
6.    public E getEgg() {
7.       return egg;
8.    }
9.    public static void main(String[] args) {
10.      Egg<Egg> egg1 = new Egg(42);
11.      Egg egg2 = new Egg<Egg>(egg1.getEgg());
12.      Egg egg3 = egg1.getEgg();
13. } }
```

Which are true? (Choose all that apply).

A. Compilation fails.

B. An exception is thrown at runtime.

C. Line 10 compiles with a warning.

D. Line 10 compiles without warnings.

E. Line 11 compiles with a warning.

F. Line 11 compiles without warnings.

53. Given:

```
2. public class Tolt {
3.    public static void checkIt(int a) {
4.      if(a == 1)  throw new IllegalArgumentException();
5.    }
6.    public static void main(String[] args) {
7.      for(int x=0; x<2; x++)
8.        try {
9.          System.out.print("t ");
10.          checkIt(x);
11.          System.out.print("t2 ");
12.        }
13.        finally { System.out.print("f "); }
14. } }
```

What is the result?

A. "t t2 f t "

B. "t t2 f t f "

C. "t t2 f t t2 f "

D. "t t2 f t ", followed by an exception.

E. "t t2 f t f ", followed by an exception.

F. "t t2 f t t2 f ", followed by an exception.

G. Compilation fails.

54. Given:

```
2. class Noodle {
3.    String name;
4.    Noodle(String n) { name = n; }
5. }
6. class AsianNoodle extends Noodle {
7.    public boolean equals(Object o) {
8.      AsianNoodle n = (AsianNoodle)o;
9.      if(name.equals(n.name))  return true;
10.      return false;
11.    }
12.    public int hashCode() { return name.length(); }
13.    AsianNoodle(String s) { super(s); }
14. }
15. public class Soba extends AsianNoodle {
```

```
16.    public static void main(String[] args) {
17.       Noodle n1 = new Noodle("bob");   Noodle n2 = new Noodle("bob");
18.       AsianNoodle a1 = new AsianNoodle("fred");
19.       AsianNoodle a2 = new AsianNoodle("fred");
20.       Soba s1 = new Soba("jill");   Soba s2 = new Soba("jill");
21.       System.out.print(n1.equals(n2) + " " + (n1 == n2) + " | ");
22.       System.out.print(a1.equals(a2) + " " + (a1 == a2) + " | ");
23.       System.out.println(s1.equals(s2) + " " + (s1 == s2));
24.    }
25.    Soba(String s) { super(s); }
26. }
```

What is the result?

A. Compilation fails.

B. true true | true true | true true

C. true false | true false | true false

D. false false | true false | true false

E. false false | true false | false false

F. false false | false false | false false

55. Given:

```
2. public class Checkout2 implements Runnable {
3.    void doStuff() { }
4.    synchronized void doSynch() {
5.       try { Thread.sleep(1000); }
6.       catch (Exception e) { System.out.print("e "); }
7.    }
8.    public static void main(String[] args) {
9.       long start = System.currentTimeMillis();
10.      new Thread(new Checkout2()).start();
11.      Thread t1 = new Thread(new Checkout2());
12.      t1.start();
13.      try { t1.join(); }
14.      catch (Exception e) { System.out.print("e "); }
15.      System.out.println("elapsed: "
                            + (System.currentTimeMillis() - start));
16.    }
17.    public void run() {
18.      for(int j = 0; j < 4; j++) {
19.         doStuff();
20.         try { Thread.sleep(1000); }
21.         catch (Exception e) { System.out.print("e "); }
22.         doSynch();
23. } } }
```

Which are true? (Choose all that apply.)

A. Compilation fails.

B. Elapsed time will be about eight seconds.

C. Elapsed time will be about nine seconds.

D. Elapsed time will be about 12 seconds.

E. Changing doSynch() to be unsynchronized will change elapsed by only a few milliseconds.

F. Changing doSynch() to be unsynchronized will change elapsed by 450 or more milliseconds.

56. Your virtual-world simulator is designed such that Grobnets can have several Ooflas, and Yazells support the contract implied by Whompers. Grobnets are a type of Yazell, and can also act as Floordums or Whompers. Which of the following code fragments legally represent this design? (Choose all that apply.)

A.
```
import java.util.*;
interface Floordum { }
interface Whomper { }
class Grobnet extends Yazell implements Floordum { List<Oofla> o; }
class Oofla { }
class Yazell implements Whomper { }
```

B.
```
import java.util.*;
class Oofla { }
class Yazell implements Whomper { }
class Floordum { }
interface Whomper { }
class Grobnet extends Yazell, Floordum { List<Oofla> o; }
```

C.
```
import java.util.*;
interface Floordum { }
interface Whomper { }
class Grobnet extends Yazell implements Floordum, Oofla { }
class Oofla { }
interface Yazell implements Whomper { }
```

D.
```
import java.util.*;
interface Floordum { }
interface Whomper { }
class Grobnet extends Yazell implements Floordum { Set<Oofla> o; }
class Oofla { }
class Yazell { Whomper w; }
```

57. Given:

```
1. import java.util.*;
2. public class Ps {
3.   public static void main(String[] args) {
4.     PriorityQueue<String> pq = new PriorityQueue<String>();
5.     pq.add("4");
6.     pq.add("7");
7.     pq.add("2");
8.     // insert code here
9. } }
```

Which code fragment(s), inserted independently at line 8, produce the output "2-4-7-"? (Choose all that apply.)

A. ```
Iterator it2 = pq.iterator();
while(it2.hasNext()) System.out.print(it2.next() + "-");
System.out.println();
```

B. ```
Arrays.sort(pq.toArray());
Iterator it3 = pq.iterator();
while(it3.hasNext()) System.out.print(it3.next() + "-");
System.out.println();
```

C. ```
Object[] pqa = pq.toArray();
Arrays.sort(pqa);
for(Object o: pqa) System.out.print(o + "-");
System.out.println();
```

D. ```
String s = pq.poll();
while (s != null) {
  System.out.print(s + "-");
  s = pq.poll();
}
```

E. ```
String s = pq.peek();
while (s != null) {
  System.out.print(s + "-");
  s = pq.peek();
}
```

**58.** Given that the current directory is bigApp, and the following directory structure:

```
bigApp
    |-- classes
    |-- source
            |-- com
                |-- wickedlysmart
                        |-- BigAppClass1.java
```
```

And the code:

```
package com.wickedlysmart;
public class BigAppClass1 {
  int doStuff() { return 42; }
}
```

And the following command-line invocations:

I. `javac -d source/com/wickedlysmart/BigAppClass1.java`

II. `javac -d classes source/com/wickedlysmart/BigAppClass1.java`

III. `javac -d classes/com/wickedlysmart source/com/wickedlysmart/BigAppClass1.java`

Which are true? (Choose all that apply.)

A. Invocation I will compile the file and place the `.class` file in the bigApp directory.

B. Invocation II will compile the file and place the `.class` file in the classes directory.

C. Invocation I will compile the file and place the `.class` file in the wickedlysmart directory.

D. Under the bigApp/classes directory, invocation II will build com/wickedlysmart subdirectories, and place the `.class` file in wickedlysmart.

E. Under the bigApp/classes directory, invocation III will build com/wickedlysmart subdirectories, and place the `.class` file in wickedlysmart.

59. Given:

```
2. class Jog implements Runnable {
3.   public void run() {
4.     for(int i = 0; i < 8; i++) {
5.       try { Thread.sleep(200); }
6.       catch (Exception e) { System.out.print("exc "); }
7.       System.out.print(i + " ");
8. } } }
9. public class Marathon {
10.   public static void main(String[] args) throws Exception {
11.     Jog j1 = new Jog();
12.     Thread t1 = new Thread(j1);
13.     t1.start();
14.     t1.sleep(500);
15.     System.out.print("pre ");
16.     t1.interrupt();
17.     t1.sleep(500);
18.     System.out.print("post ");
19. } }
```

Assuming that sleep() sleeps for about the amount of time specified in its argument, and that all other code runs almost instantly, which output is likely? (Choose all that apply.)

A. exc

B. 0 1 pre exc post

C. exc 0 1 2 3 4 5 6 7

D. pre post 0 1 2 3 4 5 6 7

E. pre exc 0 1 post 2 3 4 5 6 7

F. 0 1 pre exc 2 3 4 post 5 6 7

60. Given:

```
2. class Explode {
3.    static String s = "";
4.    static { s += "sb1 "; }
5.    Explode() { s += "e "; }
6. }
7. public class C4 extends Explode {
8.    C4() {
9.       s += "c4 ";
10.      new Explode();
11.   }
12.   static {
13.      new C4();
14.      System.out.print(s);
15.   }
16.   { s += "i "; }
17.   public static void main(String[] args) { }
18. }
```

And given the command-line invocation "java C4", what is the result?

A. e c4 i

B. e i c4

C. e sb1 i c4

D. sb1 e i c4 e

E. sb1 e c4 i e

F. Compilation fails.

G. A StackOverflowError is thrown.

H. An exception other than StackOverflowError is thrown.

QUICK ANSWER KEY

1. F
2. D
3. C
4. G
5. C
6. C, D, E, F
7. A, G
8. B
9. B, E
10. B, D, F
11. A, G
12. B, C, D
13. A, B, C
14. A, B, C, F
15. B, E
16. D, E
17. E
18. D
19. F, H
20. F

21. A
22. C
23. C
24. Drag and Drop
25. A
26. E
27. C, D, E
28. B, C, F
29. D
30. B, C, E
31. B, D
32. D, E, F, G
33. B
34. A, B, C, D
35. E
36. A, C, D, F
37. D
38. B, C, F
39. A, B, F, G
40. C

41. Drag and Drop
42. A
43. D
44. B, E, F
45. C, D, G
46. B
47. D
48. B
49. D
50. D
51. C
52. B, C, F
53. E
54. D
55. B, E
56. A
57. C, D
58. D
59. F
60. D

PRACTICE EXAM 4: ANSWERS

1. Given:

```
1. abstract class Vibrate {
2.    static String s = "-";
3.    Vibrate() {  s += "v"; }
4. }
5. public class Echo extends Vibrate {
6.    Echo() { this(7); s += "e"; }
7.    Echo(int x) { s += "e2"; }
8.    public static void main(String[] args) {
9.      System.out.print("made " + s + " ");
10.   }
11.   static {
12.     Echo e = new Echo();
13.     System.out.print("block " + s + " ");
14. } }
```

What is the result?

A. made -ve2e

B. block -ee2v

C. block -ve2e

D. made -eve2 block -eve2

E. made -ve2e block -ve2e

F. block -ve2e made -ve2e

G. block -ve2e made -ve2eve2e

H. Compilation fails

Answer (for Objective 1.5):

☑ **F** is correct. The static initialization block is the only place where an instance of Echo is created. When the Echo instance is created, Echo's no-arg constructor calls its 1-arg constructor, which then calls Vibrate's constructor (which then secretly calls Object's constructor). At that point, the various constructors execute, starting with Object's constructor and working back down to Echo's no-arg constructor.

☒ **A, B, C, D, E, G,** and **H** are incorrect based on the above.

2. Given:

```
3. public class KaChung {
4.    public static void main(String[] args) {
5.       String s = "";
6.       if(Integer.parseInt("011") == Integer.parseInt("9")) s += 1;
7.       if(021 == Integer.valueOf("17")) s += 2;
8.       if(1024 == new Integer(1024)) s += 3;
9.       System.out.println(s);
10. } }
```

What is the result?

A. 2

B. 3

C. 13

D. 23

E. 123

F. Compilation fails.

G. An exception is thrown at runtime.

Answer (for Objective 3.1):

☑ **D** is correct. On line 6, the parseInt() method assumes a radix of 10 if a radix is not specified. Line 7 is comparing an octal int to an int. Line 8 is comparing an int to an Integer, and autoboxing converts the Integer to an int to do the comparison.

☒ **A, B, C, E, F,** and **G** are incorrect based on the above.

3. Given the invocation "java GiveUp" and:

```
2. public class GiveUp {
3.    public static void main(String[] args) throws Exception {
4.       try {
5.          assert false;
6.          System.out.print("t ");
7.       }
8.       catch (Error e) {
9.          System.out.print("c ");
10.         throw new Exception();
11.      }
12.      finally { System.out.print("f "); }
13. } }
```

What is the result?

A. c

B. c f

C. t f

D. Compilation fails.

E. "c f " followed by an uncaught exception.

Answer (for Objective 2.4):

☑ **C** is correct. It's legal (although not recommended) to catch an Error. It's also legal for main() to throw an exception. The trick to this question is that assertions were not enabled, so line 5 is skipped, and no Error is thrown. If the invocation had been "java -ea GiveUp", then answer **E** would have been correct.

☒ **A, B, D,** and **E** are incorrect based on the above.

4. Given:

```
3.  import java.util.*;
4.  public class VC {
5.    public static void main(String[] args) {
6.      List<Integer> x = new ArrayList<Integer>();
7.      Integer[] a = {3, 1, 4, 1};
8.      x = Arrays.asList(a);
9.      a[3] = 2;
10.     x.set(0, 7);
11.     for(Integer i: x) System.out.print(i + " ");
12.     x.add(9);
13.     System.out.println(x);
14. } }
```

What is the result?

A. Compilation fails.

B. 3 1 4 2 [7, 1, 4, 1]

C. 3 1 4 2 [7, 1, 4, 2]

D. 7 1 4 2 [7, 1, 4, 2]

E. 3 1 4 2 [7, 1, 4, 1, 9]

F. 3 1 4 2 [7, 1, 4, 2, 9]

G. 7 1 4 2, followed by an exception.

H. 3 1 4 2, followed by an exception.

Answer (for Objective 6.5):

☑ **G** is correct. The asList() method "backs" the List to the array. In other words, changes to one are mirrored in the other. However, neither can grow, so when add() is called an exception is thrown.

☒ **A, B, C, D, E, F**, and **H** are incorrect based on the above.

5. Given:

```
3. public class Honcho {
4.    static boolean b1 = false;
5.    static int z = 7;
6.    static Long y;
7.    public static void main(String[] args) {
8.      for(int i = 0; i < 4; i++)
9.        go(i);
10.   }
11.   static void go(int x) {
12.     try {
13.       if((x == 0) && (!b1 && z == 7)) System.out.print("0 ");
14.       if(x < 2 ^ x < 10) System.out.print("1 ");
15.       if((x == 2) &&
            (y == null | (y.longValue() == 0))) System.out.print("2 ");
16.       if(z <= (x + 4)) System.out.print("3 ");
17.     }
18.     catch(Exception e) { System.out.print("e "); }
19. } }
```

What is the result?

A. 0 1 2 3

B. 1 e 1 3

C. 0 1 e 1 3

D. 0 1 1 1 1 3

E. 1 1 1 2 1 3

F. 0 1 1 1 2 1 3

G. Compilation fails.

Answer (for Objective 7.6):

☑ **C** is correct. The ^ is true only when exactly one of the tests is true. The | does NOT short circuit, so longValue() is invoked and throws a NullPointerException.

☒ **A, B, D, E, F**, and **G** are incorrect based on the above.

6. Given:

```
2. class Chilis {
3.    Chilis(String c, int h) { color = c; hotness = h; }
4.    String color;
5.    int hotness;
6.    public boolean equals(Object o) {
7.       Chilis c = (Chilis)o;
8.       if(this.color == c.color) return true;
9.       return false;
10.   }
11.   public int hashCode() { return (color.length() + hotness); }
12. }
```

If instances of class `Chilis` are to be used as keys in a `Map`, which are true? (Choose all that apply.)

A. The code will not compile.

B. The `hashCode()` and `equals()` contracts have been supported.

C. The `equals()` method is reflexive, symmetric, and transitive.

D. The `Chilis` class CANNOT be used to create keys to reliably add and retrieve entries in a `Map`.

E. If the `hashCode()` method is not considered, the `equals()` method could be an override that supports the `equals()` contract.

F. If the `equals()` method is not considered, the `hashCode()` method could be an override that supports the `hashCode()` contract.

Answer (for Objective 6.2):

☑ **C, D, E**, and **F** are correct. Taken individually, the `equals()` and `hashCode()` methods are legal, potentially contract-fulfilling overrides. The problem is that they don't match each other. In other words, two objects that are equal according to `equals()`, do not necessarily return the same result from `hashCode()`.

☒ **A** and **B** are incorrect based on the above.

7. Given:

```
2. package pack.clients;
3. import pack.banking.Bank;
4. public class Client{
5.    public static void main(String[] args){
6.       Bank bank = new Bank();
7.       System.out.println(bank.getMoney(2000L));
8. } }
```

And given that `Client.java` resides in the `$ROOT` directory and is not yet compiled. There is another class named `pack.banking.Bank`, which has a method called `getMoney(long)` that returns a value. Bank class is compiled and deployed into a JAR file called `pack.jar`, as shown in the following directory structure

```
$ROOT
    |-- Client.java
    |-- [pack.jar]
              |-- pack
                    |-- banking
                          |-- Bank.class
```

Which are correct about compiling or running the `Client` class from the `$ROOT` directory? (Choose all that apply.)

A. To compile, use `javac -cp pack.jar -d . Client.java`

B. To compile, use `javac -cp pack.jar#pack.banking.Bank -d . Client.java`

C. To compile, use `javac -cp * -d . Client.java`

D. To run, use `java -cp pack.jar pack.clients.Client`

E. To run, use `java -cp . -d pack.jar pack.clients.Client`

F. To run, use `java -cp . -cp pack.jar pack.clients.Client`

G. To run, use `java -cp .:pack.jar pack.clients.Client`

Answer (for Objective 7.5):

☑ **A** and **G** are correct. **A** is correct because it correctly specifies the classpath to `pack.jar` and the destination directory. **G** is correct because the classpath should include the JAR file and base location of the `Client` class. Note: The symbol `":"` is used for the path separation, although in real life that character depends on the platform.

☒ **B, C, D, E,** and **F** are incorrect because they don't correctly specify the classpath.

---

8. Given:

```
2. class Bird {
3.   public static String s = "";
4.   public static void fly() { s += "fly "; }
5. }
6. public class Hummingbird extends Bird {
7.   public static void fly() { s += "hover "; }
8.   public static void main(String[] args) {
9.     Bird b1 = new Bird();
10.    Bird b2 = new Hummingbird();
```

```
11.        Bird b3 = (Hummingbird)b2;
12.        Hummingbird b4 = (Hummingbird)b2;
13.
14.        b1.fly();  b2.fly();  b3.fly();  b4.fly();
15.        System.out.println(s);
16. } }
```

What is the result?

A. `fly fly fly fly`

B. `fly fly fly hover`

C. `fly fly hover hover`

D. `fly hover hover hover`

E. `hover hover hover hover`

F. Compilation fails.

G. An exception is thrown at runtime.

Answer (for Objective 5.2):

☑ **B** is correct. Remember, polymorphic invocations apply only to instance methods, not static methods.

☒ **A, C, D, E, F,** and **G** are incorrect based on the above.

9. Given two files:

```
1. package com;
2. public class Extramuros {
3.    public static void howdy() { System.out.print("howdy "); }
4.    public static final Extramuros ex = new Extramuros();
5.    public int instVar = 42;
6.    public enum avout {OROLO, JAD};
7. }
```

```
1. // insert code here
...
6. public class Theorics {
7.    public static void main(String[] args) {
8.       Extramuros.howdy();
9.       System.out.print(Extramuros.avout.OROLO + " ");
10.      howdy();
11.      System.out.print(ex.instVar + " ");
12. } }
```

Which are the minimum line(s) of code to add at `"insert code here"` for the files to compile? (Choose all that apply.)

A. `import static com.*;`

B. `import com.Extramuros;`

C. `import com.Extramuros.*;`

D. `import static com.Extramuros;`

E. `import static com.Extramuros.*;`

F. Even with correct imports, the code will not compile due to other errors.

Answer (for Objective 1.1):

☑ **B** and **E** are the `import` statements that correctly allow access to the elements in `Extramuros`.

☒ **A, C,** and **D** are incorrect. These `import` statements will not allow access to the elements of `Extramuros` invoked in `Theorics`. **F** is incorrect because with the correct `import` statements in place, the code will compile.

---

10. Given:

```
2. import java.text.*;
3. import java.util.*;
4. public class Vogue {
5.    public static void main(String[] args) {
6.      DateFormat df1 = DateFormat.getInstance();
7.      DateFormat df2 = DateFormat.getInstance(DateFormat.SHORT);
8.      DateFormat df3 = DateFormat.getDateInstance(DateFormat.FULL);
9.      DateFormat df4 = DateFormat.getDateInstance(DateFormat.EXTENDED);
10. } }
```

Which are true? (Choose all that apply.)

A. Line 2 is not necessary.

B. Line 3 is not necessary.

C. Compilation fails due to an error on line 6.

D. Compilation fails due to an error on line 7.

E. Compilation fails due to an error on line 8.

F. Compilation fails due to an error on line 9.

Answer (for Objective 3.3):

☑ **B, D,** and **F** are correct. The `DateFormat` class is in the `java.text` package. The `getInstance()` method takes no arguments, and it uses the SHORT style by default. There is no such style as EXTENDED. Note: We agree that this is largely a memorization question. For the most part the exam doesn't tend to be so memorization intensive, but this objective tends to be more so. Take the perspective that once you're done you can forget the details, and later on, when you're using these classes in practice, you'll have that nagging sensation that there are in fact a couple of gotchas in the API.

☒ **A, C,** and **E** are incorrect based on the above.

11. Given:

```
2. public class Cult extends Thread {
3.    static int count = 0;
4.    public void run() {
5.      for(int i = 0; i < 100; i++) {
6.        if(i == 5 && count < 3) {
7.          Thread t = new Cult(names[count++]);
8.          t.start();
9.          // insert code here
10.       }
11.       System.out.print(Thread.currentThread().getName() + " ");
12.     }
13.   }
14.   public static void main(String[] args) {
15.     new Cult("t0").start();
16.   }
17.   Cult(String s) { super(s); }
18.   String[] names = {"t1", "t2", "t3"};
19. }
```

And these two fragments:

I. `try { t.join(); }  catch(Exception e) { }`

II. `try { Thread.currentThread().join(); }  catch(Exception e) { }`

When each fragment is inserted independently at line 9, which are true? (Choose all that apply.)

A. With fragment I, t0 completes last.

B. With fragment I, t3 completes last.

C. With fragment II, t0 completes last.

D. With fragment II, t3 completes last.

E. With both fragments, compilation fails.

F. With fragment I, the code never completes.

G. With fragment II, the code never completes.

Answer (for Objective 4.2):

☑ **A** and **G** are correct. With fragment I, t0 joins to t1, which joins to t2, which joins to t3. Next, t3 completes and returns to t2, which completes and returns to t1, which completes and returns to t0. With fragment II, t0 starts t1 and then joins to itself. Then, t1 starts t2 and joins to itself. Then, t2 starts t3 and joins to itself. Finally, t3 runs and when it completes, t2 hangs, waiting for itself to finish.

☒ **B, C, D, E,** and **F** are incorrect based on the above.

12. Which are true? (Choose all that apply.)

A. If a class's member's values can be retrieved, but not changed, without using the class's API, the class is not cohesive.

B. If a class's member's values can be retrieved, but not changed, without using the class's API, tight coupling could occur.

C. If a class's member's values can be retrieved, but not changed, without using the class's API, the class is not well encapsulated.

D. If a class's member's values can be updated only through the use of its API, or by an inner class, the class is well encapsulated.

E. If a class's member's values can be updated only through the use of its API, or by an inner class, the class is NOT well encapsulated.

Answer (for Objective 5.1):

☑ **B, C,** and **D** are correct. B and C are correct because even just "getting" values should be done through a class's API to avoid coupling issues and to enforce encapsulation. D is correct because inner classes, by definition, are allowed to break their outer class's encapsulation.

☒ **A** is incorrect because this situation is describing encapsulation issues, not cohesion issues. **E** is incorrect based on the above.

13. Given:

```
3. public class BigData {
4.    static BigData bd;
5.    public static void main(String[] args) {
6.      new BigData().doStuff();
7.      // do lots of memory intensive stuff
...     // JVM finds an eligible BigData object for GC
...     // JVM invokes finalize()
...     // do more stuff
48.    }
49.    void doStuff() {  }
50.    // insert code here
51.      bd = this;
52.    }
53. }
54. class MyException extends Exception { }
```

and the following four fragments:

I. `protected void finalize() throws Throwable {`

II. `protected void finalize() {`

III. `protected void finalize() throws MyException {`

IV. `void finalize() {`

If the fragments are inserted, independently, at line 50, which are true? (Choose all that apply.)

A. Fragment I compiles.

B. Fragment II compiles.

C. Fragment III compiles.

D. Fragment IV compiles.

E. Of those that compile, the GC will collect any given object after the JVM has called `finalize()` on that object.

F. Because of the way `finalize()` has been overridden, the GC will never collect eligible objects of type `BigData`.

Answer (for Objective 7.4):

☑ **A, B,** and **C** are correct because Fragments I-III are legal signatures to override `finalize()`.

☒ **D** is incorrect because the access privilege is weaker. **E** is incorrect because `finalize()` copies a reference of the object to the `static` variable bd. **F** is incorrect. For a given object, the JVM will never call `finalize()` again, but it might still GC it.

14. Given:

```
2. interface Clickable {  void click();  }
3. // insert code here
```

Which code, inserted independently at line 3, will compile? (Choose all that apply.)

A. `interface Keyboard extends Clickable { }`

B. `interface Keyboard extends Clickable { void click(); }`

C. `interface Keyboard extends Clickable { void doClick(); }`

D. `interface Keyboard extends Clickable { void click() { ; } }`

E. `interface Keyboard extends Clickable { protected void click(); }`

F. `interface Keyboard extends Clickable { void click(); void doClick(); }`

Answer (for Objective 1.2):

☑ **A, B, C,** and **F** are correct. When an interface extends another interface, it doesn't have to actually implement anything—in fact, it CANNOT implement anything.

☒ **D** is incorrect because the extending interface is trying to implement a method. **E** is incorrect because interface methods can be only `public`.

15. Given:

```
1. public class Argue {
2.    static boolean b;
3.    static int x = 0;
4.    public static void main(String[] args) {
5.       int guess = (int)(Math.random() * 5);
6.       if(guess < 0) assert false;
7.       assert b = true;
8.       assert x = 0;
9.       assert x == 0;
10. } }
```

Which are true? (Choose all that apply.)

A. The code compiles.

B. The `assert` on line 6 is appropriate.

C. Compilation fails due to an error on line 6.

D. Compilation fails due to an error on line 7.

E. Compilation fails due to an error on line 8.

F. Compilation fails due to an error on line 9.

Answer (for Objective 2.3):

☑ **B** and **E** are correct. It's considered appropriate, even in `public` methods, to validate that a code block will not be reached. Line 8 fails to compile because the first expression in an `assert` statement must resolve to a `boolean` value.

☒ **A, C, D**, and **F** are incorrect based on the above.

16. Given two files:

```
1. package com.wickedlysmart2;
2. public class Utils {
3.    void do1() { System.out.print("do1 "); }
4.    protected void do2() { System.out.print("do2 "); }
5.    public void do3() { System.out.print("do3 "); }
6. }
```

```
1. import com.wickedlysmart2.*;
2. public class UPS extends Utils {
3.    public static void main(String[] args) {
4.       Utils u = new Utils();
5.       u.do1();
6.       u.do2();
7.       u.do3();
8. } }
```

What is the result? (Choose all that apply.)

A. do1 do2 do3

B. "do1 ", followed by an exception.

C. Compilation fails due to an error on line 4 of UPS.

D. Compilation fails due to an error on line 5 of UPS.

E. Compilation fails due to an error on line 6 of UPS.

F. Compilation fails due to an error on line 7 of UPS.

Answer (for Objective 7.1):

☑ **D** and **E** are correct, lines 5 and 6 will NOT compile. If the `protected` method `do2()` was invoked through inheritance (for instance, `"new UPS().do2();"`), it would compile.

☒ **A, B, C**, and **F** are incorrect based on the above.

17. Given:

```
 4. class Electricity { int getCharge() { return 24; } }
 5. public class Voltage extends Electricity {
 6.    enum volts {twelve, twentyfour, oneten};
 7.    public static void main(String[] args) {
 8.       volts v = volts.twentyfour;
 9.       switch (v) {
10.         case twelve:
11.            System.out.print("12 ");
12.         default:
13.            System.out.print(getCharge() + " ");
14.         case oneten:
15.            System.out.print("110 ");
16. } } }
```

What is the result? (Choose all that apply.)

A. 24

B. 24 110

C. 24 110 12

D. Compilation fails due to a misuse of enums

E. Compilation fails due to a non-enum issue.

Answer (for Objective 1.3):

☑ **E** is correct. The code fails because the instance method getCharge() is called from a static method. The enums are used correctly. If getCharge() was a static method, the output would be "24 110".

☒ **A, B, C,** and **D** are incorrect based on the above.

18. Given:

```
 2. import java.io.*;
 3. public class Uboat {
 4.    public static void main(String[] args) {
 5.       try {
 6.         File f1 = new File("sub1");
 7.         f1.mkdir();
 8.         File f2 = new File(f1,"sub2");
 9.         File f3 = new File(f1,"sub3");
10.         PrintWriter pw = new PrintWriter(f3);
11.       } catch (Exception e) { System.out.println("ouch"); }
12. } }
```

And, if the code compiles, what is the result if `"java Uboat"` is invoked TWICE? (Choose all that apply.)

A. Compilation fails.

B. The second invocation produces the output `"ouch"`.

C. The second invocation creates at least one new file as a peer to the new directory.

D. The first invocation creates a new directory and one new file in that directory.

E. The first invocation creates a new directory and two new files in that directory.

F. The first invocation creates a new directory and at least one new file as a peer to it.

Answer (for Objective 3.2):

☑ **D** is correct. The program creates a new directory called `"sub1"`, and adds a new file called `"sub3"` to `"sub1"`. The program creates a File object called `"sub2"`, but it is never used to create a physical file. The second invocation of the program runs without exception. The call to `mkdir()` returns a `boolean` indicating whether or not a new directory was made. The second invocation of `Uboat` truncates the file `"sub3"` to zero length, so any data added to the file before the second invocation is lost.

☒ **A, B, C, E,** and **F** are incorrect based on the above.

19. Given:

```
2. class Car {
3.    private Car() { }
4.    protected Car(int x) { }
5. }
6. public class MG extends Car {
7.    // MG(int x) { }
8.    // MG(int x) { super(); }
9.    // MG(int x) { super(x); }
10.   // private MG(int x) { super(x); }
11.   // MG() { }
12.   // MG() { this(); }
13.   // MG() { this(6); }
14.   // MG() { super(7); }
15.   public static void main(String[] args) {
16.      new MG(7);
17.      new MG();
18. } }
```

Which sets of constructors can be uncommented for the code to compile? (Choose all that apply.)

A. Line 7 and line 11.

B. Line 7 and line 14.

C. Line 8 and line 12.

D. Line 8 and line 13.

E. Line 9 and line 12.

F. Line 9 and line 13.

G. Line 10 and line 11.

H. Line 10 and line 14.

Answer (for Objective 5.3):

☑ **F** and **H** are correct. None of the constructors can chain to `Car`'s private constructor, they must all get to `Car`'s protected constructor somehow. Lines 7 and 8 won't ever work because `Car`'s protected constructor needs an argument. Line 13 would work with either line 9 or line 10. Line 14 would work with either line 9 or line 10.

☒ **A, B, C, D, E,** and **G** are incorrect based on the above.

20. Given:

```
2. interface Gadget {
3.    int patent = 12345;
4.    Gadget doStuff();
5. }
6. public class TimeMachine implements Gadget {
7.    int patent = 34567;
8.    public static void main(String[] args) {
9.      new TimeMachine().doStuff();
10.   }
11.   TimeMachine doStuff() {
12.     System.out.println( ++patent);
13.     return new TimeMachine();
14. } }
```

If `javac` is invoked twice:

```
javac -source 1.4 TimeMachine.java
javac TimeMachine.java
```

And, if "java TimeMachine" is invoked whenever TimeMachine compiles, what is the result?

A. First, compilation fails, then 12346

B. First, compilation fails, then 34568

C. First, 12346, then compilation fails.

D. First, 34568, then compilation fails.

E. First, 12346, then 34568

F. Compilation fails on both javac invocations.

Answer (for Objective 1.4):

☑ **F** is correct. Regardless of the Java version, the implementing doStuff() method must be declared public. If it was declared public, the answer would be **B**. The Java 1.4 compilation would fail because doStuff() is using a covariant return, which wasn't available until Java 5.

☒ **A, B, C, D**, and **E** are incorrect based on the above.

21. Given:

```
1. import java.util.*;
2. public class LogSplitter {
3.    public static void main(String[] args) {
4.      for(int x = 1; x < args.length; x++)
5.        System.out.print(args[0].split(args[x]).length + " ");
6. } }
```

And the command-line invocation:

```
java LogSplitter "x1 23 y #" "\d" "\s" "\w"
```

What is the result?

A. 4 4 6

B. 3 3 6

C. 5 4 6

D. 4 6 4

E. 3 6 3

F. 5 6 4

G. Compilation fails.

H. An exception is thrown at runtime.

Answer (for Objective 3.4):

☑ **A** is correct. For the "regex-related" parts of the exam you need to remember the three metacharacters `"\d"` (which means digit), `"\s"` (which means a whitespace character), and `"\w"` (which means a word character—i.e., letters, digits, or the underscore character). With that said, the calls to the `split()` method are "tokenizing" calls. In this case, we're using metacharacters as our token delimiters. In the first iteration of the `for` loop, digits are the delimiters. In the second iteration, whitespace characters are the delimiters. And in the final iteration, "word" characters are the delimiters.

☒ **B, C, D, E, F, G,** and **H** are incorrect based on the above.

22. Given this code in a method:

```
3.      int y, count = 0;
4.      for(int x = 3; x < 6; x++) {
5.        try {
6.          switch(x) {
7.            case 3: count++;
8.            case 4: count++;
9.            case 7: count++;
10.           case 9: { y = 7 / (x - 4); count += 10; }
11.         }
12.       } catch (Exception ex) { count++; }
13.     }
14.     System.out.println(count);
```

What is the result?

A. 2

B. 15

C. 16

D. 25

E. 26

F. Compilation fails.

G. An exception is thrown with no other output.

Answer (for Objective 2.1):

☑ **C** is correct. Remember that once a matching `case` is found, its code and all subsequent cases' code will be executed. When `"x"` equals 4 and the code for `case 9` is executed, an exception will be thrown, but it's caught correctly and the code will continue to run.

☒ **A, B, D, E, F,** and **G** are incorrect based on the above.

23. Given:

```
5. abstract class Thing { static String s = ""; Thing() { s += "t "; } }
6. class Steel extends Thing {
7.    Steel() { s += "s "; }
8.    Steel(String s1) {
9.       s += s1;
10.      new Steel();
11.   }
12. }
13. public class Tungsten extends Steel {
14.    Tungsten(String s1) {
15.       s += s1;
16.       new Steel(s);
17.    }
18.    public static void main(String[] args) {
19.       new Tungsten("tu ");
20.       System.out.println(s);
21. } }
```

What is the result?

A. s tu s tu s

B. t s tu t s t s

C. t s tu t t s tu t s

D. t tu t s tu t t tu t s tu t s

E. Compilation fails.

F. An exception is thrown at runtime.

Answer (for Objective 5.4):

☑ **C** is correct. The first thing is that abstract class constructors run in the constructor chain just like other constructors. After that, this question is probably trickier than what's on the real exam, but if you get this one right, you're totally ready to deal with constructor chaining questions. A few clues: When line 16 executes, what's the value of "s"? In general, what exactly does the compiler add to constructors?

☒ **A, B, D, E,** and **F** are incorrect, based on the above.

24. You want to add a capability to `MyStuff` so that collections of `MyStuff` objects can be sorted in a "natural" order. Use the fragments to fill in the blanks to create this capability. Note: Not all the fragments will be used, not all the blanks have to be filled (maybe), and you can use each fragment more than once

Second note: As in the real exam's Drag-and-Drop questions, there may be more than one correct answer. Here, give yourself bonus points if you create more than one correct answer. In the real exam, you'll get full credit for ANY correct answer.

```
import java.util.*;
class MyStuff _____  _____ {
   MyStuff(String n, int v) { name = n; value = v; }
   String name; int value;
   _____  _____  _____  _____ {
   return _____  _____ ;
   }
   public String toString() { return name + " " + value + " "; }
}
```

Fragments:

```
Comparable                  Comparator                public
Comparable<MyStuff>         Comparator<MyStuff>       protected
implements                  extends                   boolean
(MyStuff m)                 (MyStuff a, MyStuff b)     String
name.compareTo              compare                    (b.name)
value - m.value             compares                   (m.name)
m.value - value             sort                       (name, n.name)
name.equals(m.name)         compareTo                  (a.name, b.name)
a.name.compareTo            a.name.equals(b.name)      int
```

Answer (for Objective 6.5):

```
class MyStuff implements Comparable<MyStuff> {
   MyStuff(String n, int v) { name = n; value = v; }
   String name; int value;
   public int compareTo(MyStuff m) {
     return name.compareTo(m.name);  // sort alphabetically
     // return value - m.value;      // 2nd answer, to sort ascending
   }
   public String toString() { return name + " " + value + " "; }
}
```

Answer note: If you chose `"m.value - value"`, you're close. This will sort the objects in value-descending sequence, which is a perfectly fine way to sort stuff, but it isn't considered "natural."

25. Given:

```
2. public class Swanky {
3.    Swanky s;
4.    public static void main(String[] args) {
5.       Swanky s1 = new Swanky();
6.       s1.s = new Swanky();
7.       go(s1.s);
8.       Swanky s2 = go(s1);
9.       if(s2.s.equals(s1)) System.out.print("1 ");
10.      if(s2.equals(s1)) System.out.print("2 ");
11.      if(s1.s.equals(s1)) System.out.print("3 ");
12.      if(s2.s.equals(s2)) System.out.print("4 ");
13.   }
14.   static Swanky go(Swanky s) {
15.      Swanky gs = new Swanky();
16.      gs.s = s;
17.      return gs;
18. } }
```

What is the result?

A. 1

B. 1 2

C. 1 2 4

D. Compilation fails.

E. "1 ", followed by an exception.

F. "1 2 ", followed by an exception.

Answer (for Objective 7.3):

☑ **A** is correct. Swanky doesn't override `equals()`, so `equals()` returns `true` only when both references are referring to the same object. Similar to garbage collection questions, the best way to approach this question is to make a diagram of the reference variables, objects, connections between them, and when connections or references are lost.

☒ **B, C, D, E,** and **F** are incorrect, loosely based on the above.

26. Given:

```
2. import java.util.*;
3. public class AndOver {
4.    public static void main(String[] args) {
5.       List g = new ArrayList();
```

```
6.       g.add(new Gaited("Eyra"));
7.       g.add(new Gaited("Vafi"));
8.       g.add(new Gaited("Andi"));
9.       Iterator i2 = g.iterator();
10.      while(i2.hasNext()) {
11.         System.out.print(i2.next().name + " ");
12. } } }
13. class Gaited {
14.    public String name;
15.    Gaited(String n) { name = n; }
16. }
```

What is the result?

A. Vafi Andi

B. Andi Eyra Vafi

C. Andi Vafi Eyra

D. Eyra Vafi Andi

E. Compilation fails.

F. The output order is unpredictable.

Answer (for Objective 2.2):

☑ **E** is correct. Iterator's next() method returns an Object, which in this case needs to be cast to a Gaited before its name property can be used.

☒ **A, B, C, D,** and **F** are incorrect based on the above.

27. Given:

```
2. interface Plant {
3.    int greenness = 7;
4.    void grow();
5. }
6. class Grass implements Plant {
7.    // static int greenness = 5;
8.    // int greenness = 5;
9.    public static void main(String[] args) {
10.       int greenness = 2;
11.       new Grass().grow();
12.    }
13.    public void grow() {
14.       System.out.println(++greenness);
15. } }
```

Which are true? (Choose all that apply.)

A. As the code stands, the output is 3.

B. As the code stands, the output is 8.

C. As the code stands, it will NOT compile.

D. If line 7 is un-commented, the output is 6.

E. If line 8 is un-commented, the output is 6.

F. If line 7 is un-commented, the output is 8.

G. If line 7 is un-commented, the code will NOT compile.

Answer (for Objective 1.2):

☑ **C, D,** and **E** are correct. As the code stands, the `grow()` method will try to increment `Plant`'s greenness variable, which can't be changed because it's `final` by default, so the code will not compile. If either line 7 or 8 is uncommented, then the `grow()` method will use that line's greenness variable.

☒ **A, B, F,** and **G** are incorrect based on the above.

28. Given:

```
2. class Grab {
3.    static int x = 5;
4.    synchronized void adjust(Grab y) {
5.      System.out.print(x-- + " ");
6.       y.view(y);
7.    }
8.    synchronized void view(Grab z) { if(x > 0) z.adjust(z); }
9. }
10. public class Grapple implements Runnable {
11.    static Thread t1;
12.    static Grab g, g2;
13.    public void run() {
14.      if(Thread.currentThread().getId() == t1.getId()) g.adjust(g2);
15.      else g2.view(g);
16.    }
17.    public static void main(String[] args) {
18.      g = new Grab();
19.      g2 = new Grab();
20.      t1 = new Thread(new Grapple());
21.      t1.start();
22.      new Thread(new Grapple()).start();
23. } }
```

Which are true? (Choose all that apply.)

A. Compilation fails.

B. The output could be 5 4 3 2 1

C. The output could be 5 4 3 2 1 0

D. The program could produce thousands of lines of output.

E. The program could deadlock before producing any output.

F. The output could be "5 ", followed by the program deadlocking.

Answer (for Objective 4.3):

☑ **B, C**, and **F** are correct. This program could deadlock with "g" waiting to invoke `view()` while "g2" waits to invoke `adjust()`. If the code doesn't deadlock, then **B** and **C** are correct, **B** being the more common output.

☒ **A** and **D** are incorrect based on the above. **E** is incorrect because the code can't deadlock until the `y.view(y)` invocation is attempted.

29. Given:

```
3.  import java.util.*;
4.  public class Corner {
5.    public static void main(String[] args) {
6.      TreeSet<String> t1 = new TreeSet<String>();
7.      TreeSet<String> t2 = new TreeSet<String>();
8.      t1.add("b");  t1.add("7");
9.      t2 = (TreeSet)t1.subSet("5", "c");
10.     try {
11.       t1.add("d");
12.       t2.add("6");
13.       t2.add("3");
14.     }
15.     catch (Exception e) { System.out.print("ex "); }
16.     System.out.println(t1 + " " + t2);
17. } }
```

What is the result?

A. [6, 7, b] [6, 7, b]

B. [6, 7, b, d] [6, 7, b]

C. ex [6, 7, b] [6, 7, b]

D. ex [6, 7, b, d] [6, 7, b]

E. `[3, 6, 7, b, d]  [6, 7, b]`

F. `ex [6, 7, b, d]  [6, 7, b, d]`

G. Compilation fails due to error(s) in the code.

> **Answer (for Objective 6.3):**
>
> ☑ **D** is correct. The `subSet()` method is creating a "backed" collection with a certain value range. Additions to either collection that are in the backed collection's range will be added to both. Attempting to add an out-of-range entry to the backed collection throws an exception.
>
> ☒ **A, B, C, E, F,** and **G** are incorrect based on the above.

30. Given the current directory is `bigApp`, and the directory structure:

```
bigApp
    |-- classes
            |-- Cloned.class
            |-- com
                    |-- Cloned.class
                    |-- wickedlysmart
                                |-- Cloned.class
```

And the three files:

```
public class Cloned {
  public static void main(String[] args) { System.out.println("classes"); }
}
public class Cloned {
  public static void main(String[] args) { System.out.println("com"); }
}
public class Cloned {
  public static void main(String[] args) { System.out.println("ws"); }
}
```

Have been compiled into the `classes`, `com`, and `wickedlysmart` directories, respectively.

Which will produce the output `"ws"`? (Choose all that apply.)

A. `java -cp wickedlysmart:. Cloned`

B. `java -cp classes/com/wickedlysmart Cloned`

C. `java -cp classes/com/wickedlysmart:classes Cloned`

D. `java -cp classes:classes/com/wickedlysmart Cloned`

E. `java -cp .:classes/com/wickedlysmart:classes Cloned`

F. `java -cp .:classes/com:classes/com/wickedlysmart Cloned`

Answer (for Objective 7.2):

☑ **B, C,** and **E** correctly use the `classpath` option (`-cp`) to find the desired version of `Cloned.class`. The `":"` separates the various paths to search, and paths are searched in the order in which they appear in the command line.

☒ **A** will not find any `Cloned.class` file. **D** will find the `"classes"` version. **F** will find the `"com"` version.

31. Given:

```
1.  import java.io.*;
2.  public class Edgy {
3.    public static void main(String[] args) {
4.      try {
5.        wow();
6.        // throw new IOException();
7.      } finally {
8.        // throw new Error();
9.        // throw new IOException();
10.     }
11.   }
12.   static void wow() {
13.     // throw new IllegalArgumentException();
14.     // throw new IOException();
15. } }
```

And given that `IOException` is a direct subclass of `java.lang.Exception`, and that `IllegalArgumentException` is a runtime exception, which of the following, if uncommented independently, will compile? (Choose all that apply.)

A. Line 6

B. Line 8

C. Line 9

D. Line 13

E. Line 14

F. The code will NOT compile as is.

Answer (for Objective 2.5):

☑ **B** and **D** are correct. **B** will compile because Errors are "unchecked" by the compiler. **D** will compile because runtime exceptions are also "unchecked."

☒ **A** is incorrect because the `IOException` is not caught. **C** and **E** are incorrect because the `IOExceptions` are neither handled nor declared. **F** is incorrect based on the above.

32. Given two files:

```
1. package com;
2. public class MyClass {
3.    public static void howdy() { System.out.print("howdy "); }
4.    public static final int myConstant = 343;
5.    public static final MyClass mc = new MyClass();
6.    public int instVar = 42;
7. }
```

```
11. import com.MyClass;
12. public class TestImports2 {
13.    public static void main(String[] args) {
14.       MyClass.howdy();
15.       System.out.print(MyClass.myConstant + " ");
16.       System.out.print(myConstant + " ");
17.       howdy();
18.       System.out.print(mc.instVar + " ");
19.       System.out.print(instVar + " ");
20. } }
```

What is the result? (Choose all that apply.)

A. howdy 343 343 howdy 42 42

B. Compilation fails due to an error on line 14.

C. Compilation fails due to an error on line 15.

D. Compilation fails due to an error on line 16.

E. Compilation fails due to an error on line 17.

F. Compilation fails due to an error on line 18.

G. Compilation fails due to an error on line 19.

Answer (for Objective 1.1):

☑ **D, E, F,** and **G** are correct. Lines 16, 17, 18, and 19 are incorrect ways to access the elements of MyClass in package com.

☒ **A** is incorrect because the code does not compile. **B** and **C** are incorrect because those lines access the elements correctly.

33. Given this code inside a method:

```
13.    int count = 0;
14.    outer:
15.    for(int x = 0; x < 5; x++) {
```

```
16.      middle:
17.      for(int y = 0; y < 5; y++) {
18.        if(y == 1) continue middle;
19.        if(y == 3) break middle;
20.        count++;
21.      }
22.      if(x > 2) continue outer;
23.        count = count + 10;
24.    }
25.    System.out.println("count: " + count);
```

What is the result?

A. count: 33

B. count: 40

C. count: 45

D. count: 65

E. Compilation fails.

F. The code runs in an endless loop.

Answer (for Objective 2.2):

☑ **B** is correct. The `label`, `break`, and `continue` statements are all legal. A `continue` statement ends the current iteration of a loop, a `break` statement ends all iterations of a loop.

☒ **A, C, D, E,** and **F** are incorrect based on the above.

34. Given:

```
2. public class Organic<E> {
3.    void react(E e) { }
4.    static void main(String[] args) {
5.      // Organic<? extends Organic> compound = new Aliphatic<Organic>();
6.      // Organic<? super Aliphatic> compound = new Aliphatic<Organic>();
7.      compound.react(new Organic());
8.      compound.react(new Aliphatic());
9.      compound.react(new Hexane());
10. } }
11. class Aliphatic<F> extends Organic<F> { }
12. class Hexane<G> extends Aliphatic<G> { }
```

Which, taken independently, are true? (Choose all that apply.)

A. If line 5 is uncommented, compilation fails due to an error at line 7.

B. If line 5 is uncommented, compilation fails due to an error at line 8.

C. If line 5 is uncommented, compilation fails due to an error at line 9.

D. If line 6 is uncommented, compilation fails due to an error at line 7.

E. If line 6 is uncommented, compilation fails due to an error at line 8.

F. If line 6 is uncommented, compilation fails due to an error at line 9.

Answer (for Objective 6.4):

☑ **A, B, C,** and **D** are correct. The generic type of the reference <? extends Organic> says that the generic type of the instantiation can be either Organic, or a subtype of Organic. Since the compiler doesn't know this instantiation generic type (runtime type), it does NOT bind any value to its generic criteria, so **A, B,** and **C** are correct. On the other hand, the generic type of the reference <? super Aliphatic> says that the generic type of the instantiation can be either Aliphatic, or a supertype of Aliphatic. Although the compiler doesn't know the instantiation generic type, it knows that it will be either Aliphatic, or a supertype of Aliphatic—such types can bind any value that is either Aliphatic or a subtype of it. Therefore, **D** is correct.

☒ **E** and **F** are incorrect based on the above.

35. Given:

```
4. public class Hemlock {
5.    static StringBuffer sb;
6.    StringBuffer sb2;
7.    public static void main(String[] args) {
8.      sb = sb.append(new Hemlock().go(new StringBuffer("hey")));
9.      System.out.println(sb);
10.   }
11.   { sb2 = new StringBuffer("hi "); }
12.   StringBuffer go(StringBuffer s) {
13.     System.out.print(s + " oh " + sb2);
14.     return new StringBuffer("ey");
15.   }
16.   static { sb = new StringBuffer("yo "); }
17. }
```

What is the result?

A. yo ey

B. hey oh hi

C. hey oh hi ey

D. oh hi hey

E. hey oh hi yo ey

F. yo hey oh hi ey

G. Compilation fails.

H. An exception is thrown at runtime.

Answer (for Objective 1.3):

☑ **E** is correct. The final contents of sb is "yo ey". Remember that the `static` initializer runs before any instances are created.

☒ **A, B, C, D, F, G,** and **H** are incorrect based on the above.

36. Given:

```
1. class Hotel {
2.    static void doStuff(int x) {
3.       assert (x < 0) : "hotel";
4.    }
5. }
6. public class Motel13 extends Hotel {
7.    public static void main(String[] args) {
8.       doStuff(-5);
9.       int y = 0;
10.      assert (y < 0) : "motel";
11. } }
```

Which of the following invocations will run without exception? (Choose all that apply.)

A. java Motel13

B. java -ea Motel13

C. java -da:Hotel Motel13

D. java -da:Motel13 Motel13

E. java -ea -da:Hotel Motel13

F. java -ea -da:Motel13 Motel13

Answer (for Objective 2.3):

☑ **A, C, D,** and **F** are correct. When assertions are enabled, the Motel13 class will throw an AssertionError, the Hotel class will not. Invocations **A, C,** and **D** do not enable assertions for Motel13. **F** is correct because although assertions were enabled, the "-da" switch selectively disabled assertions for the Motel13 class.

☒ **B** and **E** are incorrect because assertions are enabled for Motel13.

37. Given:

```
3. class One {
4.    void go1() { System.out.print("1 ");  }
5.    final void go2() { System.out.print("2 "); }
6.    private void go3() { System.out.print("3 "); }
7. }
8. public class OneB extends One {
9.    void go1() { System.out.print("1b "); }
10.    void go3() { System.out.print("3b "); }
11.
12.    public static void main(String[] args) {
13.       new OneB().go1();
14.       new One().go1();
15.       new OneB().go2();
16.       new OneB().go3();
17.       new One().go3();
18. } }
```

What is the result?

A. 1 1 2 3 3

B. 1b 1 2 3b 3

C. 1b 1b 2 3b 3b

D. Compilation fails due to a single error.

E. Compilation fails due to errors on more than one line.

Answer (for Objective 1.4):

☑ **D** is correct. The only error is on line 17: Class OneB cannot find class One's private go3() method. Note that on line 10 we're NOT overriding class One's go3() method.

☒ **A, B, C,** and **E** are incorrect based on the above.

38. Given:

```
3. public class Gauntlet {
4.   public static void main(String[] args) {
5.     String r = "0";
6.     int x = 3, y = 4;
7.     boolean test = false;
8.     if((x > 2) || (test = true))
9.     if((y > 5) || (++x == 4))
10.    if((test == true) || (++y == 4))
11.    r += "1";
12.    else if(y == 5) r += "2";
13.    else r += "3";
14.    else r += "4";
15.    // else r += "5";
16.    System.out.println(r);
17. } }
```

And given that, if necessary you can add line 15 to make the code compile, what is the result? (Choose all that apply.)

A. At line 10, test will equal true

B. At line 10, test will equal false

C. The output will be 02

D. The output will be 03

E. The output will be 023

F. The code will compile as is.

G. The code will only compile if line 15 is added.

Answer (for Objective 2.1):

☑ **B, C,** and **F** are correct. Line 8 doesn't change the value of test because of the short circuit operator. The first two ifs are true, but the third is false (although "y" is incremented), so the "else if" is executed. The code compiles as is because not all if statements need to have matching else statements.

☒ **A, D, E,** and **G** are incorrect based on the above.

39. Given:

```
2. import rt.utils.Remote;
3. public class Controller{
4.   public static void main(String[] args){
5.     Remote remote = new Remote();
6. }   }
```

And `rt.utils.Remote` class is properly bundled into a JAR file called `rtutils.jar`.

And given the following steps:

P. Place `rtutils.jar` in the $ROOT directory.

Q. Extract `rtutils.jar` and put `rt` directory with its subdirectories in the $ROOT directory.

R. Extract `rtutils.jar` and place `Remote.class` in the $ROOT directory.

S. Place `rtutils.jar` in the $JAVA_HOME/jre/lib/ext directory.

X. Compile using: `javac -cp rtutils.jar Controller.java`

Y. Compile using: `javac Controller.java`

Z. Compile using: `javac -cp . Controller.java`

If `Controller.java` resides in the $ROOT directory, which set(s) of steps will compile the Controller class? (Choose all that apply.)

A. P -> X

B. Q -> Y

C. R -> Z

D. P -> Z

E. R -> Y

F. S -> X

G. S -> Z

Answer (for Objective 7.5):

☑ **A, B, F** and **G** are correct. When the JAR is placed in any directory other than $JAVA_HOME/jre/lib/ext directory, it should be included in the classpath. If the JAR file is in the $JAVA_HOME/jre/lib/ext directory, it's NOT necessary to include the JAR in the classpath. If the JAR file is extracted, the complete directory structure should exist on the classpath.

☒ **C, D,** and **E** are incorrect based on the above.

40. Given:

```
2. public class Boot {
3.   static String s;
4.   static { s = ""; }
5.   { System.out.print("shinier "); }
```

```
6.    static { System.out.print(s.concat("better ")); }
7.    Boot() { System.out.print(s.concat("bigger ")); }
8.    public static void main(String[] args) {
9.      new Boot();
10.     System.out.println("boot");
11. } }
```

What is the result?

A. better bigger boot

B. better bigger shinier boot

C. better shinier bigger boot

D. bigger shinier better boot

E. shinier better bigger boot

F. A NullPointerException is thrown at runtime.

G. An ExceptionInInitializationError is thrown at runtime.

Answer (for Objective 2.6):

☑ **C** is correct. static init blocks run before instance init blocks (in the order in which they appear, respectively), and init blocks run hard on the heels of a constructor's call to super().

☒ **A, B, D, E, F**, and **G** are incorrect based on the above.

41. Fill in the blanks using the following fragments, so the code compiles and produces the output: "0 4 "

Note: You might not need to fill in all of the blanks, you won't use all of the fragments, and each fragment can be used only once.

Code:

```
import _____
public class Latte {
  public static void main(String[] args) {
    Pattern p = _____
    Matcher m = p.matcher(_____);
    while(_____)
      System.out.print(_____ + " ");
} }
```

Fragments:

```
java.util.*;              Pattern.getPattern("aba");
Pattern.compile("aba");   "ab aa ba"
new Pattern("aba");       " aba baabaa ba"
m.find()                  "abaababa"
m.next()                  "abababa"
m.hasNext()               m.start()
java.regex.*;             m.match()
java.util.regex.*;
```

Answer (for Objective 3.4):

```
import java.util.regex.*;
public class Latte {
  public static void main(String[] args) {
    Pattern p = Pattern.compile("aba");
    Matcher m = p.matcher("abababa");
    while(m.find())
      System.out.print(m.start() + " ");
  }
}
```

42. Given:

```
3. public static void main(String[] args) {
4.    try {
5.      throw new Error();
6.    }
7.    catch (Error e) {
8.      try { throw new RuntimeException(); }
9.      catch (Throwable t) { }
10.   }
11.   System.out.println("phew");
12. }
```

Which are true? (Choose all that apply.)

A. The output is phew

B. The code runs without output.

C. Compilation fails due to an error on line 5.

D. Compilation fails due to an error on line 7.

E. Compilation fails due to an error on line 8.

F. Compilation fails due to an error on line 9.

Answer (for Objective 2.4):

☑ **A** is correct. It's legal to throw and handle errors and runtime exceptions. RuntimeException is a sub-subclass of Throwable.

☒ **B** is incorrect because the code produces "phew". **C**, **D**, **E**, and **F** are incorrect based on the above.

43. Given:

```
1. import java.util.*;
2. public class Analyzer {
3.   static List<Exception> me;
4.   Exception myEx;
5.   public static void main(String[] args) {
6.     Analyzer[] aa = {new Analyzer(), new Analyzer()};
7.     me = new ArrayList<Exception>();
8.     for(int i = 0; i < 2; i++) {
9.       try {
10.        if(i == 0) throw new Exception();
11.        if(i == 1) throw new MyException();
12.      }
13.      catch(Exception e) {
14.        me.add(e);
15.        aa[i].myEx = e;
16.      }
17.    }
18.    System.out.println(aa.length + " " + me.size());
19.    aa = null; me = null;
20.    // do more stuff
21. } }
22. class MyException extends Exception { }
```

When line 20 is reached, how many objects are eligible for garbage collection?

A. 2

B. 4

C. 5

D. 6

E. 7

F. 8

Answer (for Objective 7.4):

☑ **D** is correct. Line 6 creates three objects: an array and two `Analyzer` objects. Line 7 creates an `ArrayList` object. Line 10 and 11 each create some sort of `Exception` object. While it's true that each `Analyzer` also has a reference to an `Exception` object, those references are referring to the same exceptions that are in the array.

☒ **A, B, C, E,** and **F** are incorrect based on the above.

44. Given the following from the `java.io.File` API:
Field Summary: `static String separator`
Method Summary: `static File[] listRoots()`
And given:

```
2. // insert code here
3. // insert code here
4. public class Eieio {
5.    public static void main(String[] args) {
6.      try {
7.        String s = "subdir" + separator + "myFile.txt";
8.        java.io.File f = new java.io.File(s);
9.        java.io.FileReader fr = new java.io.FileReader(f);
10.       java.io.File[] r = listRoots();
11.       fr.close();
12.     }
13.     catch(Exception e) { }
14. } }
```

And the following four fragments:

I. `import java.io.*;`

II. `import static java.io.File.*;`

III. `import static java.io.File.separator;`

IV. `import static java.io.File.listRoots;`

Which set(s) of fragments, inserted independently on lines 2 and/or 3, will compile? (Choose all that apply.)

A. Fragment I

B. Fragment II

C. Fragments I and III

D. Fragments I and IV

E. Fragments II and IV

F. Fragments III and IV

Answer (for Objective 7.1):

☑ **B, E,** and **F** are correct. The code provides some fully qualified names from the `java.io` package, but the names for the `"separator"` field and the `listRoots()` method are not fully qualified. Fragment II alone is the correct "static import" syntax, and therefore **B** and **E** are correct. Fragment III provides the name for `separator`, and fragment IV provides the name for `listRoots()`, so taken together III and IV will compile.

☒ **A, C,** and **D** are incorrect based on the above.

45. Given:

```
1. import java.util.*;
2. public class Bucket {
3.    public static void main(String[] args) {
4.       Set<String> hs = new HashSet<String>();
5.       Set<String> lh = new LinkedHashSet<String>();
6.       Set<String> ts = new TreeSet<String>();
7.       List<String> al = new ArrayList<String>();
8.       String[] v = {"1", "3", "1", "2"};
9.       for(int i=0; i< v.length; i++) {
10.         hs.add(v[i]); lh.add(v[i]); ts.add(v[i]); al.add(v[i]);
11.      }
12.      Iterator it = hs.iterator();
13.      while(it.hasNext()) System.out.print(it.next() + " ");
14.      Iterator it2 = lh.iterator();
15.      while(it2.hasNext()) System.out.print(it2.next() + " ");
16.      Iterator it3 = ts.iterator();
17.      while(it3.hasNext()) System.out.print(it3.next() + " ");
18.      Iterator it5 = al.iterator();
19.      while(it5.hasNext()) System.out.print(it5.next() + " ");
20. } }
```

Which statements are true? (Choose all that apply.)

A. An exception is thrown at runtime.

B. Compilation fails due to an error on line 18.

C. `"1 3 2"` is only guaranteed to be in the output once.

D. `"1 2 3"` is only guaranteed to be in the output once.

E. `"1 3 2"` is guaranteed to be in the output more than once.

F. `"1 2 3"` is guaranteed to be in the output more than once.

G. `"1 3 1 2"` is guaranteed to be in the output at least once.

H. Compilation fails due to error(s) on lines other than line 18.

Answer (for Objective 6.1):

☑ **C, D,** and **G** are correct. The code is all legal and runs without exception. For `HashSets`, iteration order is not guaranteed. For `LinkedHashSets`, iteration order equals insertion order. For `TreeSets`, the default iteration order is ascending. For `ArrayLists`, iteration order is by index, and when using `add()`, index "kind of" equals insertion order. Of course, `Sets` don't allow duplicates.

☒ **A, B, E, F,** and **H** are incorrect based on the above.

46. Given:

```
 2. public class Maize {
 3.   public static void main(String[] args) {
 4.     String s = "12";
 5.     s.concat("ab");
 6.     s = go(s);
 7.     System.out.println(s);
 8.   }
 9.   static String go(String s) {
10.     s.concat("56");
11.     return s;
12. } }
```

What is the result?

A. ab

B. 12

C. ab56

D. 12ab

E. 1256

F. 12ab56

G. Compilation fails.

Answer (for Objective 3.1):

☑ **B** is correct. Strings are immutable. If we captured the result of line 5, we would have `"12ab"`, but we didn't capture that, so that `String` is lost. Similarly, the result of line 10 is lost.

☒ **A, C, D, E, F,** and **G** are incorrect based on the above.

47. Given:

```
4. class MySuper { protected MySuper() { System.out.print("ms "); } }
5. public class MyTester extends MySuper {
6.    private MyTester() { System.out.print("mt "); }
7.    public static void main(String[] args) {
8.      new MySuper();
9.      class MyInner {
10.        private MyInner() { System.out.print("mi "); }
11.        { new MyTester(); }
12.        { new MySuper(); }
13.      }
14.      new MyInner();
15. } }
```

What is the result?

A. ms mi mt ms

B. ms mt ms mi

C. ms mi ms mt ms

D. ms ms mt ms mi

E. Compilation fails.

F. An exception is thrown at runtime.

Answer (for Objective 5.3):

☑ **D** is correct. MyTester can access MySuper's protected constructor, and MyInner can access MyTester's private constructor. As far as the order goes, the MyInner code is invoked after it's declared. When the MyInner code does run, the instance init blocks run after MyInner's constructor's call to super(), and before the rest of the constructor runs. Remember that a new instance of MyTester calls MySuper's constructor.

☒ **A, B, C, E** and **F** are incorrect based on the above.

48. Given:

```
2. public class Tshirt extends Thread {
3.    public static void main(String[] args) {
4.      System.out.print(Thread.currentThread().getId() + " ");
5.      Thread t1 = new Thread(new Tshirt());
6.      Thread t2 = new Thread(new Tshirt());
7.      t1.start();
8.      t2.run();
9.    }
```

```
10.    public void run() {
11.       for(int i = 0; i < 2; i++)
12.          System.out.print(Thread.currentThread().getId() + " ");
13. } }
```

Which are true? (Choose all that apply.)

A. No output is produced.

B. The output could be 1 1 9 9 1

C. The output could be 1 2 9 9 2

D. The output could be 1 9 9 9 9

E. An exception is thrown at runtime.

F. Compilation fails due to an error on line 4.

G. Compilation fails due to an error on line 8.

Answer (for Objective 4.1):

☑ **B** is correct. It's legal to get the ID of the "main" thread. It's also legal to call run()
directly, but it won't start a new thread. In this case, it's just invoking run() on main's
call stack. In this code, t2 is never started, so there are only two threads (main and t1),
therefore only two IDs are in the output. **D** is incorrect because no thread's getId()
method is called more than three times.

☒ **A, C, E, F,** and **G** are incorrect based on the above.

49. Given:

```
14.    FileWriter fw1 =
          new FileWriter(new File("f1.txt"));
15.    FileWriter fw2 =
          new FileWriter(new BufferedWriter(new PrintWriter("f2.txt")));
16.    PrintWriter pw1 =
          new PrintWriter(new BufferedWriter(new FileWriter("f3.txt")));
17.    PrintWriter pw2 =
          new PrintWriter(new FileWriter(new File("f4.txt")));
```

And given the proper imports and error handling, what is the result?

A. Compilation succeeds.

B. Compilation fails due to multiple errors.

C. Compilation fails due only to an error on line 14.

D. Compilation fails due only to an error on line 15.

E. Compilation fails due only to an error on line 16.

F. Compilation fails due only to an error on line 17.

Answer (for Objective 3.2):

☑ **D** is correct. The code is using so-called "chained-methods" (or constructors) syntax. The *objects* fw1, pw1, and pw2 are created correctly. The *object* fw2 cannot be created because a FileWriter cannot be constructed using a BufferedWriter object.

☒ **A, B, C, E,** and **F** are incorrect based on the above.

50. Given:

```
2. import java.util.*;
3. public class GIS {
4.    public static void main(String[] args) {
5.       TreeMap<String, String> m1 = new TreeMap<String, String>();
6.       m1.put("a", "amy"); m1.put("f", "frank");
7.       NavigableMap<String, String> m2 = m1.descendingMap();
8.       try {
9.         m1.put("j", "john");
10.        m2.put("m", "mary");
11.       }
12.       catch (Exception e) { System.out.print("ex "); }
13.       m1.pollFirstEntry();
14.       System.out.println(m1 + "\n" + m2);
15. } }
```

What is the result?

A. {f=frank, j=john} {f=frank}

B. {f=frank, j=john} {m=mary, f=frank}

C. ex {f=frank, j=john} {f=frank}

D. {f=frank, j=john, m=mary} {m=mary, j=john, f=frank}

E. ex {f=frank, j=john, m=mary} {f=frank}

F. ex {f=frank, j=john, m=mary} {f=frank, a=amy}

G. {a=amy, f=frank, j=john, m=mary} {f=frank, a=amy}

H. Compilation fails due to error(s) in the code.

Answer (for Objective 6.3):

☑ **D** is correct. The `descendingMap()` method creates a `NavigableMap` in reverse order, which is "backed" to the map it was created from. It is NOT a subMap, so there is no worry about being outside of its range. The `pollFirstEntry()` method returns *AND* removes the "first" entry in the Map.

☒ **A, B, C, E, F, G,** and **H** are incorrect based on the above.

51. Given:

```
2. public class Clover extends Harrier {
3.    String bark() { return "feed me "; }
4.    public static void main(String[] args) {
5.      Dog[] dogs = new Dog[3];
6.      dogs[0] = new Harrier();
7.      dogs[1] = (Dog)new Clover();
8.      dogs[2] = (Dog)new Harrier();
9.      for(Dog d: dogs)  System.out.print(d.bark());
10. } }
11. class Dog { String bark() { return "bark "; } }
12. class Harrier extends Dog { String bark() { return "woof "; } }
```

What is the result? (Choose all that apply.)

A. bark bark bark

B. woof bark bark

C. woof feed me woof

D. Compilation fails due to an error on line 6.

E. Compilation fails due to an error on line 7.

F. Compilation fails due to an error on line 8.

G. Compilation fails due to an error on line 9.

Answer (for Objective 5.2):

☑ **C** is correct. All the code is legal, and line 9 is using a for-each loop. The polymorphic invocations of `bark()` use the version of `bark()` that corresponds with the object's type, not the reference variable's type.

☒ **A, B, D, E, F,** and **G** are incorrect based on the above.

52. Given:

```
1. public class Egg<E extends Object> {
2.    E egg;
3.    public Egg(E egg) {
4.       this.egg=egg;
5.    }
6.    public E getEgg() {
7.       return egg;
8.    }
9.    public static void main(String[] args) {
10.      Egg<Egg> egg1 = new Egg(42);
11.      Egg egg2 = new Egg<Egg>(egg1.getEgg());
12.      Egg egg3 = egg1.getEgg();
13. } }
```

Which are true? (Choose all that apply).

A. Compilation fails.

B. An exception is thrown at runtime.

C. Line 10 compiles with a warning.

D. Line 10 compiles without warnings.

E. Line 11 compiles with a warning.

F. Line 11 compiles without warnings.

Answer (for Objective 6.4):

☑ **B, C,** and **F** are correct. Compiler warnings are given when assigning a non-generic object to a reference with generic type. **F** is correct and **E** is incorrect, because the reference type of egg2 doesn't have any generic type specification. Line 12 assigns the return value of egg1.getEgg() to egg3. It compiles because the compiler assumes that the return value of egg1.getEgg() will be an Egg. **B** is correct because at runtime, the actual return type will be an Integer, which causes a ClassCastException to be thrown.

☒ **A, D,** and **E** are incorrect based on the above.

53. Given:

```
2. public class Tolt {
3.    public static void checkIt(int a) {
4.       if(a == 1)  throw new IllegalArgumentException();
5.    }
```

```
6.    public static void main(String[] args) {
7.       for(int x=0; x<2; x++)
8.          try {
9.             System.out.print("t ");
10.            checkIt(x);
11.            System.out.print("t2 ");
12.          }
13.          finally { System.out.print("f "); }
14. } }
```

What is the result?

A. `"t t2 f t "`

B. `"t t2 f t f "`

C. `"t t2 f t t2 f "`

D. `"t t2 f t "`, followed by an exception.

E. `"t t2 f t f "`, followed by an exception.

F. `"t t2 f t t2 f "`, followed by an exception.

G. Compilation fails.

Answer (for Objective 2.5):

☑ **E** is correct. As far as the exception goes, it's thrown during the second iteration of the for loop, and it's uncaught and undeclared (which is legal since it's a runtime exception). Remember, finally (almost) ALWAYS runs. In main(), the code is legal: the entire try-finally code is considered a single statement from the for loop's perspective, and of course the idea of a try-finally is legal; a catch statement is not required.

☒ **A, B, C, D, F,** and **G** are incorrect based on the above.

54. Given:

```
2. class Noodle {
3.    String name;
4.    Noodle(String n) { name = n; }
5. }
6. class AsianNoodle extends Noodle {
7.    public boolean equals(Object o) {
8.       AsianNoodle n = (AsianNoodle)o;
9.       if(name.equals(n.name))  return true;
10.      return false;
11.   }
```

```
12.    public int hashCode() { return name.length(); }
13.    AsianNoodle(String s) { super(s); }
14. }
15. public class Soba extends AsianNoodle {
16.    public static void main(String[] args) {
17.       Noodle n1 = new Noodle("bob");  Noodle n2 = new Noodle("bob");
18.       AsianNoodle a1 = new AsianNoodle("fred");
19.       AsianNoodle a2 = new AsianNoodle("fred");
20.       Soba s1 = new Soba("jill");  Soba s2 = new Soba("jill");
21.       System.out.print(n1.equals(n2) + " " + (n1 == n2) + " | ");
22.       System.out.print(a1.equals(a2) + " " + (a1 == a2) + " | ");
23.       System.out.println(s1.equals(s2) + " " + (s1 == s2));
24.    }
25.    Soba(String s) { super(s); }
26. }
```

What is the result?

A. Compilation fails.

B. `true true | true true | true true`

C. `true false | true false | true false`

D. `false false | true false | true false`

E. `false false | true false | false false`

F. `false false | false false | false false`

Answer (for Objective 6.2):

☑ **D** is correct. `Noodle` uses the default `equals()` method that returns `true` only when comparing two references to the same object. `AsianNoodle` overrides `equals()` (and `Soba` inherits the overridden method) and uses the `name` variable to determine equality. The `==` operator ALWAYS compares to see whether two reference variables refer to the same object.

☒ **A, B, C, E,** and **F** are incorrect based on the above.

---

55. Given:

```
2. public class Checkout2 implements Runnable {
3.    void doStuff() { }
4.    synchronized void doSynch() {
5.       try { Thread.sleep(1000); }
6.       catch (Exception e) { System.out.print("e "); }
```

```
7.     }
8.     public static void main(String[] args) {
9.       long start = System.currentTimeMillis();
10.      new Thread(new Checkout2()).start();
11.      Thread t1 = new Thread(new Checkout2());
12.      t1.start();
13.      try { t1.join(); }
14.      catch (Exception e) { System.out.print("e "); }
15.      System.out.println("elapsed: "
                            + (System.currentTimeMillis() - start));
16.    }
17.    public void run() {
18.      for(int j = 0; j < 4; j++) {
19.        doStuff();
20.        try { Thread.sleep(1000); }
21.        catch (Exception e) { System.out.print("e "); }
22.        doSynch();
23. } } }
```

Which are true? (Choose all that apply.)

A. Compilation fails.

B. Elapsed time will be about eight seconds.

C. Elapsed time will be about nine seconds.

D. Elapsed time will be about 12 seconds.

E. Changing doSynch() to be unsynchronized will change elapsed by only a few milliseconds.

F. Changing doSynch() to be unsynchronized will change elapsed by 450 or more milliseconds.

Answer (for Objective 4.3):

☑ **B** and **E** are correct. Even when doSynch() is synchronized, the two run() invocations aren't running against the same Checkout2 object. This code creates two distinct Checkout2 objects, so there is no synchronization.

☒ **A, C, D,** and **F** are incorrect based on the above.

56. Your virtual-world simulator is designed such that Grobnets can have several Ooflas, and Yazells support the contract implied by Whompers. Grobnets are a type of Yazell, and can also act as

Floordums or Whompers. Which of the following code fragments legally represent this design? (Choose all that apply.)

A.
```
import java.util.*;
interface Floordum { }
interface Whomper { }
class Grobnet extends Yazell implements Floordum { List<Oofla> o; }
class Oofla { }
class Yazell implements Whomper { }
```

B.
```
import java.util.*;
class Oofla { }
class Yazell implements Whomper { }
class Floordum { }
interface Whomper { }
class Grobnet extends Yazell, Floordum { List<Oofla> o; }
```

C.
```
import java.util.*;
interface Floordum { }
interface Whomper { }
class Grobnet extends Yazell implements Floordum, Oofla { }
class Oofla { }
interface Yazell implements Whomper { }
```

D.
```
import java.util.*;
interface Floordum { }
interface Whomper { }
class Grobnet extends Yazell implements Floordum { Set<Oofla> o; }
class Oofla { }
class Yazell { Whomper w; }
```

Answer (for Objective 5.5):

☑ **A** is correct. The phrase translations are "can have" usually means a class has an instance variable, or set of variables; "support the contract implied" should be taken to mean implementing an interface; "type of" typically means subclass; "can act as" is often another way to say implement an interface. Notice in answer **A** that Grobnet indirectly implements Whompers by extending Yazells.

☒ **B, C,** and **D** are incorrect. **B** is incorrect because a class can't extend more than one class. **C** is incorrect because implementing an interface is not the same as having an instance variable of the interface's type. In addition, interfaces can't implement interfaces. **D** is incorrect because Yazell has-a Whomper and the design calls for Yazell to implement Whompers.

57. Given:

```
1. import java.util.*;
2. public class Ps {
3.    public static void main(String[] args) {
4.       PriorityQueue<String> pq = new PriorityQueue<String>();
5.       pq.add("4");
6.       pq.add("7");
7.       pq.add("2");
8.       // insert code here
9. } }
```

Which code fragment(s), inserted independently at line 8, produce the output "2-4-7-"? (Choose all that apply.)

A.
```
Iterator it2 = pq.iterator();
while(it2.hasNext()) System.out.print(it2.next() + "-");
System.out.println();
```

B.
```
Arrays.sort(pq.toArray());
Iterator it3 = pq.iterator();
while(it3.hasNext()) System.out.print(it3.next() + "-");
System.out.println();
```

C.
```
Object[] pqa = pq.toArray();
Arrays.sort(pqa);
for(Object o: pqa) System.out.print(o + "-");
System.out.println();
```

D.
```
String s = pq.poll();
while (s != null) {
  System.out.print(s + "-");
  s = pq.poll();
}
```

E.
```
String s = pq.peek();
while (s != null) {
  System.out.print(s + "-");
  s = pq.peek();
}
```

Answer (for Objective 6.1):

☑ **C** and **D** are correct ways to determine how elements in the `PriorityQueue` would be prioritized, although **D** consumes the queue in the process.

☒ **A** is incorrect because the `Iterator` for `PriorityQueue` does NOT guarantee a sorted result. **B** is incorrect because the `toArray()` method creates a new array, it doesn't change the existing array. **E** is incorrect because `peek()` only looks at a queue's "first" element, it doesn't consume it, so an infinite loop is created. Note: If you didn't get answer **A** that's okay. Answer **A** might be a little bit on the trivia end of the spectrum. So if you got this question correct except for answer **A**, give yourself full credit.

58. Given that the current directory is `bigApp`, and the following directory structure:

```
bigApp
    |-- classes
    |-- source
            |-- com
                |-- wickedlysmart
                                |-- BigAppClass1.java
```

And the code:

```
package com.wickedlysmart;
public class BigAppClass1 {
   int doStuff() { return 42; }
}
```

And the following command-line invocations:

I. `javac -d source/com/wickedlysmart/BigAppClass1.java`

II. `javac -d classes source/com/wickedlysmart/BigAppClass1.java`

III. `javac -d classes/com/wickedlysmart source/com/wickedlysmart/BigAppClass1.java`

Which are true? (Choose all that apply.)

A. Invocation I will compile the file and place the `.class` file in the `bigApp` directory.

B. Invocation II will compile the file and place the `.class` file in the `classes` directory.

C. Invocation I will compile the file and place the `.class` file in the `wickedlysmart` directory.

D. Under the `bigApp/classes` directory, invocation II will build `com/wickedlysmart` subdirectories, and place the `.class` file in `wickedlysmart`.

E.   Under the `bigApp/classes` directory, invocation III will build `com/wickedlysmart` subdirectories, and place the `.class` file in `wickedlysmart`.

Answer (for Objective 7.2):

☑   **D** correctly describes the results that the `"-d"` option will produce.

☒   **A** and **C** will not compile. **E** inaccurately describes the directories that will be built. **B** is incorrect based on the above.

59. Given:

```
2. class Jog implements Runnable {
3.    public void run() {
4.      for(int i = 0; i < 8; i++) {
5.        try { Thread.sleep(200); }
6.        catch (Exception e) { System.out.print("exc "); }
7.        System.out.print(i + " ");
8. } } }
9. public class Marathon {
10.    public static void main(String[] args) throws Exception {
11.      Jog j1 = new Jog();
12.      Thread t1 = new Thread(j1);
13.      t1.start();
14.      t1.sleep(500);
15.      System.out.print("pre ");
16.      t1.interrupt();
17.      t1.sleep(500);
18.      System.out.print("post ");
19. } }
```

Assuming that `sleep()` sleeps for about the amount of time specified in its argument, and that all other code runs almost instantly, which output is likely? (Choose all that apply.)

A.   exc

B.   0 1 pre exc post

C.   exc 0 1 2 3 4 5 6 7

D.   pre post 0 1 2 3 4 5 6 7

E.   pre exc 0 1 post 2 3 4 5 6 7

F.   0 1 pre exc 2 3 4 post 5 6 7

Answer (for Objective 4.2):

☑ **F** is correct. Remember that `sleep()` is `static` and that when a sleeping thread is interrupted, an `InterruptedException` is thrown. In this code, the `t1` thread is started, and then the `main` thread sleeps for 500 milliseconds. While the `main` thread is sleeping, `t1` sleeps and then iterates a couple of times. When `main` wakes up, it interrupts `t1` (which is almost certainly sleeping), causing the exception, which is handled. Then, `main` goes back to sleep for a while, `t1` iterates a few more times, and `main` reawakens and completes, and finally `t1` completes.

☒ **A, B, C, D,** and **E** are incorrect based on the above.

60. Given:

```
2. class Explode {
3.    static String s = "";
4.    static { s += "sb1 "; }
5.    Explode() { s += "e "; }
6. }
7. public class C4 extends Explode {
8.    C4() {
9.       s += "c4 ";
10.      new Explode();
11.   }
12.   static {
13.      new C4();
14.      System.out.print(s);
15.   }
16.   { s += "i "; }
17.   public static void main(String[] args) { }
18. }
```

And given the command-line invocation `"java C4"`, what is the result?

A. `e c4 i`

B. `e i c4`

C. `e sb1 i c4`

D. `sb1 e i c4 e`

E. `sb1 e c4 i e`

F.   Compilation fails.

G.   A `StackOverflowError` is thrown.

H.   An exception other than `StackOverflowError` is thrown.

Answer (for Objective 5.4):

☑   **D** is correct. `Static` init blocks run once, when a class is first loaded. Instance init blocks run after a constructor's call to `super()`, but before the rest of the constructor runs. It's legal to invoke `new()` from within a constructor, and when a subclass invokes `new()` on a superclass no recursive calls are implied.

☒   **A, B, C, E, F, G**, and **H** are incorrect based on the above.

Analyzing Your Results

First, we have to come clean. We tried to make this last exam the toughest one in the book.

Table 7-1 is based partly on the assumption that this last exam is a bit tougher than the real thing. We hear from a lot of candidates, and we understand that everyone has different goals. If your goal is to score over 90 percent on the real exam, then you have to analyze your results differently than if your goal is to pass comfortably. The following table is based on a couple of assumptions:

- This last exam is a bit tougher than the real thing.
- Your goal is to pass comfortably. By that, we mean that when you take the real exam you don't just barely squeak (squeal?) by with a passing score, but that you're also pleased even if you don't get 90 percent.

As we've said several times, as of this writing, a passing score on the OCP Java SE Programmer exam is 58.33 percent (35 out of 60 questions).

| TABLE 7-1 | What Your Score Means If You Want to Pass Comfortably |

Number of Correct Answers	Recommended Plan
0–30	You should do a LOT of studying before taking the real exam.
31–35	You should do more studying before taking the real exam.
36–44	You're right on the "passing" boundary. Our guess would be that you'd pass at this point, but not by a lot.
45–60	We suspect that you'll pass comfortably.

More Study Tips, One Last Time

We're probably stating the obvious when we say that the practice exams in this book can only be used so often. If you keep taking them over and over again, you run the risk of memorizing the questions and answers and possibly not understanding the underlying Java concepts. So our advice is this: You can probably take each of these exams only a couple of times before they start to lose their value.

On the other hand, as we mentioned in Chapter 4, almost all of these questions CAN be used as jumping off points for your own exploration. If you want to do more studying (or if you're sick of studying, but still need to do more of it ☺), then a fantastic way to study is to find the questions in this book that focus on the topics with which you're struggling. Take those questions, and type in the code. Compile the code, fix the errors, and run the code. Then, change the code. Ask yourself "what if" questions about the code… "What if doStuff() was static?", "What if I did a peek() instead of a poll()?"… Try it! That's how the exam creation team created the exam, and that's how we created most of the questions in this book.

Good luck, and let us know on JavaRanch.com how you're doing.

A

Objectives Index

U se this appendix when you want to look up questions for a particular objective. Each objective has two sets of page numbers. The "Q" rows refer to the pages where a question is first presented. The "A" rows refer to the pages where a question AND its answer are presented.

Obj.	Description	Page Numbers
	Section 1: Declarations, Initialization, and Scoping	
1.1	Declare classes (abstract, nested), interfaces, enums, packages, imports.	Q: 32, 58, 65, 159, 240, 250, 329, 343 A: 44, 93, 104, 195, 276, 289, 370, 389
1.2	Declare interfaces and abstract classes. Implement interfaces, extend abstract classes.	Q: 60, 76, 161, 162, 245, 333, 340 A: 95, 119, 197, 199, 282, 374, 385
1.3	Declare primitives, arrays, enums, and objects as static, instance, and local variables.	Q: 3, 68, 71, 168, 242, 249, 334, 345 A: 13, 108, 113, 207, 278, 288, 376, 392
1.4	Given code, determine correct overrides or overloads, identify legal returns (and co-vars).	Q: 63, 74, 156, 169, 247, 255, 336, 346 A: 101, 117, 190, 210, 285, 296, 379, 393
1.5	Given classes and superclasses, understand constructors. Instantiate nested classes.	Q: 8, 35, 80, 170, 173, 250, 254, 325 A: 19, 48, 125, 211, 215, 290, 295, 363
	Section 2: Flow Control	
2.1	Develop if and switch statements, and identify their legal argument types.	Q: 5, 59, 72, 172, 241, 252, 337, 347 A: 15, 95, 114, 213, 276, 292, 380, 394
2.2	Develop loops and iterators: for, for-each, do, while, labels… explain loop counters.	Q: 66, 69, 168, 174, 245, 253, 339, 344 A: 105, 109, 208, 216, 282, 294, 384, 390
2.3	Develop assertions code and distinguish appropriate and inappropriate usage.	Q: 37, 80, 82, 171, 179, 251, 252, 271, 333, 346 A: 50, 126, 129, 212, 223, 290, 292, 319, 375, 393
2.4	Develop exceptions (try, catch, finally), and declare methods and overrides with exceptions.	Q: 36, 71, 76, 161, 244, 271, 326, 349 A: 48, 112, 120, 198, 280, 319, 365, 398
2.5	Recognize effects of exceptions including runtime, checked, and errors.	Q: 6, 61, 85, 182, 248, 258, 343, 356 A: 17, 98, 132, 229, 285, 300, 388, 407
2.6	Recognize common exceptions including ArrayIndex, ClassCast, NullPointer…	Q: 74, 157, 167, 176, 239, 256, 270, 348 A: 116, 192, 205, 219, 273, 298, 318, 396

Obj.	Description	Page Numbers
	Section 3: API Contents	
3.1	Use primitive wrapper classes and autoboxing. Strings, StringBuffer...	Q: 5, 57, 81, 156, 178, 262, 325, 352 A: 16, 92, 126, 190, 223, 306, 364, 401
3.2	Use java.io to navigate file systems, and to create, read, and write files.	Q: 31, 67, 75, 158, 169, 260, 334, 354 A: 42, 107, 117, 193, 209, 303, 377, 404
3.3	Use java.text to format and parse dates, numbers, and currency. Use java.util.Locale.	Q: 60, 167, 177, 244, 261, 330 A: 96, 207, 221, 281, 305, 371
3.4	Use java.util, java.util.regex, and String.split() to format, parse, and tokenize.	Q: 9, 33, 78, 85, 162, 250, 263, 336, 349 A: 21, 44, 123, 133, 199, 288, 308, 380, 397
3.X	Serialization	Q: 160 A: 196
	Section 4: Concurrency	
4.1	Define, instantiate, and start new threads using the Thread and Runnable types.	Q: 4, 62, 157, 180, 254, 260, 353 A: 14, 99, 191, 225, 295, 304, 403
4.2	Recognize thread states and transitions using sleep(), join(), interrupt()...	Q: 8, 35, 57, 73, 170, 243, 262, 331, 360 A: 20, 47, 91, 115, 210, 279, 307, 372, 414
4.3	Write code that performs object locking to protect against concurrent access problems.	Q: 38, 38, 79, 89, 163, 184, 251, 265, 341, 357 A: 51, 52, 124, 138, 200, 231, 291, 311, 386, 409
	Section 5: OO Concepts	
5.1	Develop code with tight encapsulation, loose coupling, and high cohesion.	Q: 8, 64, 81, 179, 181, 249, 264, 331 A: 20, 103, 127, 223, 227, 287, 309, 372
5.2	Develop polymorphic code. Determine when to cast and understand casting-related errors.	Q: 61, 84, 163, 172, 246, 267, 329, 355 A: 97, 131, 201, 214, 284, 315, 369, 405
5.3	Explain how modifiers and inheritance affect constructors, and static and instance members.	Q: 38, 78, 88, 165, 183, 240, 335, 352 A: 51, 122, 137, 203, 230, 275, 378, 402
5.4	Develop overridden/overloaded code. Call superclasses or overloaded constructors.	Q: 3, 34, 67, 82, 179, 269, 337, 361 A: 12, 46, 106, 128, 224, 317, 381, 415
5.5	Develop code that implements "is-a" or "has-a" relationships.	Q: 70, 86, 174, 182, 258, 265, 358 A: 111, 133, 217, 228, 301, 311, 410

Obj.	Description	Page Numbers
	Section 6: Collections/Generics	
6.1	Determine which collections should implement a design. Use Comparable.	Q: 67, 73, 180, 185, 239, 263, 351, 359 A: 106, 114, 226, 234, 274, 307, 401, 412
6.2	Understand the hashCode() and equals() contract. Distinguish equals() vs. ==	Q: 6, 64, 83, 183, 185, 261, 266, 328, 356 A: 18, 102, 129, 230, 233, 304, 313, 367, 408
6.3	Use generic versions of Collections: Set, List, Map. Use the "Navigable" interfaces.	Q: 7, 70, 158, 166, 176, 269, 341, 354 A: 18, 111, 193, 205, 220, 318, 387, 405
6.4	Use generics type parameters for classes, variables, and methods. Use wildcard types.	Q: 37, 88, 184, 186, 255, 345, 355 A: 49, 136, 232, 234, 297, 391, 406
6.5	Use java.util to sort and search Lists and arrays. Use Comparables and Comparators.	Q: 31, 77, 87, 175, 259, 326, 338 A: 41, 121, 135, 219, 301, 366, 382
	Section 7: Fundamentals	
7.1	Use access modifiers, packages, and imports (via access or inheritance) to interact with code.	Q: 10, 32, 77, 164, 257, 333, 350 A: 22, 43, 120, 202, 299, 375, 400
7.2	Given a class and a command line, determine the expected behavior.	Q: 34, 65, 84, 167, 175, 248, 342, 359 A: 45, 104, 130, 206, 218, 286, 388, 413
7.3	Determine the effects on references and variables when passed to methods.	Q: 58, 69, 155, 171, 242, 259, 264, 339 A: 94, 110, 189, 213, 277, 302, 310, 383
7.4	Determine when objects become eligible for garbage collection. Use finalize().	Q: 63, 87, 155, 181, 252, 267, 332, 350 A: 100, 135, 188, 227, 293, 314, 373, 399
7.5	Use JAR files. Determine if given code and a given classpath will compile.	Q: 86, 166, 178, 246, 268, 328, 347 A: 134, 204, 222, 283, 316, 368, 395
7.6	Use operators: assignment, arithmetic, relational, instanceof. Determine equality.	Q: 4, 62, 75, 159, 165, 244, 257, 327 A: 14, 100, 118, 194, 203, 280, 299, 366

GET YOUR FREE SUBSCRIPTION TO *ORACLE MAGAZINE*

Oracle Magazine is essential gear for today's information technology professionals. Stay informed and increase your productivity with every issue of *Oracle Magazine*. Inside each free bimonthly issue you'll get:

- Up-to-date information on Oracle Database, Oracle Application Server, Web development, enterprise grid computing, database technology, and business trends

- Third-party news and announcements

- Technical articles on Oracle and partner products, technologies, and operating environments

- Development and administration tips

- Real-world customer stories

If there are other Oracle users at your location who would like to receive their own subscription to *Oracle Magazine*, please photo-copy this form and pass it along.

Three easy ways to subscribe:

① Web
Visit our Web site at **oracle.com/oraclemagazine**
You'll find a subscription form there, plus much more

② Fax
Complete the questionnaire on the back of this card and fax the questionnaire side only to **+1.847.763.9638**

③ Mail
Complete the questionnaire on the back of this card and mail it to **P.O. Box 1263, Skokie, IL 60076-8263**

ORACLE®

Want your own FREE subscription?

To receive a free subscription to *Oracle Magazine*, you must fill out the entire card, sign it, and date it (incomplete cards cannot be processed or acknowledged). You can also fax your application to +1.847.763.9638. **Or subscribe at our Web site at oracle.com/oraclemagazine**

O **Yes, please send me a FREE subscription** *Oracle Magazine.*   O No.

O From time to time, Oracle Publishing allows our partners exclusive access to our e-mail addresses for special promotions and announcements. To be included in this program, please check this circle. If you do not wish to be included, you will only receive notices about your subscription via e-mail.

O Oracle Publishing allows sharing of our postal mailing list with selected third parties. If you prefer your mailing address not to be included in this program, please check this circle.

If at any time you would like to be removed from either mailing list, please contact Customer Service at +1.847.763.9635 or send an e-mail to oracle@halldata.com. If you opt in to the sharing of information, Oracle may also provide you with e-mail related to Oracle products, services, and events. If you want to completely unsubscribe from any e-mail communication from Oracle, please send an e-mail to: unsubscribe@oracle-mail.com with the following in the subject line: REMOVE [your e-mail address]. For complete information on Oracle Publishing's privacy practices, please visit oracle.com/html/privacy/html

X
signature (required)   date

name   title

company   e-mail address

street/p.o. box

city/state/zip or postal code   telephone

country   fax

Would you like to receive your free subscription in digital format instead of print if it becomes available? O Yes O No

---

YOU MUST ANSWER ALL 10 QUESTIONS BELOW.

① WHAT IS THE PRIMARY BUSINESS ACTIVITY OF YOUR FIRM AT THIS LOCATION? (check one only)

- ☐ 01 Aerospace and Defense Manufacturing
- ☐ 02 Application Service Provider
- ☐ 03 Automotive Manufacturing
- ☐ 04 Chemicals
- ☐ 05 Media and Entertainment
- ☐ 06 Construction/Engineering
- ☐ 07 Consumer Sector/Consumer Packaged Goods
- ☐ 08 Education
- ☐ 09 Financial Services/Insurance
- ☐ 10 Health Care
- ☐ 11 High Technology Manufacturing, OEM
- ☐ 12 Industrial Manufacturing
- ☐ 13 Independent Software Vendor
- ☐ 14 Life Sciences (biotech, pharmaceuticals)
- ☐ 15 Natural Resources
- ☐ 16 Oil and Gas
- ☐ 17 Professional Services
- ☐ 18 Public Sector (government)
- ☐ 19 Research
- ☐ 20 Retail/Wholesale/Distribution
- ☐ 21 Systems Integrator, VAR/VAD
- ☐ 22 Telecommunications
- ☐ 23 Travel and Transportation
- ☐ 24 Utilities (electric, gas, sanitation, water)
- ☐ 98 Other Business and Services _____

② WHICH OF THE FOLLOWING BEST DESCRIBES YOUR PRIMARY JOB FUNCTION? (check one only)

CORPORATE MANAGEMENT/STAFF
- ☐ 01 Executive Management (President, Chair, CEO, CFO, Owner, Partner, Principal)
- ☐ 02 Finance/Administrative Management (VP/Director/ Manager/Controller, Purchasing, Administration)
- ☐ 03 Sales/Marketing Management (VP/Director/Manager)
- ☐ 04 Computer Systems/Operations Management (CIO/VP/Director/Manager MIS/IS/IT, Ops)

IS/IT STAFF
- ☐ 05 Application Development/Programming Management
- ☐ 06 Application Development/Programming Staff
- ☐ 07 Consulting
- ☐ 08 DBA/Systems Administrator
- ☐ 09 Education/Training
- ☐ 10 Technical Support Director/Manager
- ☐ 11 Other Technical Management/Staff
- ☐ 98 Other

③ WHAT IS YOUR CURRENT PRIMARY OPERATING PLATFORM (check all that apply)

- ☐ 01 Digital Equipment Corp UNIX/VAX/VMS
- ☐ 02 HP UNIX
- ☐ 03 IBM AIX
- ☐ 04 IBM UNIX
- ☐ 05 Linux (Red Hat)
- ☐ 06 Linux (SUSE)
- ☐ 07 Linux (Oracle Enterprise)
- ☐ 08 Linux (other)
- ☐ 09 Macintosh
- ☐ 10 MVS
- ☐ 11 Netware
- ☐ 12 Network Computing
- ☐ 13 SCO UNIX
- ☐ 14 Sun Solaris/SunOS
- ☐ 15 Windows
- ☐ 16 Other UNIX
- ☐ 98 Other
- 99 ☐ None of the Above

④ DO YOU EVALUATE, SPECIFY, RECOMMEND, OR AUTHORIZE THE PURCHASE OF ANY OF THE FOLLOWING? (check all that apply)

- ☐ 01 Hardware
- ☐ 02 Business Applications (ERP, CRM, etc.)
- ☐ 03 Application Development Tools
- ☐ 04 Database Products
- ☐ 05 Internet or Intranet Products
- ☐ 06 Other Software
- ☐ 07 Middleware Products
- 99 ☐ None of the Above

⑤ IN YOUR JOB, DO YOU USE OR PLAN TO PURCHASE ANY OF THE FOLLOWING PRODUCTS? (check all that apply)

SOFTWARE
- ☐ 01 CAD/CAE/CAM
- ☐ 02 Collaboration Software
- ☐ 03 Communications
- ☐ 04 Database Management
- ☐ 05 File Management
- ☐ 06 Finance
- ☐ 07 Java
- ☐ 08 Multimedia Authoring
- ☐ 09 Networking
- ☐ 10 Programming
- ☐ 11 Project Management
- ☐ 12 Scientific and Engineering
- ☐ 13 Systems Management
- ☐ 14 Workflow

HARDWARE
- ☐ 15 Macintosh
- ☐ 16 Mainframe
- ☐ 17 Massively Parallel Processing

- ☐ 18 Minicomputer
- ☐ 19 Intel x86(32)
- ☐ 20 Intel x86(64)
- ☐ 21 Network Computer
- ☐ 22 Symmetric Multiprocessing
- ☐ 23 Workstation Services

SERVICES
- ☐ 24 Consulting
- ☐ 25 Education/Training
- ☐ 26 Maintenance
- ☐ 27 Online Database
- ☐ 28 Support
- ☐ 29 Technology-Based Training
- ☐ 30 Other
- 99 ☐ None of the Above

⑥ WHAT IS YOUR COMPANY'S SIZE? (check one only)

- ☐ 01 More than 25,000 Employees
- ☐ 02 10,001 to 25,000 Employees
- ☐ 03 5,001 to 10,000 Employees
- ☐ 04 1,001 to 5,000 Employees
- ☐ 05 101 to 1,000 Employees
- ☐ 06 Fewer than 100 Employees

⑦ DURING THE NEXT 12 MONTHS, HOW MUCH DO YOU ANTICIPATE YOUR ORGANIZATION WILL SPEND ON COMPUTER HARDWARE, SOFTWARE, PERIPHERALS, AND SERVICES FOR YOUR LOCATION? (check one only)

- ☐ 01 Less than $10,000
- ☐ 02 $10,000 to $49,999
- ☐ 03 $50,000 to $99,999
- ☐ 04 $100,000 to $499,999
- ☐ 05 $500,000 to $999,999
- ☐ 06 $1,000,000 and Over

⑧ WHAT IS YOUR COMPANY'S YEARLY SALES REVENUE? (check one only)

- ☐ 01 $500, 000, 000 and above
- ☐ 02 $100, 000, 000 to $500, 000, 000
- ☐ 03 $50, 000, 000 to $100, 000, 000
- ☐ 04 $5, 000, 000 to $50, 000, 000
- ☐ 05 $1, 000, 000 to $5, 000, 000

⑨ WHAT LANGUAGES AND FRAMEWORKS DO YOU USE? (check all that apply)

- ☐ 01 Ajax
- ☐ 02 C
- ☐ 03 C++
- ☐ 04 C#
- ☐ 05 Hibernate
- ☐ 06 J++/J#
- ☐ 07 Java
- ☐ 08 JSP
- ☐ 09 .NET
- ☐ 10 Perl
- ☐ 11 PHP
- ☐ 12 PL/SQL
- ☐ 13 Python
- ☐ 14 Ruby/Rails
- ☐ 15 Spring
- ☐ 16 Struts
- ☐ 17 SQL
- ☐ 18 Visual Basic
- ☐ 98 Other

⑩ WHAT ORACLE PRODUCTS ARE IN USE AT YO[UR] SITE? (check all that apply)

ORACLE DATABASE
- ☐ 01 Oracle Database 11*g*
- ☐ 02 Oracle Database 10*g*
- ☐ 03 Oracle9*i* Database
- ☐ 04 Oracle Embedded Database (Oracle Lite, Times Ten, Berkeley DE[B])
- ☐ 05 Other Oracle Database Release

ORACLE FUSION MIDDLEWARE
- ☐ 06 Oracle Application Server
- ☐ 07 Oracle Portal
- ☐ 08 Oracle Enterprise Manager
- ☐ 09 Oracle BPEL Process Manager
- ☐ 10 Oracle Identity Management
- ☐ 11 Oracle SOA Suite
- ☐ 12 Oracle Data Hubs

ORACLE DEVELOPMENT TOOLS
- ☐ 13 Oracle JDeveloper
- ☐ 14 Oracle Forms
- ☐ 15 Oracle Reports
- ☐ 16 Oracle Designer
- ☐ 17 Oracle Discoverer
- ☐ 18 Oracle BI Beans
- ☐ 19 Oracle Warehouse Builder
- ☐ 20 Oracle WebCenter
- ☐ 21 Oracle Application Express

ORACLE APPLICATIONS
- ☐ 22 Oracle E-Business Suite
- ☐ 23 PeopleSoft Enterprise
- ☐ 24 JD Edwards EnterpriseOne
- ☐ 25 JD Edwards World
- ☐ 26 Oracle Fusion
- ☐ 27 Hyperion
- ☐ 28 Siebel CRM

ORACLE SERVICES
- ☐ 28 Oracle E-Business Suite On Demand
- ☐ 29 Oracle Technology On Demand
- ☐ 30 Siebel CRM On Demand
- ☐ 31 Oracle Consulting
- ☐ 32 Oracle Education
- ☐ 33 Oracle Support
- ☐ 98 Other
- 99 ☐ None of the Above

0801 4004

The Best Fully Integrated Study System Available for OCP Java SE 6 Programmer Exam (Exam 1Z0-851)

Written by the lead developers of the SCJP (now OCP Java SE 6 Programmer) exam, *SCJP Sun Certified Programmer for Java 6 Study Guide* features hundreds of practice questions and hands-on exercises. It's the perfect companion to *OCP Java SE 6 Programmer Practice Exams!*

On the CD:

- Complete MasterExam practice testing engine, featuring:
  - Full practice exams
  - Detailed answers with explanations
  - Score Report performance assessment tool
- Ebook
- Bonus coverage of the SCJD exam
- Additional downloadable practice test with free online registration

Available everywhere computer books are sold, in print and ebook formats.